£6

D0307254

REMAINS

Historical and Literary

CONNECTED WITH THE PALATINE COUNTIES OF

Lancaster and Chester

VOLUME XXV—THIRD SERIES

MANCHESTER:

Printed for the Chetham Society

1978

The publication of this book has been assisted by an award from the
Twenty-Seven Foundation

THE LANCASHIRE
GENTRY
AND THE GREAT
REBELLION
1640 60

by

B. G. BLACKWOOD

MANCHESTER
Printed for the Chetham
Society
1978

© The Chetham Society 1978

Published for the Society by
Manchester University Press
Oxford Road, Manchester M13 9PL

ISBN 0 719 0 1334 8

Distributed in the USA by
Humanities Press Inc
Atlantic Highlands, N.J. 07716

British Library cataloguing-in-publication data

Blackwood, B G
  The Lancashire gentry and the Great
Rebellion, 1640–60.—(Remains historical
and literary connected with the Palatine
counties of Lancaster and Chester: 3rd
series; vol. 25).
  1. Lancashire—Gentry—History
  I. Title   II. Series
  301.44′1   HT657

ISBN 0–7190–1334–8

Printed in Great Britain by Butler & Tanner Ltd, Frome and London

CONTENTS

PREFACE

This book is a shortened and revised version of my Oxford D.Phil. thesis entitled 'The Lancashire gentry, 1625–60: a social and economic study', submitted and approved in 1973. It deals with the Lancashire gentry in general, and the Royalist and Parliamentarian gentry in particular, during the period of the Great Rebellion. It is primarily a social and economic study of the gentry, and is concerned only to a limited extent with their political, military and religious history. The book has two main aims: first and foremost, to examine the social and economic condition of the Royalist and Parliamentarian gentry before and after the Civil War; and, secondly, to investigate the long-term trends in patterns of land ownership, wealth and social mobility among the gentry as a whole during the seventeenth century, and the extent to which existing trends were affected by the mid-seventeenth-century crisis.

I am grateful to Lord Clitheroe for allowing me to examine his court rolls of the manor of Downham, 1645–55. Many public bodies also helped me to find and to use manuscripts in their care. I am thinking of the staffs of the Public Record Office, British Library, Guildhall Library, House of Lords Record Office, Inner Temple Library, Bodleian Library, Cambridge University Library, Lancashire Record Office, Manchester Central Library, Chetham's Library, John Rylands Library, Liverpool Record Office and the Wigan Central Library, Extracts from Crown-copyright records in the Public Record Office appear by permission of the Controller of H.M. Stationery Office.

I am indebted to a number of scholars in the preparation of this work. I have greatly benefited from discussions with Professor Owen Ashmore, Professor G. E. Aylmer, Dr J. T. Cliffe, Mr R. N. Dore, Professor A. M. Everitt, Mr G. C. F. Forster, Professor I. G. Gentles, Mr Richard Grassby, Sir John Habakkuk, Dr R. W. K. Hinton, Dr K. J. Lindley, Dr Brian Manning, Dr J. S. Morrill, Mr D. H. Pennington, Dr C. B. Phillips, Professor Austin Woolrych, Dr K. E. Wrightson and Brigadier Peter Young. Several of these provided me with useful information or references, for which acknowledgement is made in the footnotes. I have also benefited from the helpful criticisms of my doctoral examiners, Professor H. R. Trevor-Roper and Dr Christopher Hill. I am grateful to Professors J. S. Roskell and W. H. Chaloner for help in preparing this work for publication. Above all, I must thank Dr Joan Thirsk, who supervised my thesis at Oxford and encouraged me to publish. Needless to say, none of these persons is responsible for any errors which appear in this book.

I am very grateful to the Twenty-Seven Foundation Awards Committee for an extremely generous grant which has assisted the publication of this book.

Finally I would like to record my immense debt to my wife and parents for all their moral and practical support during the preparation of the work.

B.G.B.

September 1976

ABBREVIATIONS

Agric. Hist Rev.	*Agricultural History Review*
Al. Cant.	J. and J. A. Venn, eds., *Alumni Cantabrigienses to 1751*, 4 vols., 1922–27
Al. Oxon.	J. Foster, ed. *Alumni Oxonienses: the Members of the University of Oxford, 1500–1714*, 4 vols., 1891–92
Amer. H.R.	*American Historical Review*
A. & O.	C. H. Firth and R. S. Rait, eds., *Acts and Ordinances of the Interregnum*, 3 vols., 1911
B.I.H.R.	*Bulletin of the Institute of Historical Research*
B.L.	British Library, London
Add. MS.	Additional Manuscript
Harl. MS.	Harleian Manuscript
Blackwood, 'Agrarian Unrest'	B. G. Blackwood, 'Agrarian Unrest and the early Lancashire Quakers', J.F.H.S., li, 1966
Blackwood, B.Litt. thesis	B. G. Blackwood, 'Social and Religious Aspects of the History of Lancashire, 1635–55', Oxford Univ. B.Litt. thesis, 1956
Blackwood, 'Catholic and Protestant Gentry'	B. G. Blackwood, 'The Catholic and Protestant Gentry of Lancashire during the Civil War period', Trans. Hist. Soc. L. & C., Vol. 126, 1976
Blackwood, 'Cavalier and Roundhead Gentry'	B. G. Blackwood, 'The Cavalier and Roundhead Gentry of Lancashire', Trans. L. & C. Antiq. Soc., Vol. 77, 1967
Blackwood, D.Phil. thesis	B. G. Blackwood, 'The Lancashire Gentry, 1625–1660: A Social and Economic Study', Oxford Univ. D.Phil. thesis, 1973
Blackwood, 'Economic State'	B. G. Blackwood, 'The Economic State of the Lancashire Gentry on the Eve of the Civil War', North. Hist., xii, 1976
Blackwood, 'Lancs. Cavaliers'	B. G. Blackwood, 'The Lancashire Cavaliers and their Tenants', Trans. Hist. Soc. L. & C., Vol. 117, 1965
Blackwood, 'Marriages'	B. G. Blackwood, 'The Marriages of the Lancashire Gentry on the Eve of the Civil War', *The Genealogists' Magazine*, xvi, 1970
Bod. Lib.	Bodleian Library, Oxford
Broxap	E. Broxap, *The Great Civil War in Lancashire, 1642–51*, 2nd edn., Manchester, 1973
C.A.M.	M. A. E. Green, ed., *Calendar of the Proceedings of the Committee for Advance of Money, 1642–1656*, 3 vols., 1888

C.C.C.	M. A. E. Green, ed., *Calendar of the Proceedings of the Committee for Compounding with Delinquents, 1643–1660*, 5 vols., 1889–92
Chet. Lib.	Chetham's Library, Manchester
Chet. Soc.	Chetham Society
C.J.	*Journal of House of Commons*
Clarendon, *Rebellion*	Edward Hyde, earl of Clarendon, *History of the Rebellion*, ed. W. D. Macray, 6 vols., Oxford, 1888
Cliffe	J. T. Cliffe, *The Yorkshire Gentry from the Reformation to the Civil War*, 1969
C.R.S.	Catholic Record Society
C.S.P.D.	*Calendar of State Papers Domestic*
C.W.T.	G. Ormerod, ed., *Tracts relating to Military Proceedings in Lancashire during the Great Civil War*, Chet. Soc., O.S., Vol. 2, 1844
Discourse	E. Beamont, ed., *A Discourse of the Warr in Lancashire*, Chet. Soc., O.S., Vol. 62, 1864
D.N.B.	*Dictionary of National Biography*
Ec.H.R.	*Economic History Review*
E.H.R.	*English Historical Review*
Everitt, *Change*	A. M. Everitt, *Change in the Provinces: the Seventeenth Century*, Univ. of Leicester, Dept. of Local History Occasional Papers, 2nd Ser., i, 1969
Everitt, *Kent*	A. M. Everitt, *The Community of Kent and the Great Rebellion, 1640–60*, Leicester, 1966
Everitt, *Local Community*	A. M. Everitt, *The Local Community and the Great Rebellion*, Historical Association Pamphlet G.70, 1969
Fletcher	Anthony Fletcher, *A County Community in Peace and War: Sussex 1600–1660*, 1975
GI. Adm. Reg.	J. Foster, ed., *Register of Admissions to Gray's Inn, 1521–1889*, 1889
Glamorgan County Hist., iv	Glanmor Williams, ed., *Glamorgan County History*, Vol. iv: *Early Modern Glamorgan*, Cardiff, 1974
Guild. Lib.	Guildhall Library, London
Habakkuk, 'Landowners'	H. J. Habakkuk, 'Landowners and the Civil War', Ec.H.R., 2nd Ser., xviii, 1965
H.L.R.O.	House of Lords Record Office, Houses of Parliament
HMC	Historical Manuscripts Commission Reports
Holiday, 'Land sales'	P. G. Holiday, 'Land Sales and Repurchases in Yorkshire after the Civil Wars, 1650–1670', North. Hist., v, 1970
Holmes	Clive Holmes, *The Eastern Association and the English Civil War*, Cambridge, 1974
IT. Adm. Reg.	'Admissions to the Inner Temple to 1659' (typescript, Inner Temple Library, 1954)

James	Mervyn James, *Family, Lineage and Civil Society: A Study of Society, Politics and Mentality in the Durham Region, 1500–1640*, Oxford, 1974
J.F.H.S.	*Journal of the Friends' Historical Society*
J. Ry. Lib.	John Rylands Library, Manchester
L. & C. Rec. Soc.	Lancashire and Cheshire Record Society
LI. Adm. Reg.	J. Foster, ed., *The Records of the Honourable Society of Lincoln's Inn, Admissions . . . 1420 to A.D. 1799*, 1896
L.J.	*Journal of the House of Lords*
L.R.O.	Lancashire County Record Office, Preston
DD	Deposited Deeds
DDAl	Alison of Park Hall
DDBl	Blundell of Little Crosby
DDBr	Braddyll of Portfield
DDCl	Clifton of Lytham
DDF	Farington of Worden
DDGe	Gerard of Ashton-in-Makerfield
DDHp	Hopwood of Hopwood
DDIn	Blundell of Ince Blundell
DDK	Stanley of Knowsley
DDLx	Trappes-Lomax of Clayton-le-Moors
DDM	Molyneux of Sefton
DDN	National Trust
DDPt	Petre of Dunkenhalgh
DDSc	Scarisbrick of Scarisbrick
DDTa	Tatton of Cuerden
DDTo	Towneley of Towneley
DDX	Smaller Deposits
DP	Documents Purchased
DX	Ancient Deeds
QDD	Quarter Sessions Deeds of Bargain and Sale
QSC	Quarter Sessions Commissions of the Peace
QSR	Quarter Sessions Rolls
Manch. Cen. Ref. Lib.	Manchester Central Reference Library
L3	Radcliffe Papers
M35	Carill Worsley Papers
Morrill, *Cheshire*	J. S. Morrill, *Cheshire 1630–1660: County Government and Society during the 'English Revolution'*, Oxford, 1974
Morrill & Dore	J. S. Morrill and R. N. Dore, 'The Allegiance of the Cheshire Gentry in the Great Civil War', Trans. L. & C. Antiq. Soc., Vol. 77, 1967
MT. Adm. Reg.	H. A. C. Sturgess, ed., *Register of Admissions to the Honourable Society of the Middle Temple, from the Fifteenth Century to the Year 1944*, vol. i, 1949

North. Hist.	*Northern History*
N.S.	New Series
O.S.	Old Series
P.R.O.	Public Record Office, London
C	Chancery
C54	Close Rolls
C181	Crown Office, Miscellaneous Books
C193	Ditto
C231	Crown Office, Docquet Books
CRES	Crown Estate Office
CRES6	Entry Books and Registers: Surveyor-General's Book of Constats, 1660–61
DL	Duchy of Lancaster
DL1	Pleadings
DL4	Depositions and Examinations
DL5	Entry Books of Decrees and Orders
DL7	Inquisitions post-mortem
DL42	Miscellaneous Books
E	Exchequer
E121	King's Remembrancer, Certificates as to the Sale of Crown Lands
E134	K.R., Depositions
E179	K.R., Lay Subsidy Rolls, Schedule of Contributors to the 'Free and Voluntary Gift', Hearth Tax Assessments
E190	K.R., Port Books
E377	Lord Treasurer's Remembrancer, Recusant Rolls, Pipe Office Series
E379	L.T.R., Sheriffs' Accounts of Seizures
LC	Lord Chamberlain's Office
LC4	Entry Books of Recognisances
LR	Land Revenue Office
LR2	Miscellaneous Books
PL	Palatinate of Lancaster
PL6	Chancery Bills
PL17	Prothonotary's Records, Feet of Fines
PROB	Prerogative Court of Canterbury
PROB 11	Registered Copy Wills, 1384–1858
SP	State Papers Domestic
SP12	Elizabeth I
SP16	Charles I
SP18	Interregnum
SP19	Committee for Advance of Money
SP23	Committee for Compounding
SP28	Commonwealth Exchequer Papers
SP29	Charles II
Wards	Court of Wards and Liveries
Wards 5	Feodaries' Surveys
Wards 9	Miscellaneous Books

Rec. S.J.	H. Foley, ed., *Records of the English Province of the Society of Jesus*, 7 vols., 1875–83
Roy. Comp. Papers	J. H. Stanning, J. Brownbill, eds., *Lancashire Royalist Composition Papers*, 6 vols. in 7 parts, L. & C. Rec. Soc., Vols. 24, 26, 29, 36, 72, 95, 96, 1891–1942
Stone, *Causes*	Lawrence Stone, *The causes of the English Revolution, 1529–1642*, 1972
Stone, *Crisis*	Lawrence Stone, *The Crisis of the Aristocracy, 1558–1641*, Oxford, 1965
Stone, 'Social mobility'	Lawrence Stone, 'Social Mobility in England, 1500–1700', in Paul S. Seaver, *Seventeenth Century England: Society in an Age of Revolution*, New York, 1976
Thirsk, 'Agriculture and social change'	Joan Thirsk, 'Seventeenth-Century Agriculture and Social Change', in ibid.
Thirsk, 'Restoration land settlement	Joan Thirsk, 'The Restoration Land Settlement', *Journal of Modern History*, xxvi, 1954
Thirsk, 'Sale of lands'	Joan Thirsk, 'The Sale of Royalist Lands during the Interregnum', Ec.H.R., 2nd Ser., v, 1953
Trans. Cumb. & West. Ant. & Arch. Soc.	*Transactions of the Cumberland and Westmorland Antiquarian and Archaeological Society*
Trans. Hist. Soc. L. & C.	*Transactions of the Historic Society of Lancashire and Cheshire*
Trans. L. & C. Antiq. Soc.	*Transactions of the Lancashire and Cheshire Antiquarian Society*
Trans. Roch. Lit. & Sci. Soc.	*Transactions of the Rochdale Literary and Scientific Society*
T.R.H.S.	*Transactions of the Royal Historical Society*
Underdown, *Somerset*	David Underdown, *Somerset in the Civil War and Interregnum*, Newton Abbot, 1973
V.C.H.	W. Farrer & J. Brownbill, eds., *Victoria History of the County of Lancaster*, 8 vols., 1906–14
Watts	S. J. Watts, *From Border to Middle Shire. Northumberland 1586–1625*, Leicester, 1975
Wigan Cen. Lib.	Wigan Central Library
D/D/An	Anderton Deeds

NOTES

'Lancashire' refers to the area which constituted the county before the boundary changes in April 1974.

In quotations from contemporary sources the original spelling has been generally retained.

The year is taken to begin on 1 January and not on 25 March, which was still the practice in the seventeenth century.

Place of publication of a book is London, unless otherwise stated. All Chetham Society volumes have been published in Manchester. Full references to books, articles and theses are given either in the List of Abbreviations above or in the first citation in the footnotes; elsewhere abbreviated references are used.

CHAPTER I

LANCASHIRE ON THE EVE OF THE CIVIL WAR: ECONOMY, POPULATION AND GENTRY

I AGRICULTURE, INDUSTRY AND POPULATION

Lancashire was a county of contrasts on the eve of the Civil War. Physically the palatinate was divided into highland and lowland zones. The highland zone embraced the Pennine country of the south-east, part of Bowland Forest and most of the north Lonsdale peninsula. The lowland plain covered the central and western regions of Lancashire.

Agriculturally the county was predominantly pastoral in the early seventeenth century. Yet it is possible to divide Lancashire into three distinct farming regions: the central mixed farming area, stretching from the Lune to the Mersey, and the pastoral districts of the coastal plain and the highland zone. The mixed farming area covered the eastern half of the Lancashire plain. Between 55 and 62 per cent of the cultivated land was in arable and a fair variety of crops was grown.[1] Nevertheless cattle rearing was also important in this part of Lancashire. Agriculturally the eastern plain, and especially the Ribble valley and the Central Fylde, was probably the richest part of Lancashire. By contrast, the western coastal plain was one of the poorest parts of the county. It was a predominantly pastoral region and a glance at John Blaeu's map of Lancashire, dated 1645,[2] enables us to understand why. The large areas of undrained marshes and mosses, such as Marton and Pilling mosses, were hardly conducive to arable farming. The mosses yielded turf for fuel and grazing for stock, but these were poor compensations for the loss of land and the barrier to communication which they caused. The second pastoral region of Lancashire covered the highland zone. There cattle rearing and selling prevailed until the beginning of the seventeenth century, when some farmers, at least in the Rossendale region, turned to dairying.[3]

It was largely, though not entirely, in the highland zone that industries were to be found. The peasants of south-east Lancashire and north Lonsdale supplemented their agricultural earnings by spinning and weaving. North Lonsdale formed part of the Westmorland textile area; but the cloth trade in this region had seriously declined since the late Tudor period, and on the eve of the Civil War it seems to

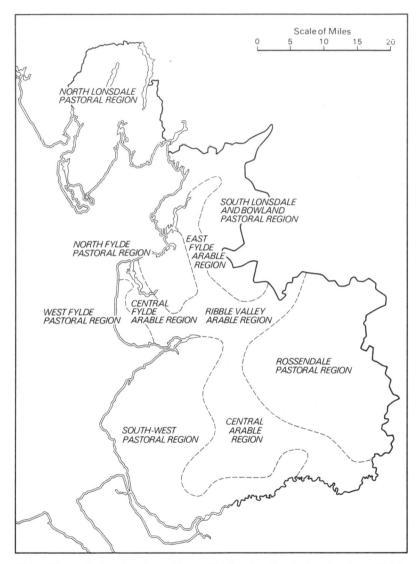

Fig. 1. The agricultural regions of Lancashire in 1642. For further details see T. W. Freeman, H. B. Rodgers and R. H. Kinvig, *Lancashire, Cheshire and the Isle of Man* (London, 1966), p. 48.

have been in a depressed state.[4] On the other hand, the textile industries of south Lancashire seem to have been in a somewhat healthier condition. During the first half of the seventeenth century woollens, linens, fustians and 'cottons' were being increasingly manufactured,[5] and in 1654 it was said that 20,000 people were employed in the manufacture of fustians.[6] Textiles were, of course, the main industries of early seventeenth century Lancashire. But we should not overlook the revival of the Furness iron industry at this time, although its expansion was very limited and its output was probably small.[7] Copper mining, too, was in progress near Coniston during the early seventeenth century, but trade depression and the Civil War eventually ruined the industry.[8] The early Stuart period also saw the growth of metal trades in south-west Lancashire, especially in the Wigan and Leigh areas.[9] Coal mining was also developing south of the Ribble, although its growth in the south-west region was slow and spasmodic.[10] Finally, the early Stuart period saw the rise of the port of Liverpool. Although its real prosperity came after the Restoration, Liverpool was apparently developing a considerable trade, based on Lancashire coal and cotton goods and Cheshire salt and cheese, even before the Civil War.[11] It is important, however, not to overstress these economic trends. Ernest Broxap only slightly exaggerated when he described Lancashire on the eve of the Civil War as an 'isolated, remote and backward part of England'.[12] According to the Ship Money valuation of 1636, admittedly an imperfect guide, Lancashire was the poorest county in England, apart from Cumberland.[13] Other fiscal records also reveal the poverty of the county.[14] Nevertheless, the textile and metal industries were gradually increasing the palatinate's wealth during the seventeenth century and slowly laying the foundations for Lancashire's industrial 'take-off' in the eighteenth century.

The population of the county was also expanding during the seventeenth century. Professor W. K. Jordan reckons that in 1600 Lancashire had between 105,000 and 120,000 inhabitants, his bias being clearly towards the lesser figure.[15] By 1664 the number of people had risen to 150,669, according to the Hearth Tax assessment (Ladyday) of that year.[16] By 1690 the population had reached 180,909,[17] according to John Houghton's statistics.[18] Demographic growth was not continuous, however, and it is likely that the population of Lancashire was approximately the same in 1642 as in 1664. The Civil War must have reduced it during the 1640s, or at least prevented its growth. Thomas Hobbes spoke of 'the killing of 100,000' persons in the conflict.[19] Few historians today would accept such a high estimate, for 'the Great Rebellion was far from being a total war'.[20] Nevertheless in Lancashire the Civil War seems to have been bloodier and fiercer than elsewhere and the casualty rate may have been very high. Nearly half the population of Bolton may have been killed in the siege of 1644,[21] and the capture of Liverpool by Prince Rupert also cost many lives.[22] However, more people in Lancashire probably died from plague and famine than from war wounds. The plague was particularly prevalent between 1644 and 1657. 'During that period there were few years in which some part of the county was not stricken with greater or lesser degrees of severity.'[23] Moreover many Lancastrians must have died of starvation because of the serious harvest failures of 1646–50 and 1657–61 in other parts of England.[24] In short, the high death rate of the 1640s and 1650s[25] seems to justify the use of the 1664 (Ladyday) Hearth Tax Assessment to estimate the population of Lancashire in 1642.[26]

2 THE GENTRY: IDENTIFICATION, NUMBERS AND DISTRIBUTION

The population of Lancashire in 1642 was divided on an hierarchical basis. At the top of the social scale stood three peers: James Stanley, seventh Earl of Derby; Henry Parker, thirteenth Baron Morley and Mounteagle; and Richard Molyneux of Sefton, who held the second viscountcy of Maryborough in Ireland. These men were extremely powerful in 1642,[27] far more so than noblemen in many other regions.[28] Moreover the Lancashire peers had nation-wide interests, possessing large estates in many counties besides Lancashire.[29] This means that, despite their historical importance, they cannot receive the same detailed treatment as the Lancashire gentry, whose estates were largely confined to the palatinate.

Who were the Lancashire gentry? Until we define the term 'gentry' we cannot possibly say. Unfortunately this is easier said than done. In theory the gentry were those bearing the title of 'baronet, knight, esquire or gentleman'. In practice, 'esquire' and especially 'gentleman' were often vague and meaningless terms, and were too readily applied to some, such as town officials or even men of lower status,[30] who had no claims to gentility. This was especially the case during the period 1640–60.[31] Faced with this problem, some historians have considered that the heralds' visitation lists are the most reliable guides to gentle status and have defined the gentry in the armigerous sense.[32] Unfortunately these visitation lists are not always accurate and in any case seldom give a complete catalogue of those generally recognised as gentry by their contemporaries.[33] If we are to identify the gentry we must depend mainly on official records. But here again we run into difficulties, because the term 'gentleman' is found more frequently in some documents (e.g. lawsuits) than in others (e.g. tax rolls). In wills or lawsuits many men assumed gentle status because it seemed advantageous, while in fiscal records many downgraded themselves to avoid higher taxes. However, let us not be too sceptical. Some official sources are reasonably trustworthy. Mr J. P. Cooper has convincingly argued that the freeholders' books are a reliable index of status.[34] To the Lancashire Freeholders' List of 1600,[35] together with the Amounderness Freeholders' List of 1633,[36] we may add the Muster Rolls, 1632,[37] and, despite some reservations, the Knighthood Composition Lists, 1631–32,[38] the Lay Subsidy Rolls, 1641,[39] and the Protestation returns, 1642.[40] These are the main sources which have been used to establish the total number of Lancashire gentry families in 1642.

The gentry—those *consistently* described as such in official documents—fluctuated in numbers throughout the seventeenth century, and gradually decreased in proportion to the rest of the Lancashire population. In 1600 763 gentry families were recorded in the Freeholders' List,[41] which means that if we use the multiplier of 4·5 persons to a household[42] they formed 3·2 per cent of a total population of 105,000. In 1642 Lancashire had 774 gentry families, and these comprised only 2·3 per cent of a population based on the 1664 (Ladyday) Hearth Tax Assessment. Even if we relied on Professor Jordan's alternative estimate of the population in 1600—120,000—and applied it to 1642, the gentry would still form less than 3 per cent of the Lancashire people. During the English Revolution the numbers of Lancashire gentry declined absolutely as well as relatively. At the time of the 1664 (Ladyday) Hearth Tax Assessment only 627 gentry families can be found,[43] and these comprised a mere 1·8 per cent of the palatinate's population. By 1695 the number of Lancashire gentry had risen to 662, but this was well below the pre-war level.[44] Moreover, these 662 gentry families formed only 1·6 per cent of the Lancashire people.[45] Thus during the seventeenth century Lancashire's gentry population declined at the very time that its total population increased.[46]

At the end of the seventeenth century Lancashire had a smaller proportion of gentry families than such counties as Glamorgan.[47] Yet around 1600, if not earlier, Lancashire may have had a larger gentry community than most other regions.[48] Lancashire certainly had a higher proportion of gentle families than Yorkshire and Kent in 1600. In Lancashire 763 gentry families comprised 3·2 per cent of the population. In Kent about 700 gentry families[49] formed only 2·1 per cent of a total population of approximately 145,000.[50] In Yorkshire the 641 gentry families[51] comprised less than 1 per cent of the county's 300,000 estimated inhabitants.[52] Some English counties, of course, had more gentry than Lancashire. Writing shortly before 1600, William Camden remarked that Cheshire 'alwaies bred and reared more Gentry' than any other shire.[53] Dr J. S. Morrill discovered that Cheshire had about 800 gentry families in the period 1625–42.[54] This was a very large number indeed considering that the population of Cheshire was almost certainly much less than that of Lancashire.

Just as the gentry were unevenly distributed *between* counties, so they were unevenly spread *within* counties. In Lancashire some hundreds had a higher proportion of gentry than others in 1642, as Table 1 shows. It will be noticed that the proportion of gentry was highest in the lowland hundreds of West Derby, Leyland and Amounderness and lowest in the highland hundreds of Salford, Blackburn and Lonsdale. The highland hundreds were more pastoral and industrial than the lowland hundreds. Economic factors probably affected the social structure. Mr Julian Cornwall has suggested that where the cloth trade flourished men of great wealth were described as clothiers who elsewhere might have preferred the role of gentleman.[55] This may partly explain the low proportion of gentry in 'industrial' Salford hundred. On the other hand status and pedigree seem to matter more in economically backward regions, hence perhaps the fairly high proportion of gentry in Leyland hundred.[56]

Not only were the Lancashire gentry usually more numerous in agricultural than in semi-industrial areas. Like the gentry of Glamorgan,[57] they seem to have been rather more abundant in arable than in pastoral regions in 1641–42.[58] In Blackburn hundred the arable and lowland township of Walton-le-Dale included a baronet, an esquire and two gentlemen, while the pastoral and highland districts of Pendle and Barrowford had only one gentleman each.[59] In Amounderness hundred some predominantly arable townships had several gentry. Whittingham had one esquire and six gentlemen[60] and Weeton-with-Preese had one esquire and two gentlemen.[61] On the other hand some pastoral townships had no gentry. Bleasdale township, forming part of Bowland Forest, was squireless, and so were the mossland districts of Bispham, Carleton, Marton and Stalmine.[62] In Leyland hundred the story is the same: more arable land, more gentry; more pastoral land, few or no gentry. The largely arable township of Chorley had one esquire and seven gentlemen.[63] Leyland, with slightly less arable land, had one esquire and two gentlemen.[64] The pastoral township of Hesketh-with-Becconsall had no esquires and only one gentleman. But some other pastoral and mossland townships, like Much Hoole, Little Hoole, Longton and Tarleton, had no gentry whatever.[65] However, let us not exaggerate or oversimplify. The gentry were also absent from some arable townships like Kirkham, and dominant in certain pastoral districts, like Lytham, where the wealthy Clifton family reigned supreme.[66]

The distribution of the gentry in Lancashire was not unrelated to political and religious divisions. It is significant that the hundreds with the highest proportion of gentry—West Derby, Leyland and Amounderness—were also the most Royalist and pro-Catholic during the Civil War, while the hundred with the lowest proportion of gentry—Salford—was a Parliamentarian and Puritan stronghold.[67] Moreover, Table 2 shows that towns with several gentry families were more likely to support the king than those with only a few. The contrast between Preston and Bolton is particularly striking. Preston,

TABLE 1

THE GENTRY AND THE HUNDREDAL POPULATIONS OF LANCASHIRE IN 1642

Hundreds	Total No. of households[a]	Total population (using 4.5 multiplier)	Total No. of gentry families[b]	Total gentry population (using 4.5 multiplier)	Gentry as a percentage of total population
Salford	10,767	48,451·5	196	382·0	1·8
Blackburn	4,740	21,330·0	110	495·0	2·3
West Derby	6,935	31,207·5	198	891·0	2·8
Leyland	2,368	10,656·0	71	319·5	3·0
Amounderness	3,926	17,667·0	107	481·5	2·7
Lonsdale	4,746	21,357·0	92	414·0	1·9
Totals	33,482	150,669·0	774	3,483·0	2·3

a These are taken from the Hearth Tax Assessment, Ladyday 1664 (P.R.O., E,179/250/11).
b These are the numbers in 1642.

TABLE 2

THE GENTRY, TOWN POPULATIONS (1642) AND CIVIL WAR ALLEGIANCES

Towns[a]	Total No. of households[b]	Total population (using 4·5 multiplier)	Total No. of gentry families[c]	Total gentry population (using 4·5 multiplier)	Gentry as a percentage of total population	Civil War allegiance of town[d]
Blackburn	233	1,048·5	3	13·5	1·2	Parliamentarian
Bolton	353	1,588·5	3	13·5	0·8	Ditto
Bury	343	1,543·5	3	13·5	0·8	Ditto ?
Lancaster	211	949·5	6	27·0	2·8	Parliamentarian
Liverpool	286	1,287·0	3	13·5	1·0	Ditto
Manchester	820	3,690·0	27	121·5	3·2	Ditto
Preston	410	1,845·0	27	121·5	6·5	Royalist
Salford	248	1,116·0	8	36·0	3·2	Ditto
Warrington	398	1,791·0	2	9·0	0·5	Parliamentarian ?
Wigan	458	2,061·0	11	49·5	2·2	Royalist

a A town is defined as any place with over 1,000 inhabitants. Cf. L. Stone in *Past and Present*, No. 28 (1964), 59. Although not quite satisfying this criterion, Lancaster has been included in the table in view of its status as a county town.
b These are taken from the Hearth Tax Assessment, Ladyday 1664 (P.R.O., E179/250/11).
c These are the numbers in 1642.
d For details and documentation see Blackwood, B.Litt. thesis, 11–32.

Fig. 2. The hundreds and towns of Lancashire in 1642.

which had 'an abundance of gentry in it',[68] was loyal to Charles I,
'the Townes men' being 'generally disaffected to the Parliament'.[69]
But Bolton, which had hardly any gentry families, was called 'The
Geneva of Lancashire'[70] and was sacked by Prince Rupert.[71]

The number of urban gentry in Lancashire should not be exaggerated. In 1642 only 93 (12·0 per cent) out of a total of 774 families
were town dwellers. This is similar to the situation in Yorkshire, where
70 (10·3 per cent) out of 679 gentry families were urban.[72] In Lancashire, as in Yorkshire, many urban gentry had close links with the
land.[73] Several, like the Haworths and Worthingtons of Manchester
and the Morts of Preston, stemmed from local landed families,[74]
although others, like the Marklands of Wigan, were from families long
settled in the towns.[75] Many urban gentry were also landed gentry.
In the 1641 lay subsidy rolls 46 urban gentlemen were assessed on
the value of their lands and only 22 on the value of their goods.[76]
The landed possessions of the urban gentry were generally modest[77]
and lay in or near the towns. Nevertheless, the mere ownership of
land had considerable social importance. It distinguished most urban
gentry from their fellow townsmen and linked them with the country
gentry to form Lancashire's ruling class.

3 STATUS AND POWER

During the seventeenth century the main division in lay society was
between gentlemen and plebeians. But the gentry also had their own
internal stratification. From 1611, when the order of baronetcy was
created, they embraced four distinct social categories: baronets,
knights, esquires and plain gentlemen. Table 3 shows the basic

TABLE 3

THE STATUS OF HEADS OF LANCASHIRE
GENTRY FAMILIES, 1642[a]

Baronets	7 (0·9%
Knights	6 (0·8%)[b]
Esquires	140 (18·1%)
Gentlemen	621 (80·2%)
Total	774 (100·0%)

a For sources see below, p. 30 n. 35–40.
b This figure excludes Sir Gilbert Gerard of Halsall, a younger son.

structure of the Lancashire gentry in 1642. It would seem that only
one-fifth of the Lancashire gentry were 'county' or greater gentry—

baronets, knights and esquires—and that four-fifths were 'parochial' or lesser gentry: plain gentlemen.[78]

A major distinction between the greater gentry and the lesser gentry was that many of the former exercised considerable power within the shire, while most of the latter did not. To be sure, the lesser gentry usually supplied the high constables of hundreds and the grand juries at quarter sessions. But the real governors of Caroline Lancashire, those who bore the main responsibility for executing the king's commands, were drawn almost entirely from the ranks of the greater gentry. Between 1625 and 1642 all justices of the peace (80),[79] deputy lieutenants (14), sheriffs (17) and militia officers (29) were chosen from the greater Lancashire gentry, and so were all but seven of the 63 men who served as commissioners for sewers, lay subsidies and knighthood compositions.[80] The key figures in local government during the seventeenth century were the justices of the peace. They not only dealt with criminal offences, both individually and collectively, at petty and quarter sessions, but also had a wide range of administrative duties, including the binding of poor children as apprentices, the relief of the aged and impotent poor, the regulation of the corn supplies and the fixing of wages. Most of the 80 Lancashire magistrates who served at some time or other between 1625 and 1642 were apparently active men, and only 22 seldom appeared at quarter sessions.[81] If we include both the active and the passive justices, it would seem that 67 (43 per cent) of the 153 greater gentry families supplied Lancashire with magistrates between 1625 and 1642. Thus while all magistrates were greater gentry, not all the greater gentry were magistrates. Why were so many important Lancashire families excluded from the Bench? In some cases it may have been because the families were headed by minors, who were too young to serve. But in a majority of cases there would seem to have been a religious explanation. During our period Roman Catholics were legally disqualified from royal service.[82] It is therefore significant that 54 (63 per cent) of the 86 non-magisterial families were Papist, as compared with only six (9 per cent), or possibly ten (15 per cent), of the 67 magisterial families.[83] The law was no respecter of persons. Thus some Catholics excluded from the Bench were men of great social prestige, like Thomas Clifton of Lytham, Esquire, and Thomas Tyldesley of Myerscough, Esquire, perhaps the two most important men in Amounderness. Clearly there was no exact correlation between status and power in Lancashire on the eve of the Civil War.

4 THE INCOMES OF THE GENTRY

In wealth, as in status and power, the Lancashire gentry were far from being a homogeneous group. Basing our assessments of annual landed income mainly on the lay subsidy rolls, but also occasionally

on other sources, such as the Duchy of Lancaster Pleadings, the feodaries' certificates of the Court of Wards, the papers of the Committee
for Compounding and family muniments,[84] it would seem that the
wealth of the Lancashire gentry in 1642 was distributed as in Table
4. Although we are ignorant of the landed incomes of 37 per cent

TABLE 4

THE INCOMES OF THE LANCASHIRE GENTRY, 1642[a]

Annual income from land in 1642 £	Number of families within each income bracket
3,000 and over	2
2,000–2,999	6
1,000–1,999	16
750–999	8
500–749	24
250–499	57
100–249	168
Under 100	204
Unknown	289
Total	774

a Where there is more than one estimate of income for an individual gentleman, the highest has been chosen.

TABLE 5

THE INCOMES OF THE LANCASHIRE AND YORKSHIRE GENTRY, 1642

Annual income from land in 1642 (£)	Lancashire gentry families	Yorkshire gentry families[b]
1,000 and over	24 (3·1%)	73 (10·8%)
250–999	89 (11·5%)	244 (35·9%)
Under 250	372 (48·1%)	362 (53·3%)
Unknown	289 (37·3%)[a]	–
Total	774 (100·0%)	679 (100·0%)

a Since only 11 of these 289 families belonged to the esquire class and the rest were
mostly obscure gentlemen, it is likely that in Lancashire the percentage of poor gentry
(under £250 p.a.) was considerably higher than that suggested in this table.
b Cliffe, 29.

of the Lancashire gentry,[85] the table suggests that it is extremely difficult to speak of them as a single class. An enormous gap separated
the richest from the poorest gentleman in Lancashire. Apart from the
three peers,[86] the wealthiest person in Lancashire seems to have been
Sir Robert Bindloss of Borwick, Baronet. With an annual income of
£3,240,[87] he could have had little in common with a humble gentleman
like Rowland Beckingham of Hornby, worth only £8 a year.[88]

The Lancashire gentry were not only economically heterogeneous;
they also seem to have been poor by comparison with other northern
gentry. Table 5 shows that there were far fewer rich and middling
gentry in Lancashire than in Yorkshire. The very small percentage
of rich gentry in Lancashire is particularly striking. Even in the
remote Lake Counties over 4 per cent of the gentry had annual incomes of over £1,000, while the proportion of very poor gentlemen
(under £100 p.a.) was not as high as in Lancashire.[89]

The poverty among the Lancashire gentry becomes even more
pronounced if we include younger sons in our survey.[90] Although our
knowledge of the economic state of younger sons is very limited,
enough evidence exists to suggest that it was, in most cases, unenvi-
able. Since the custom of primogeniture endowed the eldest son with
all or most of the family estate, most younger sons during our period
had to be content with either a small life estate or, more commonly,
an annuity. Table 6 shows that most of these annuities were trifling
sums.

TABLE 6

ANNUITIES OF SOME YOUNGER SONS[a]

Annuities (£)	No. of younger sons
50 and over	5
40–49	5
30–39	4
20–29	18
10–19	8
Under 10	14
Total	54

a Main sources are *Roy. Comp. Papers*, i–vi, pt. ii; G. J. Piccope, ed., *Lancs. & Cheshire Wills*, Chet. Soc., O.S. Vols. 51, 54 (1860–61); J. P. Earwaker, ed., ibid., Chet. Soc., N.S., Vols. 3, 28 (1884, 1893); P.R.O., PROB 11; and wills among the probate records and family archives in the L.R.O.

5 LAND OWNING, FARMING AND INDUSTRY

From where did the Lancashire gentry derive their incomes on the eve of the Civil War? In most cases it was from the land, or, more specifically, from rents, entry fines, tithes, demesne farming and minerals. For many of the gentry rent was by far the most important source of income. The total annual landed income of John Calvert of Cockerham was £913 5s. 3d., of which £850 6s. 3d. came from the rents of his 111 tenants.[91] Thomas Nelson of Fairhurst had lands worth £195 17s. 2d. per annum, £146 6s. 0d. consisting of rent.[92]

It was usually difficult for landlords to raise rents, for they were generally fixed by manorial custom or by the terms of long leases. Hence many landlords tried to augment their revenue by levying high entry fines when granting or renewing leases. In south-west Lancashire and the Fylde the tenants held long leases for three lives or 99 years, paying low annual rents. However, Table 7 shows that very heavy entry fines were charged in return. It will be noted that some of the families shown above levied much higher fines than others. Moreover, these exactions varied considerably from one year to another and from one holding to another, even when imposed by the same landlord. Nevertheless, the average fine seems to have been almost 35 times the annual rent.

TABLE 7

FINES EXACTED BY SOME LANCASHIRE GENTRY FAMILIES, 1600–42[a]

Lessor	No. of leases	Total rents £ s. d.	Total fines £ s. d.	Average fine as multiple of rent
Blundell of Crosby	14	7 19 3	312 0 0	39·1
Chorley of Chorley	20	11 9 2	514 0 0	44·8
Clifton of Lytham	32	16 2 10	615 19 10	38·1
Hesketh of Rufford	74	41 3 11	1,135 4 4	27·5
Scarisbrick of Scarisbrick	25	14 17 4	622 16 8	41·8
Totals	165	91 12 6	3,200 0 10	34·9

a See leases among family muniments in L.R.O. For those of the Chorley family see R. D. Radcliffe, ed., 'The Chorley Survey', *Miscellanies*, III, L. & C. Rec. Soc., Vol. 33 (1896), 11–49.

Although imposing heavy entry fines, landlords in south Lancashire and the Fylde do not seem to have been unduly harsh towards their tenants during the early seventeenth century. On the contrary, several appear to have been kindly, considerate landlords. William Blundell of Crosby, a Catholic Royalist in the Civil War, seems to have exacted higher fines from old tenants than from strangers.[93] The younger Sir Ralph Assheton of Whalley ordered his steward to abate the rents of those tenants who had suffered in the year 1648.[94] The younger John Atherton of Atherton was in a general way 'very respectful' to his tenants and 'by them highly honoured and reverenced'.[95] However, landlords such as these seem to have been rare in Lonsdale hundred. There some of the Royalist and Catholic gentry were imposing excessive 'gressoms' or fines, reinforcing their claims to labour services and other servile dues, and refusing to recognise the tenant's right of inheritance.[96] Sir George Middleton of Leighton told his Yealand tenants that they were merely 'tenants at will without any obliging Custome', and demanded entry fines of up to thirty years' rent. His tenants argued that he was not entitled to receive fines of more than four years ancient rent. Middleton seems also to have strongly insisted upon the payment of food rents and the performance of boon works or labour services. Another Lonsdale landlord who endeavoured to enforce antiquated labour services was John Brockholes of Lancaster. His tenants accused him of forcing them to take leases for lives involving 'most unreasonable services by plowing, harrowing, shearing, mowing and other psonall and slavish burthens (which they had never before answered)'.[97] It was not only the Lonsdale gentry, however, who demanded food rents and labour services. Landlords in south-west Lancashire and the Fylde generally insisted upon them when granting leases,[98] for such boons and services offered them a certain protection against inflation.

Some of the Lancashire gentry had other sources of income besides entry fines, money rents and food rents. At least 66 families derived some of their wealth from spiritual sources.[99] As impropriators of Church lands they were entitled to receive income from glebe lands, Easter offerings and tithes. The Tyldesleys of Myerscough had an annual income of £1,505 in 1654, of which £648 came from tithes.[100] Sometimes lay impropriators profited at the expense of the clergy. Richard Urmston was in 1636 lay rector and tithe farmer of Leigh and as such drew an income of £636 a year. By contrast the vicar got a mere £18 1s. 4d. per annum, plus a house valued at another £10.[101]

A far more important source of income than tithes was demesne farming. Indeed, for a large number of gentlemen, especially of the humbler sort, farming profits formed the major part of their income. The total annual income of John Hoghton of Park Hall was £77, of which £60 came from lands belonging to the home farm.[102] Edward Butler of Rawcliffe, a younger son, had an annual income of £54, of which £38 came from his demesne.[103]

Another major source of income for some of the Lancashire gentry was coal mining. This was, of course, far less important to the gentry in Lancashire than to their brethren in the Durham region.[104] At a conservative estimate 43 (5 per cent) of our 774 gentry families had coal-mining interests during the early seventeenth century.[105] However, a minority of these 43 families seem to have derived a considerable proportion of their income from coal mining. Thomas Charnock of Astley had a colliery at Bradford, near Manchester, which a private survey of 1662 valued at £150.[106] This was exactly half his 1641 income.[107] Abraham Langton of Lowe may have obtained as much as two-thirds of his income from coal mining in 1641.[108] But if the profits of coal mining were sometimes great, so also were the losses. During the early seventeenth century coal mining was a highly risky and speculative activity and, as in Nottinghamshire and Durham,[109] some Lancashire gentlemen suffered serious financial losses. This was because they sometimes engaged in projects which they could ill afford. John Braddyll of Portfield was outlawed for debt in 1633,[110] and one reason may have been that during the previous eleven years he had 'made divers shafts and colepitts' and had 'bestowed £300 or thereabouts for the making of a Sough'.[111] Thomas Charnock apparently invested several hundreds of pounds in his Bradford colliery under James I.[112] This may partly explain his heavy debts and land sales under Charles I.[113] The Gerards of Ince were even greater gamblers and adventurers, for they apparently invested £3,000 in their cannel mine at Aspull.[114] Such heavy expenditure may possibly explain why their debts were between £1,244 and £2,000.[115] These were heavy burdens for a family whose annual income was probably only about £250 in 1641.[116] Thus it would seem that for the Lancashire gentry coal mining was a highly precarious source of wealth.

6 THE PURSUIT OF A CAREER

How many elder and younger sons of the Lancashire gentry derived income from non-agricultural sources other than coal mining? The answer would be 'very few'. Despite the small landed incomes of many elder sons and the landlessness of many younger sons, few Lancashire gentlemen alive in 1642 had apparently pursued careers. Details are as in Table 8.

The careers that offered the best prospects during the early seventeenth century were the law, office-holding and trade. Several Lancashire gentlemen lawyers prospered. Among them was Robert Blundell of Ince Blundell. A bencher of Gray's Inn in 1618,[117] Blundell invested at least £5,400 in land between 1619 and 1632.[118] Although it cannot be *proved* that Blundell's purchases were the result of his legal activities, it is hard to think of any other explanation. Another prosperous gentleman lawyer was Alexander Rigby of Goosnargh, who had 'a Chamber, in Graies Inne, in Holobourne' in 1642.[119] Although possessed of a good estate,[120] he reckoned in 1646 that 'my profession [was] form'lie as profitable to mee annuallie as my estate'.[121] Another

TABLE 8

CAREERS OF THE LANCASHIRE GENTRY[a]

	First sons	Younger sons
Total number of gentry in 1642	774	1,000 (at least)
Total number of gentry in 1642 who were or had been		
(a) Doctors		
(i) Apothecary	–	1 (0·1%)
(ii) Physicians	3 (0·4%)	4 (0·4%)
(b) Clergymen		
(i) Catholic	–	54 (5·4%)
(ii) Protestant	4 (0·5%)	12 (1·2%)
(c) Mercenary soldiers	2 (0·3%)	1 (0·1%)
(d) Lawyers		
(i) Counsellors at law, recorders, attorneys	15 (1·9%)	7 (0·7%)
(ii) Crown lawyers	4 (0·5%)	7 (0·7%)
(e) Holders of offices of profit		
(i) Public officials	21 (2·7%)	4 (0·4%)
(ii) Officials of nobility	4 (0·5%)	1 (0·1%)
(f) Merchants or traders	34 (4·4%)	15 (1·5%)
Total	87 (11·2%)	106 (10·6%)

a The figures given here supersede those in Blackwood, 'Economic State', 68. Information about doctors and mercenary soldiers from miscellaneous sources. Catholic clergy from G. Anstruther, The Seminary Priests (Great Wakering, 1975), vol. ii; Rec S.J., i–vii; H. N. Birt, Obit Book of the English Benedictines, 1600–1912 (Edinburgh, 1913); G. Dolan, 'Lancashire and the Benedictines', Trans. Hist. Soc., L. & C., Vol. 49 (1897), 123–30; R. Trappes-Lomax, ed., Franciscana, C.R.S., Vol. 24 (1923); J. Gillow, Bibliographical Dictionary of English Catholics, 5 vols. (1885–1903). Protestant clergy from parish clergy lists in V.C.H., iii–viii; list of curates and lecturers in D. Lambert, 'The Lower Clergy in the Anglican Church in Lancashire, 1558–1642', Liverpool Univ. M.A. thesis, 1964, Appendix II; A. G. Matthews, ed., Walker Revised (Oxford, 1948), 228–31; E. Calamy, Nonconformists' Memorial, ed. S. Palmer (1775), ii, 79–111. Lawyers from R. Somerville, Office-Holders in the Duchy and County Palatine of Lancaster from 1603 (Chichester, 1972); B. L., Harl. MS. 1912, fos. 181–3, 200–26, 247–8 and miscellaneous sources. Office holders from Somerville, op. cit., P.R.O., Docquet Books, Indexes 6601–11; P.R.O., Duchy of Lancaster Index to Patents, 1558–1760, fos. 138–67. Merchants from family and parish histories; W. A. Abram, ed., Preston Guild Rolls, 1397–1682, L. & C. Rec. Soc., Vol. 9 (1884); R. J. A. Shelley, 'Wigan and Liverpool Pewterers', Trans. Hist. Soc. L. & C., Vol. 97 (1945), 21–6; P.R.O., E190/1336/11 (Liverpool 1640–41); DL1/302–72; PL6/8–16; Guild. Lib., Guildhall MS. 5576/1; 11593/1; and miscellaneous sources.

wealthy lawyer was his younger brother George. In 1627 George Rigby became Clerk of the Peace and in 1634 rebuilt Peel Hall.[122] This may have been possible because the clerkship of the peace was reckoned to be worth £200 per annum to its holder.[123] The law seems to have been more prosperous than office-holding. This was partly because so few Lancashire office-holders in 1642 held or had held posts in the central government.[124] Most Lancashire public servants held local offices such as feodary, escheator, bailiff, master forester and local receiver of the Duchy of Lancaster. These local officials, like the bureaucrats in London, held offices of profit and are therefore to be distinguished from unpaid officials like the justice of the peace, the deputy lieutenant, the sewers commissioner and others associated with county government. Yet in practice the financial differences between paid and unpaid officials were not great. Most local offices of profit were really part-time posts and, apart from local receiverships, 'could only offer a supporting income with opportunities for incidental profit'.[125] Indeed, apart from legal officers, only two local officials alive in 1642—Thomas Preston of Holker and Robert Curwen of Cark—could be said to have enriched themselves.[126] On the whole, local office-holding seems to have been more prestigious than profitable for the Lancashire gentry.[127] This may also have been true of private office-holding. The Faringtons of Worden, the Greenhalghes of Brandlesome and the Tyldesleys of Myerscough served the Earls of Derby as councillors, household officers and captains of the Isle of Man.[128] But it is hard to say whether they enriched themselves in these posts.

For the Lancashire gentry trade seems to have been more profitable than office-holding. The most successful gentleman merchant of Caroline Lancashire was undoubtedly Humphrey Chetham, the clothier and money-lender, who between 1620 and 1628 invested £9,800 in land.[129] Others who greatly enriched themselves included Francis Sherrington of Boothes, an importer of French wine, and John Hartley, a Manchester draper. Both invested heavily in real estate, the former spending £5,450 and the latter £3,423.[130] Chetham, Sherrington and Hartley were not the only successful gentlemen merchants, and at least seven others bought considerable land under Charles I. However, let us not exaggerate the success or affluence of the Lancashire mercantile gentry. The vast majority purchased little or no land and most were only modest provincial traders. Few engaged in overseas commerce or became London merchants.

7 THE RISING AND DECLINING GENTRY

So far we have studied the wealth of the Lancashire gentry. We must now consider their economic health, in other words whether they were rising or declining during the early seventeenth century. Professor Lawrence Stone has recently argued that 'both relatively and absolutely there was an impressive rise of the gentry as a status group in terms of numbers and wealth'.[131] Were the Lancashire gentry also rising in terms of numbers and wealth? They do not seem to have been. Lancashire had 763 gentry families in 1600 and 774 in 1642.[132] In terms of absolute numbers the Lancashire gentry rose very slightly. But since the population of Lancashire seems to have increased from just over 100,000 in 1600 to about 150,000 in 1642,[133] the gentry *relatively* declined.

In wealth the Lancashire gentry also seem to have slightly declined during the early seventeenth century, though this was more in terms of property transactions than of income. In terms of average and median incomes the Lancashire gentry appear to have remained almost stationary, to judge by the lay subsidy rolls. In 1593, 520 gentry families apparently had an aggregate income of £110,418, an average income of £212 and a median income of £100.[134] In 1641, 438 gentry families had an aggregate income of £91,397, an average of £208 and a median income of £100.[135] Property transactions give slightly more evidence of a declining Lancashire gentry. Between 1600 and 1642 74 gentry families considerably added to their estates,[136] purchasing 42 manors and 157 non-manors for a total of £93,881 5s. 3d.[137] But during the same period another 74 families alienated a large amount of their land,[138] selling 45 manors and 130 non-manors for the high total of £116,824 10s. 0d.[139] Thus in terms of the value, though not the number, of the properties conveyed, the Lancashire gentry apparently lost more than they gained.

Let us now turn our attention to the rising and declining families among the Lancashire gentry. There are three main groups of families to consider briefly: those who entered the gentry, those who left the gentry and those who remained gentry throughout the period from 1600 to 1642. The third group—the *socially* perdurable gentry—comprised 485 families. Only small numbers of these experienced upward or downward *economic* mobility during the early Stuart period. Table 9 gives details. It will be seen that the 'rising gentry' those whose total outlay on property between 1600 and 1642 was at least three times their gross annual landed income—formed under 10 per cent of the 485 families.[140] This is hardly surprising. The Lancashire gentry

TABLE 9

FAMILIES RISING AND DECLINING WITH THE LANCASHIRE GENTRY,
1600-42

(a) Total number of families who were gentry in both 1600 and 1642	485
(b) Families buying considerable property, 1600-42[a]	48 (9·9%)
(c) Families selling considerable property, 1600-42[a]	34 (7·0%)
(b) Families heavily in debt, 1600-42,[b] but avoiding heavy sales	35 (7·2%)

a For sources see below, p. 34 n. 139.

b Apart from family papers, particulars of loans in the pre-Civil War period are to be found in P.R.O., C54 (Recognisances); C193/41; LC4/196–202. In calculating the numbers of indebted gentry, cancelled statutes in the last named source have been ignored, and so have uncancelled bonds unless they are followed by the words '*cert. in canc.*'. Apart from these sources much evidence about the indebtedness of the gentry can be found in P.R.O., DL1; PL6; SP23; Wards 5.

were mostly poor and had little surplus wealth to invest in real estate. Of the tiny minority of families who did rise *within* the gentry, most were 'mere' gentry depending entirely on agriculture for their livelihood. Only 19 (40 per cent) of the 48 rising gentry were merchants, lawyers or office-holders. Nevertheless, it was these who bought the most extensively. Indeed, every Lancashire gentry family spending £5,000 or more on land under the early Stuarts belonged to the mercantile–legal–bureaucratic gentry. These families included lawyers, like the Blundells of Ince Blundell, office-holders, like the Mosleys of Hough, and merchants like the Chethams and the Sherringtons.[141]

Let us now consider those who declined *within* the gentry. I have classed the following as economically declining gentry: those whose total, unpaid, private debts at any time between 1600 and 1642 were at least three times their gross annual landed income;[142] and those who lost their patrimonial estates and/or whose total receipts from property sales between 1600 and 1642 were at least three times their gross annual landed income.[143] On the basis of these criteria it would seem that only 69 (14·2 per cent) of the 485 Lancashire families 'declined' between 1600 and 1642.

Why did so few families decline? It is extremely difficult to say, and only the most tentative suggestions can be made. One reason may have been that in Lancashire, as in Yorkshire, general taxation was fairly light.[144] Some knighthood fines were certainly heavy, but other taxes, such as subsidies, forced loans and ship money, seem to have had little adverse effect on the Lancashire gentry, to judge by their lack of opposition to them under Charles I.[145] Secondly, discriminatory taxes, such as recusancy and wardship payments, do not seem to have been very onerous. Between 1625 and 1648 only 22 (10 per cent) out of at least 220 Catholic gentry families appear to have paid recusancy fines, and just two of these—the Towneleys of Towneley and the Middletons of Leighton—were heavily mulcted. Between 1629 and 1641, 106 Catholic gentry paid composition rents but only 19 of these paid heavily. Of the 19, just four were adversely affected.[146] Moreover, compared with other northern gentry, a very small proportion of the Lancashire gentry seem to have suffered from the exactions of the Court of Wards.[147] Between 1600 and 1642 only 161 out of a total of 1,052 families had first hand experience of the system of wardship.[148] Of these 161 families, only 30 were severely mulcted, and among the latter a mere two—Thornborough of Hampsfield and Nowell of Read—appear to have been ruined.[149] But perhaps the main reason for the economic health of most of the Lancashire gentry was their thrift. Writing shortly before 1600, William Camden contrasted the 'provident moderation' and 'simplicity' of the Lancashire and other northern gentry with the 'riotous expense and superfluity' which had quickly ruined so many southern families.[150] Of course, spendthrift gentlemen were by no means unknown in early Stuart

Lancashire. The father of John Penketh of Penketh apparently 'squandered all his property and left little at his death'.[151] Sir Edward Tarbock of Tarbock is supposed to have lost his lands to Lady Molyneux by a throw of the dice.[152] The Towneleys of Towneleys had enormous debts of £6,396 in 1642, probably caused by their extensive building activities in 1628.[153] But Penketh, Tarbock and Towneley were fairly exceptional, and the overwhelming majority of Lancashire gentry seem to have avoided extravagance.

If the Lancashire gentry were so thrifty, why did as many as 278 families lose their gentility between 1600 and 1642?[154] It is very hard to say. Thirty-five of these families sold out and were obviously in economic difficulties.[155] However, there is little sign that any of the other 243 families were financially ruined. At least 20 of these failed in the male line.[156] About a dozen left the county, and not because of economic difficulties. The social eclipse of the remaining 211 families is hard to explain, but it would seem that many of them lacked the wealth to sustain their gentility. In short, poverty rather than insolvency was perhaps the main reason for the disappearance of so many Lancashire gentry families.[157]

There was considerable upward as well as downward social mobility in early Stuart Lancashire, despite an apparently inactive land market. Not only did 278 families leave the gentry between 1600 and 1642, but 210 families acquired gentle status for the first time, and another 79 may also have done during those years.[158] Only 25 of these 289 families can be shown to have bought their way into the gentry,[159] and it is difficult to account for the rise of the other 264 families. But since only 52 of the new families were town dwellers, it seems reasonable to assume that most of them may have risen on the profits of yeoman farming.[160]

8 THE ANTIQUITY OF THE GENTRY

Despite the rise of many new families under the early Stuarts, the majority of the Lancashire gentry in 1642 were not *parvenus*. A quarter of the 774 Lancashire families had risen to gentility under the Tudors and 36 per cent were of mediaeval gentle stock. In Yorkshire 39 per cent of the gentry were of mediaeval origins.[161] The gentry of Lancashire and Yorkshire were not as ancient as those of Kent. In that southern county between 80 and 90 per cent of the gentry as a whole, including virtually all the 'county' families, were reckoned gentle well before the Tudor period. Moreover, in Kent the number of new families was abnormally small.[162] Clearly the situation in Lancashire was markedly different from that in Kent. Nevertheless, if we concentrate on the greater Lancashire gentry (baronets, knights and esquires) and ignore the lesser gentry (plain gentlemen), we find that the palatinate did resemble Kent. Table 10 shows that the greater

TABLE 10

LINEAGE OF THE LANCASHIRE GENTRY[a]

Gentry origins	All gentry families	Greater gentry families
Middle Ages	281 (36·3%)	110 (71·9%)
Tudor period	204 (26·4%)	25 (16·3%)
Stuart period	210 (27·1%)	7 (4·6%)
Uncertain	79 (10·2%)	11 (7·2%)
Total	774 (100·0%)	153 (100·0%)

a Main sources for the Stuart gentry are given at p. 30 n. 36–40. For families of mediaeval and Tudor gentle stock see especially the following: V.C.H., iii–viii; W. D. Pink and A. B. Beavan, *The Parliamentary Representation of Lancashire, 1258–1885* (1889); H. Hornyold-Strickland, *Members of Parliament of Lancashire, 1290–1550*, Chet. Soc., N.S., Vol. 93 (1935); J. S. Roskell, *The Knights of the Shire of the County Palatine of Lancaster 1377–1460*, Chet. Soc., N.S., Vol. 96 (1937); R. Hollingworth, *Mancuniensis*, ed. W. Willis (Manchester, 1839), 39–40; Wm. Camden, *Britain* (trans. Philemon Holland, 1637) 790; P.R.O., *List of Sheriffs*, ix, 72–3; J. Brierley Watson, 'The Lancashire Gentry and Public Service, 1529–1558', Trans. L. & C. Antiq. Soc., Vol. 73–74 (1963–64), 56–8; R. Somerville, 'The Lancashire Justices of the Peace in the fifteenth and sixteenth centuries', Trans. Hist. Soc., L. & C. Vol. 102 (1950), 183–9; P.R.O., SP12/104/63; DL42/96, f. 209; B. L. Lansdowne MS. 1228: Commission of the Peace, 1561; Royal MS. 18.D.iii: Lancashire Justices of the Peace, c. 1592; L.R.O., QSC 1 (1598), 2 (1602); J. P. Rylands, 'Two Lancashire rolls of arms, temp. Edward III and Henry VIII', Trans. Hist. Soc. L. & C., Vol. 37 (1885), 149–60; The musters of soldiers in the county of Lancaster 1574, in M. Gregson, *Portfolio of Fragments* (1869), 26–31; The names of all the gentlemen of the best calling in the county of Lancaster, 1588, *Chetham Miscellanies*, III, ed. W. Langton, Chet. Soc., O.S., Vol. 57, 1862, 5–9; List of the Freeholders in Lancashire in 1600, in Earwaker, ed., *Miscellanies*, I, 229–51.

gentry—comprising 153 families—were largely of mediaeval gentle stock.

The greater gentry in Lancashire were not quite as deeply rooted as those in Cheshire, where all but 16 out of 106 leading families were established before the Reformation.[163] Yet some of the greater Lancashire gentry were very ancient indeed. The Osbaldestons of Osbaldeston, the Towneleys of Towneley and the Traffords of Trafford could reasonably claim pre-Norman ancestry.[164] More typical, however, were those families which had emerged as gentry in the high Middle Ages. Many of these took their name from the land they held. William Camden singled out 'Aston of Aston,[165] Atherton of Atherton, Tildesley of Tildesley, Standish of Standish, Bold of Bold, Hesketh of Hesketh, Worthington of Worthington and Tarbock of Tarbock'.[166]

Length of residence as well as length of gentility characterised the greater gentry of Lancashire. Table 11 shows that the vast majority of county families had been settled in the palatinate since mediaeval times and that a mere handful had taken up residence since the accession of James I.[167] The greater gentry of Lancashire were slightly more deeply rooted than those of Cheshire, Kent and Sussex and consider-

TABLE 11

THE INDIGENOUSNESS OF THE GREATER LANCASHIRE GENTRY[a]

Settled in the county	Nos. of greater gentry families in 1642
Pre-1485	124 (81·0%)
Post-1485	20 (13·1%)
Post-1603	6 (3·9%)
Unknown	3 (2·0%)
Total	153 (100·0%)

a Sources as p. 22 n.

ably more so than the leading gentry of the eastern counties. Table 12 gives details. Professor Everitt has suggested that gentry families who had been settled in their counties for centuries tended to be more locally than nationally minded.[168] Indeed, local feelings and local loyalties were likely to be strong among all groups in an age when transport facilities and communications were poor and when a journey from Manchester to London might take anything up to a week. Moreover, an insular outlook must have been strengthened by local education and local marriages.

TABLE 12

INDIGENOUSNESS OF GREATER GENTRY IN VARIOUS COUNTIES, 1642

			The percentage of those whose families had settled in the county in question		
Ref.[a]	Gentry of:	No. in group	before 1485	1485–1603	after 1603
a	Lancashire	153	81·0	13·1	3·9 (or 5·9?)
b	Cheshire	106	80·2	9·4	10·4
c	Kent	170	75·0	12·5	12·5
d	Sussex	44	77·3	27·7	−
e	Essex	59	15·2	50·9	33·9
	Hertfordshire	40	10·0	47·5	42·5
	Norfolk	59	42·4	44·1	13·5
	Suffolk	59	30·5	50·9	18·6

a References are: (a) as above, p. 22 n.; (b) Morrill, *Cheshire*, 3; (c) Everitt, *Kent*, 36; (d) Fletcher, 25; (e) Holmes, 231.

Note. For Cheshire the relevant dates are: before 1500, after 1500 and since 1600.

9 THE EDUCATION OF THE GENTRY

Let us first briefly examine the kinds of education received by the
Lancashire gentry. These and other English gentry lived in an age
of 'educational revolution'. Between 1560 and 1640 many grammar
and other schools were founded, while higher education greatly
expanded as large numbers of gentry and other social groups flocked
to the universities and the inns of court.[169] Unfortunately very little
indeed is known about the school education of the Lancashire
gentry.[170] Of the Catholic gentry alive in 1642, at least 17, and probably considerably more, were educated at St Omer, the leading Catholic 'preparatory' school on the continent.[171] But how many sons of
the Catholic gentry were educated at schools inside Lancashire it is
impossible to say. Of the Lancashire Protestant gentry alive in 1642,
only 13 are known to have attended schools outside the county.[172]
Indeed, the vast majority of the Protestant gentry must have been

TABLE 13

THE HIGHER EDUCATION OF THE LANCASHIRE GENTRY[a]

	First sons	Younger sons
(a) Total number of gentry in 1642	774	1,000 (at least)
(b) Attending university only	46 (5·9%)	21 (2·1%)
(c) Attending inn of court only	38 (4·9%)	9 (0·9%)
(d) Attending university and		
inn of court	31 (4·0%)	15 (1·5%)
(e) Attending Catholic seminary	3 (0·4%)	34 (3·4%)
(f) Attending Catholic seminary,		
university and inn of court	–	1 (0·1%)
Total	118 (15·2%)[b]	80 (8·0%)

a Sources: Bod. Lib., Oxford Univ. Archives, Matriculation Register PP, 1615–47; A. Clark,
ed., *Register of the Univ. of Oxford*, Oxford Hist. Soc., Vol. 11 (1887); *Al. Oxon.*; *Brasenose College
Register, 1509–1909*, Oxford Hist. Soc., Vol. 55 (1910); C. L. Shadwell, ed., *Registrum Orielense* (1893),
vol. i; *Al. Cant.*; J. Peile, ed., *Biographical Register of Christ's College* (Cambridge, 1910), vol. i; T. A.
Walker, ed., *Biographical Register of Peterhouse Men* (Cambridge, 1930), vol. ii; J. E. Mayor, ed.,
Admissions to the College of St. John the Evangelist (Cambridge, 1882), vol. i; W. W. Rouse Ball and
J. A. Venn, eds., *Admissions to Trinity College, Cambridge* (1913), vol. ii; Gonville and Caius College,
Cambridge, MS. 'Liber Matriculationis', 1560–1678; Sidney Sussex College, Cambridge, MS.
Register, vol. i (1598–1706); E. Peacock, *Index . . . Leyden University* (1883); *Gl. Adm. Reg.*; *Ll. Adm.
Reg.*; *MT. Adm. Reg.*; IT. Adm. Reg.; E. H. Burton and T. L. Williams, eds., *Douay College Diaries*,
C.R.S., Vol. 10 (1911); E. Henson, ed., *Registers of the English College at Valladolid, 1589–1862*, C.R.S.,
Vol. 30 (1930); A. Kenny, ed., *Responsa Scholarum*, 2 vols., C.R.S., Vols. 54, 55 (1962–63); W.
Croft, *Historical Account of Lisbon College* (1902).

b The Lancashire gentry were apparently worse educated than other northern gentry. In 1642
36 per cent of heads of Yorkshire families and 20 per cent of heads of Cumberland and Westmorland
families had received higher education. In 1615 20 per cent of eldest sons of Northumberland gentry
families had had an advanced education (Cliffe, 73; C. B. Phillips, 'The Gentry in Cumberland
and Westmorland, 1600–1665', Lancaster Univ. Ph.D. thesis, 1974, 10, 158; Watts, 91).

educated locally, for by 1640 Lancashire contained 113 schools, including 64 grammar schools.[173]

Far more is known about the higher than the secondary education
of the Lancashire gentry. But Table 13 shows that only a very small
number of Lancashire gentry alive in 1642 had left the palatinate to
receive an advanced education. It will be observed that Lancashire
gentlemen attending Catholic seminaries, such as Douai, Valladolid
and the English College of Rome, were mainly younger sons. Most
of them subsequently became priests and so could be said to have
moved out of the gentry and joined a different social order. Of those
Lancashire gentlemen attending the universities and the inns of court,
a majority were eldest sons and most sought social *cachet* rather than
degrees or legal careers. Nevertheless, a substantial minority seem to
have taken their studies seriously. Forty-three (37 per cent) out of
114 university educated gentlemen obtained degrees[174] and 29 (31
per cent) of the 94 gentlemen law students later became barristers.[175]
Eighty-three of the 94 law students were educated at Gray's Inn.[176]
Among the 114 university educated gentry, 52 went to Cambridge
and 59 to Oxford.[177] Twenty-one of the Cambridge men chose St
John's College, perhaps because of its north-country associations.
Thirty-nine of the 59 Oxford men chose Brasenose, 'the Lancashire
college', probably because, in the words of one contemporary, it had
'many peculiar privileges in favour of Lancashire men'.[178] Brasenose
College in fact drew a high proportion of its undergraduates from
north-west England. It is indeed an open question whether the 39
Lancashire gentlemen attending Brasenose had their horizons broad-
ened by a university education, or whether the regional bias of the
college merely strengthened their local loyalties.[179]

10 THE MARRIAGES OF THE GENTRY

Any local patriotism among the Lancashire gentry should have been
considerably strengthened by their marriages.[180] For geographical
reasons perhaps, over 70 per cent of the brides of the Lancashire
gentry alive in 1642 came from the same county as their husbands.
John Blaeu's map of Lancashire shows that the county was almost
isolated by its natural boundaries—the sea, the river Mersey and the
Pennines—from the outside world. Thus it is not surprising that less
than 15 per cent of the marriages contracted by the Lancashire gentry
were with women from the four neighbouring counties of Cumberland, Westmorland, Yorkshire and Cheshire, and that about the same
percentage were with women from more distant regions. In a less
self-contained county like Dorset just under half the gentry married
within the shire.[181] Indeed, the Lancashire gentry seem to have been
more endogamous than most other gentry whose marriages are
known, as Table 14 shows.

TABLE 14

THE MARRIAGE CONNECTIONS OF GENTRY IN VARIOUS COUNTIES, *c.*
1642

Ref.[a]	Gentry of:	No. of marriages	Percentage of marriages within the home county
a	Lancashire	459	71·2
b	Cheshire	371	65·0
c	Cumberland and Westmorland	120	62.5
d	Dorset	280	49·3
e	Kent	170 ?	82·0
f	Essex	263	43·3
	Hertfordshire	123	37·4
	Norfolk	282	71·6
	Suffolk	329	69·0

[a] References are: (a) Blackwood, 'Marriages', 327; (b) Morrill, *Cheshire*, 4; (c) Phillips, thesis, 31; (d) J. P. Ferris, 'The Gentry of Dorset on the Eve of the Civil War', *Genealogists' Magazine*, xv, 1965, 108; (c) Everitt, *Kent*, 42–3, 328; (f) Holmes, 11–15, 229.

Note. Figures for Kent and the four eastern counties refer to esquires and gentlemen only and exclude baronets and knights. Figures for Cheshire refer to marriages contracted by the more important families.

The marriages of the Lancashire gentry were socially as well as geographically restricted. The social status of slightly over a quarter of the brides of the Lancashire gentry alive in 1642 is unknown to us, although we cannot rule out the possibility that many of these were of 'the middling sort' (i.e. daughters of yeomen or merchants). However, there is no positive evidence to show this and the general impression is that on the eve of the Civil War socially mixed marriages were rare. If we exclude those of unknown parental status, over 90 per cent of the wives of the Lancashire gentry were themselves of gentle stock.[182] The narrow social range of their marriages would suggest that the Lancashire gentry were extremely status conscious on the eve of the Civil War.

II THE LOYALTIES AND RELIGION OF THE GENTRY

With their socially and geographically restricted marriages, not to mention their mainly local education,[183] one might expect the Lancashire gentry to have had a strong sense of provincial loyalty and of social solidarity. Especially would one expect to find a sense of county community, of local patriotism, among the greater gentry, with their long pedigrees and long associations with Lancashire. These expectations do not seem unreasonable when we remember that the Kentish gentry were also endogamous and indigenous and at the same time extremely provincial in outlook. Parochial feelings and status consciousness were certainly strong among the Lancashire gentry.[184] Yet it is a striking fact that they did not display anything like the strong sense of cohesion and intense local patriotism of the Kentish gentry. In Kent the local loyalties and conservatism of the community united the county in opposition first to the 'despotism' of Charles I and later to the centralising government of the Protectorate.[185] But in Lancashire there seems to have been little concerted opposition by local officials to governmental centralisation between 1625 and 1660.[186] Moreover, during the Civil War local issues loomed far larger in Kent than in Lancashire.[187] In Kent the Second Civil War of 1648 was 'a great local insurrection',[188] but in Lancashire the 1648 rebellion was a genuine royalist revival, with no provincial overtones. The same may be said of the Earl of Derby's rising in 1651.[189] Why, then, did the Lancashire gentry form a less cohesive and introverted community than the Kentish gentry? There is no simple answer to this problem, but one reason must surely have been that many of the Lancashire gentry were deeply and bitterly divided on religious grounds.

What exactly was the religious state of Lancashire and its gentry in 1642?[190] It is probably true to say that Lancashire was more sharply divided in religion than any other English county. Historians are generally agreed that Lancashire had a higher proportion of Catholics than any other shire, except Monmouth, and that in response to the challenge from Rome Puritanism rapidly gained in strength between 1600 and 1642, especially in Salford hundred.[191] Of course not all Lancastrians were Papists or Puritans. Apart from an unknown number of Anglicans,[192] many were apparently indifferent to religion, and in some parts of the county there was a fair amount of paganism, irreligion and doctrinal ignorance, not to mention witchcraft.[193] As for the 774 gentry families, we have no idea how many were believing, let alone practising, Anglicans. Nor do we know how many were indifferent or perhaps even hostile to Christianity. Only 221 of the gentry families can be confidently called Catholic, while only 114 were clearly Puritan. Yet despite their small numbers, Catholics and Puritans were the main religious protagonists among the Lancashire upper classes.

The following gentry have been classed as Puritans: those appointing or financially assisting Puritan ministers;[194] builders of chapels used for Puritan worship; members of puritanical religious committees; elders of Presbyterian classical assemblies; members of Independent congregations; and, finally, those shown to be Puritans by their wills,[195] correspondence or the opinions of their contemporaries.[196] Catholics are more easily identified by means of the recusant rolls, lay subsidy rolls, state papers and various miscellaneous sources.[197]

TABLE 15

RELIGIOUS AFFILIATIONS OF LANCASHIRE GENTRY FAMILIES, *c.* 1642[a]

Hundred	Catholic families	Puritan families	Anglican or indifferent families	Total number of families
Salford	9 (4·6%)	47 (24·0%)	140 (71·4%)	196 (100·0%)
Blackburn	30 (27·2%)	16 (14·6%)	64 (58·2%)	110 (100·0%)
West Derby	73 (36·9%)	21 (10·6%)	104 (52·5%)	198 (100·0%)
Leyland	28 (39·4%)	8 (11·3%)	35 (49·3%)	71 (100·0%)
Amounderness	51 (47·7%)	9 (8·4%)	47 (43·9%)	107 (100·0%)
Lonsdale	30 (32·6%)	13 (14·1%)	49 (53·3%)	92 (100·0%)
Total	221 (28·6%)	114 (14·7%)	439 (56·7%)	774 (100·0%)

a This table refers to heads of families.

Table 15 shows the numbers and geographical distribution of the various religious groups in Lancashire during the Civil War period. It will be observed that the Catholic gentry were most numerous in the lowland and more arable hundreds of West Derby, Leyland and Amounderness, while the Puritan gentry were strongest in the highland and more pastoral hundreds of Salford, Blackburn and Lonsdale.[198] Perhaps even more sociologically significant is that in 'industrial' Salford hundred Puritans were at their strongest and Catholics at their weakest.[199]

Salford was the only hundred in Lancashire where the Puritan gentry outnumbered the Catholic gentry. Indeed, there seems to have been a higher proportion of Catholic gentry in Lancashire than in other northern counties in 1642. In Yorkshire 24 per cent, in Northumberland 21 per cent, and in the Lake Counties a mere 19 per cent of gentry families were Papist.[200] Even so, Catholics were less numerous among the Lancashire gentry than has often been supposed: a mere 28 per cent. Puritans formed an even smaller proportion of the Lancashire gentry: less than 15 per cent. Even in Yorkshire the Puritans comprised 20 per cent of the gentry.[201] Yet, though small in numbers, the Catholic and Puritan gentry were to play a vital and dominating role in the Great Rebellion in Lancashire. It is to this rebellion and its aftermath that we must now turn.

NOTES

[1] Joan Thirsk, ed., *The Agrarian History of England and Wales* (Cambridge, 1967), iv, 81.

[2] There is a copy in L.R.O.

[3] Thirsk, op. cit., 80–9; T. W. Freeman, E. B. Rodgers and R. H. Kinvig, *Lancashire, Cheshire and the Isle of Man* (1966), 46–9; G. Youd, 'The Common Fields of Lancashire', *Trans. Hist. Soc. L. & C.*, Vol. 113 (1961), 1–40.

[4] A. P. Wadsworth and J. de L. Mann, *The Cotton Trade and Industrial Lancashire* (Manchester, 1931), 25; C. M. L. Bouch and G. P. Jones, *The Lake Counties, 1500–1830* (Manchester, 1961), 132 seq.; G. Elliott, 'The Decline of the Woollen Trade in Cumberland, Westmorland and Northumberland in the late Sixteenth Century', *Trans. Cumb. & West. Ant. & Arch. Soc.*, N.S., Vol. 61 (1961), 112–19.

[5] See early chapters of Wadsworth and Mann, op. cit.; J. J. Bagley, 'Matthew Markland, a Wigan Mercer', *Trans. L. & C. Antiq. Soc.*, Vol. 68 (1958), 45–68.

[6] C.S.P.D., 1654, p. 73

[7] See A. Fell, *The Early Iron Industry of Furness* (Ulverston, 1908), 191 seq. Of all the iron industries in seventeenth century England, that in the North-west (which included Furness) seems to have been the least progressive (H. R. Schubert, *Hist. of the British Iron and Steel Industry* (1957), 175, 191–2).

[8] Bouch and Jones, op. cit., 124–5.

[9] G. H. Tupling, 'The Early Metal Trades and the Beginnings of Engineering in Lancashire', *Trans. L. & C. Antiq. Soc.*, Vol. 61 (1951), 16 seq.; R. J. A. Shelley, 'The Wigan and Liverpool Pewterers', *Trans. Hist. Soc. L. & C.*, Vol. 97 (1946), 1–26; 'Lancashire Nail Makers, 1597–1747', *L.R.O. Report for 1957*, 7–13.

[10] J. U. Nef, *The Rise of the British Coal Industry* (1932), i, 61–4; A. P. Wadsworth, 'Hist. of Coalmining in the Rochdale District', *Trans. Roch. Lit. and Sci. Soc.*, Vol. 23 (1949), 105 seq.; F. A. Bailey, 'Early Coalmining in Prescot', *Trans. Hist. Soc. L. & C.*, Vol. 99 (1947), 1–20; J. H. M. Bankes, 'Records of Mining in Winstanley and Orrell', *Trans. L. & C. Antiq. Soc.*, Vol. 54 (1939), 31 seq.; J. Langton, 'Coal Output in South-west Lancashire, 1590–1799', *Ec.H.R.*, 2nd Ser., xxv, 1972, 34, 38, 51, 53–4.

[11] G. Chandler, *Liverpool Shipping* (1960), 22. Liverpool's export trade in the 1630s also included Lancashire manufactures (G. D. Ramsay, *English Overseas Trade during the Centuries of Emergence* (1957), 154). Our evidence contradicts a recent view that 'At the beginning of the Restoration, Liverpool was an insignificant seaport' (P. G. E. Clemens, 'The Rise of Liverpool, 1665–1750', *Ec.H.R.*, 2nd. Ser., xxix, 1976, 211).

[12] Broxap, 1.

[13] J. E. T. Rogers, *Hist. of Agriculture and Prices in England* (Oxford, 1887), v, 70, 104–5.

[14] The Monthly Assessments for the years 1648, 1649, 1652, 1657 and 1660 place Lancashire among the thirteen poorest counties in England (A. & O., i, 1107–10; ii, 290, 653–6, 1058–61, 1355–8). According to the Hearth Tax Assessments, 1662, only ten English counties were poorer than Lancashire (Everitt, *Change*, 55).

[15] *The Social Institutions of Lancashire, 1480–1660*, Chet. Soc., 3rd. Ser., Vol. 11, 1962, 2.

[16] P.R.O., E179/250/11. I have used the generally accepted multiplier of 4·5 persons to a house to arrive at this figure. Mr Peter Laslett has recently suggested that the household size stayed fairly constant at 4·75 from the late sixteenth century to 1910 (*Household and Family in Past Time* (Cambridge, 1972), 139). This figure seems too high, as he himself almost admits, and it may have some validity for the larger towns. Using the 4·75 multiplier, Lancashire's estimated population in 1664 would be 159,039.

[17] Our evidence for 1664 and 1690 does not support the view that the population of Lancashire declined or stagnated during the late seventeenth century (J. D. Marshall, *Lancashire* (Newton Abbot, 1974), 45–7, 50; W. G. Howson, 'Plague, Poverty and Population in Parts of North-west England, 1580–1720', *Trans. Hist. Soc. L. & C.*, Vol. 112 (1960), 38–9, 42–3, 45–9).

[18] Houghton reckoned that Lancashire had 40,202 houses in 1690. I have again used the 4·5 multiplier to calculate the population of the palatinate. Houghton may have obtained his statistics from the Hearth Books. See D. V. Glass, 'Two Papers on Gregory King', in D. V. Glass and D. E. C. Eversley, eds., *Population in History* (1965), 217–18. Davenant, who may have used the same evidence, reckoned that Lancashire had

46,961 households in 1690 (ibid., 218). I have preferred to rely on Houghton's more conservative estimates.

[19] F. Tönnies, ed., *Behemoth* (2nd edn., 1969), 95.

[20] Everitt, *Local Community*, 25.

[21] Broxap estimated that between 1,200 and 1,500 died in the Royalist attack on Bolton in 1644 and that 'the larger number' of these belonged to the town (Broxap, 122). Thus a conservative estimate of civilian casualties would be between 700 and 800. The Bolton population was 1,588 in 1664 (P.R.O., E179/250/11), and if it was approximately the same in 1642, then a 44–50 per cent death roll does not seem too high a figure.

[22] G. Chandler, *Liverpool under Charles I* (Liverpool, 1965), 21, 336.

[23] R. Sharpe France, 'A Hist. of the Plague in Lancs.', *Trans. Hist. Soc. L. & C.*, Vol. 90 (1938), 89. See also pp. 86–134 for details and Howson, art. cit., 39.

[24] See especially W. G. Hoskins, 'Harvest Fluctuations and English Economic History, 1620–1759', *Agric. Hist. Rev.*, xvi, 1968, 18. As a predominantly pastoral region, Lancashire must have depended frequently on large corn imports.

[25] Little is known about the birth rate in Lancashire during these two decades.

[26] The Protestation returns, 1641–42, cannot be used for this purpose because for Lancashire they are incomplete. There are no extant returns for Lonsdale hundred, for example. Nor are there any extant poll taxes for Lancashire for 1641.

[27] See below, Chapter II.

[28] For peers in other counties see Cliffe, 2–3; Everitt, *Kent*, 35; Fletcher, 22–4, 231; Holmes, 19, 21–5; James, 51, 79, 147; Morrill, *Cheshire*, 17; C. B. Phillips, 'The Gentry in Cumberland and Westmorland, 1600–1665', Lancaster Univ. Ph.D. thesis, 1974, 343; Underdown, *Somerset*, 19; Watts, 55 seq.; *Glamorgan County Hist.*, iv, 82, 197 seq.

[29] The Earl of Derby had lands in Cheshire, Cumberland, Derbyshire, Essex, Flintshire, Middlesex, Northamptonshire, Oxfordshire, Staffordshire, Sussex, Warwickshire, Westmorland and Yorkshire (L.R.O., DDK 12/4). He also owned the Isle of Man, being king thereof. See his *Hist. of the Isle of Man* in F. R. Raines, ed., *The Stanley Papers, Part III*, Chet. Soc., O.S., Vol. 70, 1867. Baron Morley and Mounteagle held various manors and lands in Essex, Hertfordshire, Somerset, Sussex and Yorkshire (V.C.H., viii, 195; C.C.C., iii, 2282). Viscount Molyneux had extensive estates in Sussex (L.R.O., DDM 1/60). But he apparently held no land in Ireland (C. R. Mayes, 'The Early Stuarts and the Irish Peerage', E.H.R., lxxiii (1958), 246).

[30] 'Gentleman' might be applied to husbandmen, drovers and alehouse keepers. See J. Tait, ed., *Lancs Quarter Sessions Records, 1590–1606*, Chet. Soc., N.S., Vol. 77, 1917, p. xv.

[31] See G. E. Aylmer, *The State's Servants* (1973), 394–5, and below, p. 163 n. 5.

[32] See especially Cliffe, 3–5.

[33] Sir Anthony Wagner has said, 'though only a gentleman could bear arms by right, a man with no right to bear arms could still be a gentleman' (*English Genealogy* (Oxford, 1960), 113).

[34] 'The Social Distribution of Land and Men in England, 1436–1700', Ec.H.R., 2nd Ser., xx, 1967, 426–30. For a similar opinion see Robin Jeffs in *Past and Present*, No. 32 (1965), 5.

[35] J. P. Earwaker, ed., *Miscellanies*, I, L. & C. Rec. Soc., Vol. 12 (1885), 229–51.

[36] L.R.O., DDN 64, fos. 92–5.

[37] Ibid., fos. 78–80.

[38] Earwaker, ed., *Miscellanies*, I, 211–23.

[39] P.R.O., E179/131/334; 131/335; 132/336; 132/337; 132/339; 132/340. These rolls cover every hundred in Lancashire except Blackburn, for which the roll for 1626 has been used (P.R.O., E179/131/317).

[40] See either the originals in H.L.R.O. or the Bailey Transcripts, Bundle 17, in Chet. Lib. The returns of some parishes have been printed, mainly by the Chetham Society.

[41] Earwaker, ed., *Miscellanies*, I, 229–51.

[42] For all calculations in this and subsequent paragraphs the 4·5 multiplier has been used.

[43] Many Lancashire gentry families are of course recorded in the Hearth Tax Assessment, Ladyday 1664 (P.R.O., E179/250/11). Many are also to be found in the following sources: P.R.O., E179/250/5: Voluntary Gift, 1661; E179/132/349; 132/350: Lay Subsidy Rolls, 1663 (Lonsdale and Blackburn hundreds); L.R.O., DDX 3/96; 3/97: Lay Subsidy Rolls, 1663 & 1664 (Salford hundred). See also the Lancashire Lay Subsidy Commissioners, 1663, in *Statutes of the Realm*, 15 Car. II, cap. 9. Fiscal records

such as these underestimate the numbers of gentry, but this cannot be a complete explanation for the drastic fall in the numbers of gentle families between 1642 and 1664. See below, Chapters III, IV and V.

⁴⁴ L.R.O., DDK 1704/2: List of Lancashire Freeholders, 1695. For full details of gentry numbers in Lancashire during the seventeenth century, see below, Appendix I.

⁴⁵ The population of Lancashire can have been little different in 1695 from what it was in 1690. See above, p. 3.

⁴⁶ The possible reasons for this decline will be considered in subsequent chapters.

⁴⁷ Glamorgan's 219 gentry families in 1690 formed between 2·1 and 2·4 per cent of a population calculated at between 40,874 and 45,415 in 1670 (M. I. Williams in *Glamorgan County Hist.*, iv, 311, 315).

⁴⁸ Dr Christopher Haigh has said that in Lancashire in the 1560s 'the gentry formed a much smaller proportion of the total population than in most other areas', having '1 gentleman for every 800 people'. But by relying solely on the heralds' visitation lists, he may have greatly underestimated the numbers of late Tudor gentry (*Reformation and Resistance in Tudor Lancashire* (Cambridge, 1975), 107).

⁴⁹ I am grateful to Professor A. M. Everitt for this (conservative) estimate.

⁵⁰ W. K. Jordan, *Social Institutions in Kent, 1480–1660*, Archaeologia Cantiana, Vol. 75, 1961, 3.

⁵¹ This was actually the number of armigerous families in 1604 (Cliffe, 189).

⁵² W. K. Jordan, *The Charities of Rural England, 1480–1660* (1961), 217. Yorkshire's estimated gentry population is small because it is based on Dr Cliffe's rather narrow (armigerous) definition of gentry. Hugh Aveling reckons that during the sixteenth and seventeenth centuries Yorkshire had 'a hard core of some 600–700 families of armorial gentry', and at least as many non-armigerous gentry ('Some Aspects of Yorkshire Catholic Recusant History, 1558–1791', in G. J. Cuming, ed., *Studies in Church Hist.* (Leiden, 1967), iv, 117). But even if we accept a possible total of 1,400 households in 1600, the gentry would only comprise 2·1 per cent of the Yorkshire population.

⁵³ Wm. Camden, *Britain*, trans. Philemon Holland (1637), 601.

⁵⁴ *Cheshire*, 14–15. The author included both the armigerous and non-armigerous gentry in his calculations. So did Everitt in *Kent*, 34.

⁵⁵ 'The Early Tudor Gentry', Ec.H.R., 2nd Ser., xvii, 1965, 457.

⁵⁶ The late W. Ogwen Williams argued that the poverty of Wales in the sixteenth century 'meant that many of the gentry, circumscribed in their scope for material ostentation, made much more of their pedigrees than would otherwise have been the case', and that the Welsh obsession with pedigrees was 'linked with the existence of a numerically large class of gentry ... in relation to the size of the population' ('The Social Order in Tudor Wales', *Trans. Honourable Society of Cymmrodorion*, Part 2, 1967, 168, 170).

⁵⁷ M. I. Williams in *Glamorgan County Hist.*, iv, 315.

⁵⁸ The distinction between arable and pastoral districts was not absolute during the seventeenth century. Nor did it always correspond with the 'distinction' between agricultural and industrial regions. Some pastoral districts, like the mossland areas of south-west Lancashire, had no industries other than the domestic manufacture of linen for home use (F. Walker, *An Historical Geography of South-west Lancashire*, Chet. Soc., N.S., Vol. 103, 1939, 61). On the other hand some arable parishes, like Wigan, Leigh and Prescot, had important coal and metal industries. See above, p. 3.

⁵⁹ See Protestation returns, 1642.

⁶⁰ Ibid.

⁶¹ P.R.O., E179/132/336.

⁶² Ibid.

⁶³ See Protestation returns.

⁶⁴ P.R.O., E179/131/335.

⁶⁵ Ibid.

⁶⁶ P.R.O., E179/132/336.

⁶⁷ For details of Civil War allegiances see Broxap, passim.

⁶⁸ These were the words used by Dr Edmund Calamy to describe Preston in 1709. They are just as apposite for 1642. See Calamy, *An Historical Account of My Own Life*, ed. J. T. Rutt (1829), ii, 221.

⁶⁹ *Discourse*, 29. Our argument is not invalidated by the fact that Preston had more Parliamentarian than Royalist gentry. See map, fig. 3. In any case the Royalist and neutral gentry in the town together outnumbered the Parliamentary gentry.

[70] *Mercurius Belgicus*, 28 May 1644, B.L., E. 1099(3).

[71] For details see Broxap, 121–4.

[72] Cliffe, 25.

[73] For Yorkshire see ibid.

[74] For the Haworths see J. P. Earwaker, ed., *Manchester Court Leet Records* (Manchester, 1887), iv, 73. For the Worthingtons see J. Crossley, ed., *The Diary and Correspondence of Dr. John Worthington*, Chet. Soc., O.S., Vol. 13, 1847, 1–2. For the Morts see H. Fishwick, *Hist of Preston* (Rochdale, 1900), 319–20; E. Axon, 'The Mort Family', *Trans. Unitarian Hist. Soc.*, Vol. 3 (1923), 135–47.

[75] The Marklands had held property in Wigan since 1327 and been prominent in town affairs since 1600 (A. W. Boyd, 'The Markland Family Deeds and Papers', *Trans. L. & C. Antiq. Soc.*, Vol. 47 (1930–31), 27).

[76] P.R.O., E179/131/334; 132/336; 132/337; 132/340.

[77] Thirty-eight of the 46 urban gentlemen had annual landed incomes of less than £250, according to the 1641 lay subsidy rolls (ibid.). For a full discussion of the value of these rolls see Blackwood, 'Economic State', pp. 55–7.

[78] I adopt Professor G. E. Aylmer's definitions of greater and lesser gentry (*State's Servants*, 179).

[79] We are only concerned with J.P.s who were resident lay gentry with most of their property in Lancashire. The following J.P.s are ignored: peers, non-Lancastrians, clergy and ex-officio members of the Bench, such as mayors of boroughs.

[80] For those nominated to the magistracy see L.R.O., QSC 5–37 (1625–42); for magistrates attending quarter sessions see L.R.O., QSR 22–39 (1625–42). For deputy-lieutenants see D. P. Carter, 'The Lancashire Lieutenancy: an Aspect of County Administration in the period 1625–1640', Manchester Univ. M.A. thesis, 1973, Appendix III. For sheriffs see P.R.O., *List*, ix, 73. For militia officers for 1628, 1634 and 1640 see L.R.O., DDN 64, fos. 47–9, 112, 164; for those named in 1636 see P.R.O., SP16/337/81. For sewers commissioners see P.R.O., C181/4 (1629–34); records covering the years 1620–29 and 1636–46—C181/3 and C181/5—have no entries for Lancashire. For lay subsidy commissioners for 1628 see B.L., Add. MS. 36924, f. 98 (West Derby hundred) and Leyland Hundred Lay Subsidy Roll, in J. P. Earwaker, ed., *Miscellanies*, I, 164; for the 1626 and 1641 commissioners see P.R.O., E179/131/312; 131/313; 131/314; 131/315; 131/316; 131/317; 131/334; 131/335; 132/336; 132/337; 132/339; 132/340. For knighthood commissioners see Earwaker, ed., *Miscellanies*, I, 211, 219, 222–3.

[81] Activity is defined in terms of attending at least one quarter sessions per annum.

[82] An Act of 1606 forbad recusants or husbands of recusants to hold any kind of public office (*Statutes of the Realm*, 3 Jac. I, cap. 5). But see below, p. 57.

[83] For the purging of the Lancashire magistracy of Catholic elements under Charles I, see P. R. Long, 'The Wealth of the Magisterial Class in Lancashire, c. 1590–1640', Manchester Univ. M.A. thesis, 1968, 22–4. For sources regarding Lancashire Catholics see below, p. 36 n. 197.

[84] The reliability of all these sources—listed in the Bibliography—is discussed in detail in Blackwood, 'Economic State', 54–7.

[85] The total *known* aggregate income of the Lancashire gentry was £111,146.

[86] For the incomes of the peers see below, pp. 58, 69 n. 91.

[87] According to C.A.M., i, 413. I am grateful to Dr J. T. Cliffe for this reference.

[88] P.R.O., SP23/174/201–5.

[89] Forty-one (22·7 per cent) of the 180 Lakeland gentry families had less than £100 p.a. from land in 1642 (Phillips, thesis, 10, 19). 204 (26·3 per cent) of the 774 Lancashire families had annual landed incomes of under £100.

[90] There must have been at least 1,000 younger sons of the Lancashire gentry alive in 1642, but for only 480 is there any biographical information.

[91] L.R.O., DP 391: survey of Cockerham manor, July 1653.

[92] P.R.O., SP23/58/167–82: survey 1653.

[93] Blackwood, 'Lancs. Cavaliers', 21.

[94] Chet. Lib., MS. A.3, 90 (Letter Book of Sir Ralph Assheton 1648): Assheton to B. Driver, 19 Sept. 1648.

[95] Rev. John Livesay, *Catastrophe Magnatum* (1657), 284, B.L., E.1582(2).

[96] Blackwood, art. cit., 24–31. The harshness of the Royalist and Catholic landlords in Lonsdale contrasts sharply with the benevolence of their brethren in other parts of Lancashire (ibid., 17–31). Landlords in Lonsdale acted similarly to those in Northumberland, Cumberland and Westmorland. See Watts, 159–69; Andrew B. Appleby,

'Agrarian Capitalism or Seigneurial Reaction? The Northwest of England, 1500–1700', Amer H.R., lxxx, 1975, 578, 587 seq.

[97] P.R.O., SP23/129/199.

[98] See Long, thesis, 113–16.

[99] Forty-one of these were magisterial families (ibid., 121–6). Apart from family papers, information about spiritual income is derived from H. Fishwick, ed., *Commonwealth Church Surveys*, L. & C. Rec. Soc., Vol. 1 (1879); W. A. Shaw, ed., *Plundered Ministers Accounts, 1643–1660*, L. & C. Rec. Soc., Vols. 28, 34 (1893, 1896); *Roy. Comp. Papers*, i–vi, pt. ii.

[100] J. Lunn, *Hist. of the Tyldesleys of Lancashire* (Altrincham, 1966), 193–5.

[101] C. Hill, *Economic Problems of the Church* (Oxford, 1956), 140–1, 329.

[102] J. Ry. Lib., English MS. 213, f. 41 : A particular or real estate ... August, 1653.

[103] P.R.O., SP23/58A/550: survey Feb. 1654.

[104] James, 62–71, 86–93. In Yorkshire at least 80 (8 per cent) of the 963 gentry families had coal-mining interests in the period 1558–1642 (Cliffe, 57).

[105] Figures from family histories and archives; Nef. op. cit., vols. i–ii; V.C.H., iii–vi; H. T. Crofton, 'Lancs. and Cheshire Coalmining Records', *Trans. L. & C. Antiq. Soc.*, Vol. 7 (1889), 53 seq.; Bankes, art. cit., 38–9; Bailey, art. cit., 16 seq.; W. Bennett, *Hist. of Burnley* (Burnley, 1947), ii, 90—1; P.R.O., DL1/302 72 (1625 42); PL6/8–16 (1625–41).

[106] L.R.O., DDTa 265.

[107] P.R.O., E179/131/335.

[108] For details see Blackwood, 'Economic State', p. 65.

[109] Stone, *Crisis*, 341; James, 69, 93, 179.

[110] P.R.O., E379/73, f. 6. See also L.R.O., DDBr 18/7.

[111] P.R.O., DL1/341; 348.

[112] Nef, op. cit., i, 350.

[113] See below, Chapter II.

[114] P.R.O., DL4/17/13. See also *Roy. Comp. Papers*, iii, 35.

[115] P.R.O., DL1/329; 336; 340.

[116] P.R.O., E179/132/340.

[117] *Al. Cant.*, i, 170.

[118] T. E. Gibson, *Lydiate Hall* (Edinburgh, 1876), 114; L.R.O., DDIn 16/11; 47/4, 49/21, 55/48, 61/32, 35, 36, 38, 41, 44.

[119] J. Harland, ed., *The Lancs. Lieutenancy*, Chet. Soc., O.S., Vol. 50. 1859, 297.

[120] J. P. Rylands, ed., *Lancs. Inquisitions, 1603–25*, L. & C. Rec. Soc., Vol. 17 (1888), 456–60.

[121] Alex Rigby to Thos. Sandys, M.P., 25 Jan. 1646, in *Palatine Note Book* (Manchester, 1883), iii, 200–1.

[122] Ibid., (Manchester, 1884), iv, 144; J. J. Bagley, 'Kenyon v. Rigby', Trans. Hist. Soc., L. & C., Vol. 106 (1954), 41.

[123] Ibid., 54

[124] See below, p. 56.

[125] Long, thesis, 157; also pp. 147–8, 158–9.

[126] But see above, p. 20. For further information on Preston and Curwen see Blackwood, 'Economic State', p. 71.

[127] As it seems to have been for the Glamorgan gentry (*Glamorgan County Hist.*, iv), 40–2).

[128] Long, op. cit., 162–5. Several Lancashire gentry families were in the service of the Molyneuxes of Sefton in about 1620, but in an unknown capacity, hence they have not been counted for statistical purposes. See below, p. 48.

[129] F. R. Raines and C. W. Sutton, *The Life of Humphrey Chetham*, Chet. Soc., N.S., Vol. 49, 1903, 19, 30–1.

[130] For Sherrington see R. Parkinson, ed., *The Life of Adam Martindale*, Chet. Soc., O.S., Vol. 4, 1845, 30; H. V. Hart-Davis, *Wardley Hall* (Manchester, 1908), 86; P.R.O., E190/1336/11; C54/2930/5; PL17/122/1; L.R.O., QDD 42/7. For Hartley see QDD 36/21; 37/10d; 38/9d; 42/4, 6; 43/20; 45/3; 47/8.

[131] *Causes*, 74.

[132] For references and details see above, p. 30 n. 35–40 and below, Appendix I.

[133] See above, p. 3.

[134] L.R.O., DDF 2430: Lay subsidy roll for all Lancashire hundreds, 1593. The status of the taxpayers is seldom given but this can be discovered with the aid of the 1600 Freeholders' list. See above, p. 30 n. 35.

[135] For references see above, p. 30 n. 39. For gentry in Blackburn hundred the 1626 lay subsidy roll has been used.

[136] Forty-eight of these families belonged to the socially perdurable gentry, 25 to the new gentry and one to the disappearing gentry.

[137] In the case of 11 of the 175 transactions the purchase price is unknown.

[138] Thirty-four of these families belonged to the socially perdurable gentry, 35 to the disappearing gentry and five to the new gentry.

[139] In the case of 22 of the 158 transactions the sale price is unknown. We are not concerned with families whose estates were only slightly increased or diminished. Apart from the V.C.H., iii–viii, family histories and family muniments, the best sources of evidence for property transactions in the pre-Civil War period are L.R.O., QDD 12–48 (1600–42); Guild. Lib., Royal Contract Estates: Sales Contracts 1628–77; also Draft Deeds 52 and 53. Of more limited value are P.R.O., PL17; C54 (deeds of bargain and sale).

[140] But at least another twenty (4·1 per cent) of the 485 families increased their estates by marriage.

[141] See above, pp. 16, 18, and below, pp. 58–9.

[142] This is roughly the criterion of indebtedness used by Professor Lawrence Stone. See *Crisis*, 540–1.

[143] Only seven families apparently parted with their patrimonial lands between 1600 and 1642. For details see Blackwood, D.Phil. thesis, 49, 58–9, 61, 323, 330, 333, 336–8.

[144] For Yorkshire see Cliffe, 139–42.

[145] See Blackwood, 'Cavalier and Roundhead Gentry', 88.

[146] For details see Blackwood, 'Catholic and Protestant Gentry', pp. 6–7.

[147] For wardship exactions affecting the gentry of Yorkshire and the Lake Counties see Cliffe, 128–35; Phillips, thesis, 227–38.

[148] These 1,052 families comprise 774 living in 1642 and 278 who left the gentry between 1600 and 1642. The names of the families suffering at least one wardship are in the Alphabetical list in P.R.O., Wards 9/197. For details of their wardships see Wards 5/21; 5/22; Wards 9/203–9. Wardships are often found in family muniments.

[149] For details see Blackwood, 'Economic State', pp. 79–80.

[150] Wm. Camden, *Britain*, 748.

[151] *The Responsa Scholarum, Part two*, ed. A. Kenny, C.R.S., Vol. 55 (1963), 530.

[152] T. Helsby, 'Torbock of Torbock', *Reliquary*, xi, 1870, 98. See also below, p. 59.

[153] Their debts were well over three times their annual income of £1,500 in 1632. For details see Blackwood, 'Economic State', pp. 77, 81.

[154] These 278 families are mentioned in the Lancashire freeholders list, 1600 (Earwaker, ed., *Miscellanies*, I, 229–51). But most had disappeared from the gentry by the accession of Charles I.

[155] Many of the other families sold land but not enough to impair their status thereby. For sources of evidence for land transactions see above, n. 139.

[156] This figure—which is a very conservative estimate—excludes two families who failed in the male line and also sold out. Evidence for failure in the male line is to be found in V.C.H., iii–viii, and various parish and family histories.

[157] For a fuller discussion see Blackwood, art. cit.

[158] It is not absolutely certain when the 79 families attained their gentility, but it is more likely to have been under James I or Charles I than under the Tudors. For sources concerning the origins of gentility, see above, p. 22 n. See also above, p. 30 n. 35–40.

[159] Many of the other 264 families bought land during the early seventeenth century, but apparently not enough to raise their status thereby. For sources see above, n. 139.

[160] Fewer than 20 of the 289 new gentry families seem to have been of non-Lancashire origins. For a fuller discussion see Blackwood, art. cit. See also below, p. 163 n. 4.

[161] Cliffe, 13.

[162] Everitt, *Kent*, 36.

[163] Morrill, *Cheshire*, 3.

[164] W. W. Longford, 'Some Notes on the Family of Osbaldeston', Trans. Hist. Soc., L. & C., Vol. 87 (1935), 62; G. C. Yates, 'The Towneleys of Towneley', Trans. L. & C. Antiq. Soc., Vol. 10 (1892), 87; Gregson, op. cit., 169; H. T. Crofton, *Hist. of Stretford*, Chet. Soc., N.S., Vol. 51, 1903, 99–101.

[165] Camden was obviously thinking of the Asshetons of Middleton.

[166] *Britain*, 747–8.

[167] The degree of indigenousness among the lesser gentry families of Lancashire is unknown.

[168] See especially Everitt, *Kent*, passim; *Change*, passim.

[169] See especially K. Charlton, *Education in Renaissance England* (1965); Joan Simon, *Education and Society in Tudor England* (Cambridge, 1966); L. Stone, 'The Educational Revolution in England, 1560–1640', *Past & Present*, No. 28 (1964), 41–80; L. Stone, ed., *The University in Society* (Oxford, 1975), vol. i; H. Kearney, *Scholars and Gentlemen* (1970); W. R. Prest, *The Inns of Court under Elizabeth I and the Early Stuarts, 1590–1640* (1972).

[170] The Irelands of Hutt seem to have been privately tutored at home (Blackwood, D.Phil. thesis, 71–2). But how many other Lancashire gentlemen had been similarly educated, it is impossible to say.

[171] Those named in the St Omer Composition Lists are difficult to identify. See B.L., Add. MS. 9354.

[172] For details see Blackwood, op. cit., 72–3.

[173] P. J. Wallis, 'A Preliminary Register of Old Schools in Lancashire and Cheshire', *Trans. Hist. Soc., L. & C.*, Vol. 120 (1968), 10–17.

[174] A higher proportion of younger than of elder sons graduated, 22 (59 per cent) out of 37 of the former, and only 21 (27 per cent) out of 77 of the latter. Academically, the Lancashire gentry could stand comparison with some of the Welsh gentry. Of the 132 gentlemen from south-west Wales who matriculated at Oxford between 1540 and 1640, at least 50 (37 per cent) took degrees (H. A. Lloyd, *The Gentry of South-West Wales* (Cardiff, 1968), 194).

[175] Fourteen of the 29 barristers (some of whom later held crown appointments) were younger sons. For sources concerning barristers see above, p. 17 n.

[176] Of the remaining eleven, six attended Lincoln's Inn, three the Inner Temple, one the Middle Temple and one Staple Inn.

[177] One Lancashire gentleman was educated at Edinburgh University and two at Leyden University. No Lancashire gentleman alive in 1642 seems to have been educated by means of the Grand Tour of Europe.

[178] T. Heywood, ed., *The Moore Rental*, Chet. Soc., O.S., Vol. 12, 1847, 6–7.

[179] Victor Morgan denies that a university education weakened local attachments. See 'Cambridge University and "The Country" 1560–1640', in *The University in Society*, i, 189 245. For opposing views see Kearney, op. cit., 169; Prest., op. cit., 39 40.

[180] For full details see Blackwood, 'Marriages', 321–28.

[181] J. P. Ferris, 'The Gentry of Dorset on the Eve of the Civil War', *The Genealogists' Magazine*, xv, 1965, 108.

[182] For details see Blackwood, op. cit., 323–5, 328.

[183] Even some of those educated at the universities may have come under local influences. See above, p. 25.

[184] See Blackwood, D.Phil. thesis, 181–2, 190–2, 221–2.

[185] Everitt, *Kent*, passim.

[186] See Blackwood, op. cit., 87–93, 221–2. Before the Civil War there is no evidence of any attempt by Lancashire's Lords Lieutenant and their deputies 'knowingly to obstruct the crown's policies' (D. P. Carter, 'The "Exact Militia" in Lancashire, 1625–1640', North. Hist., xi, 1975, 87).

[187] For local issues in the Civil War in Lancashire see Blackwood, 'Cavalier and Roundhead Gentry', 92–3.

[188] Everitt, *Kent*, 241; also p. 16 and the whole of Chapter VII.

[189] For an account of the Second and Third Civil Wars in Lancashire see Broxap, Chapters IX and X.

[190] For a full account of the religion of the gentry see Blackwood, 'Catholic and Protestant Gentry'.

[191] See especially R. C. Richardson, *Puritanism in North-west England* (Manchester, 1972); C. Haigh, *Reformation and Resistance in Tudor Lancashire* (Cambridge, 1975). There are many references to Lancashire in J. Bossy, *The English Catholic Community, 1570–1850* (1975).

[192] Dr Haigh writes: 'there are few hints of a substantial Anglican presence in Lancashire, except in the sense of mere passive conformity, until after the Civil War' (Haigh, op. cit., 332).

[193] Richardson, op. cit., 3–5, 156, 164. One of those executed for witchcraft at Lancaster in 1612 was a gentlewoman, Alice Nutter of Roughlee (Mildred Tonge, 'The Lancashire Witches, 1612 and 1634', Trans. Hist. Soc. L. & C., Vol. 83 (1931), 156).

[194] The evidence of presentations generally needs to be corroborated by other information.

[195] Wills must, of course, be used cautiously, since they sometimes reflect the views of the scribe rather than of the testator.

[196] Sources include: V.C.H., iii–viii; Fishwick, ed., *Commonwealth Church Surveys*; Jordan, *Social Institutions of Lancs.*; C.W.T., 91; A. & O., ii, 972; W. A. Shaw, ed., *Minutes of Manchester Presbyterian Classis*, 3 vols., Chet. Soc., N.S., Vols. 20, 22, 24 (1890–91); id., *Minutes of Bury Presbyterian Classis*, 2 vols., Chet. Soc., N.S., Vols. 36, 41 (1896, 1898); H. Fishwick, ed., *Jolly's Note Book*, Chet. Soc., N.S., Vol. 33 (1894); Parkinson, ed., *Life of Adam Martindale*; T. Heywood, ed., *Diary of Henry Newcome*, Chet. Soc., Vol. 18 (1849); R. Parkinson, ed., *Autobiography of Henry Newcome*, Chet. Soc., O.S., Vol. 26 (1852); R. Halley, *Lancashire: its Puritanism and Nonconformity*, 2 vols. (1869); B. Nightingale, *Lancs. Nonconformity*, 6 vols. (Manchester, 1891–93); Richardson, op. cit.; and various wills in print and in manuscript.

[197] See P.R.O., E377/34A–49; E179/131/317, 131/334, 131/335, 132/336, 132/337; 132/339; 132/340; SP19/21/232; 22/244; 93/122; 114/36; 158/139; SP23/58A; 61 et seq.; SP28/211; 218; B.L., Harl. MS. 2112, fos. 56–63; Chet. Lib., Bailey Transcripts, Bdle 17; G. Anstruther, 'Lancashire Clergy in 1639', *Recusant History*, iv, 1957, 40–6.

[198] But Dr C. Haigh, though not Dr J. Bossy, rejects any 'straightforward link between the pattern of religious allegiance and the pattern of agriculture' in Lancashire (Haigh, op. cit., 307, 323–4; Bossy, op. cit., 91–3).

[199] Dr Bossy has indeed argued that 'in the sixteenth and seventeenth centuries any sort of sustained industrial development in the North was a practically absolute barrier to the persistence of Catholicism' (ibid., 88).

[200] Cliffe, 186; Watts, 82–3; Phillips, thesis, 46. The Northumberland figures are for 1615.

[201] Cliffe, 262.

CHAPTER II

THE CAVALIER AND ROUNDHEAD
GENTRY

INTRODUCTION

Contemporaries believed that far more gentry were Royalists than
Parliamentarians during the Civil War. Richard Baxter, a Puritan
divine, observed that, outside the Home Counties and East Anglia,
'a very great part of the Knights and Gentlemen ... adhered to the
king' and that Parliament's support came from 'the smaller part (as
some thought) of the Gentry in most of the Counties, and the greatest
part of the Tradesmen and Free-holders and the middle sort of Men'.[1]
The Royalist Edward Hyde, Earl of Clarendon, stressed that 'most
of the gentry ... throughout the kingdom' were 'engaged against' Parliament.[2] It should be noted that both Baxter and Clarendon are
emphasising numerical, not economic, differences between the Royalist and Parliamentarian gentry. This accords with the findings of
recent research. In his book on the Yorkshire gentry Dr J. T. Cliffe
has shown that the only major economic distinction between the two
sides was that indebtedness was more noticeable among the Royalists
than among the Parliamentarians. He has also suggested that religion
was an important reason for choosing sides.[3]

What was the situation in Lancashire? It has been shown that the
towns were mainly Parliamentarian,[4] and that many of the rural
'middle sort' strongly resisted the king's forces during the Civil War.[5]
But so far the gentry have received little attention. This chapter will
therefore attempt to answer three main questions. First, how many
of the Lancashire gentry were to be found on either or neither side?
Secondly, what part did the gentry play in the Civil War, both inside
and outside the palatinate?[6] Thirdly, how did the Royalist and Parliamentarian gentry compare from a social, economic and religious
standpoint?

I POLITICAL LOYALTIES

Who were the Royalist and Parliamentarian gentry? They were those
who, at some time or other between 1642 and 1648, served either the
king or Parliament in a military or civil capacity. A Lancashire Royalist was one who fought for King Charles I either in the First Civil
War (1642–46) or in the Second Civil War (1648), or in both wars.

The Royalists also included such officials as commissioners of array, collectors of the subsidy in 1642 and members of the Earl of Derby's Council. The Lancashire Parliamentarians included soldiers, civilian officials like county committeemen, sequestration agents, assessors, collectors and magistrates, and also those who voluntarily contributed men or money to the Parliamentary cause. Besides Royalist and Parliamentarian gentry there were a number who changed sides. Yet Side-changers appear to have been far fewer in Lancashire than in many other English counties, although I have excluded from this category those few who only changed sides in or after 1646.[7]

Well over half the 774 Lancashire gentry families cannot be placed in any of the three above-mentioned categories. We are ignorant as to the possible Civil War allegiances or sympathies of 482 families.[8] The overwhelming majority of these were minor gentry (plain gentlemen), and only 32—a mere 6 per cent—belonged to the greater gentry: the baronets, knights and esquires. The landed income of only 237 out of the 482 is discoverable and the average was as low as £115 per annum.[9] Indeed, most of these 482 families were so poor and obscure that they might almost, to use Professor W. G. Hoskins's phrase, be termed 'peasant gentry'. Like the common people, the bulk of them may have remained neutral during the Civil War.[10]

What about the other gentry families? How many were Royalists and Parliamentarians, and how many changed sides or belonged to politically divided families? The existing evidence would suggest that in Lancashire the Royalists greatly outnumbered the Parliamentarians.[11] Excluding the three peers—James Stanley, seventh Earl of Derby, Viscount Richard Molyneux of Sefton, and Henry, Lord Morley and Mounteagle—who were all Royalists, 177 (22·9 per cent) of the Lancashire gentry families supported the King, while only 91 (11·7 per cent) aided Parliament. Even if we added those who supported the Republic from 1649 to 1660 but did not apparently participate in either the First or Second Civil War, the number of Parliamentarian families would rise to only 117. In every hundred, except Salford, the Royalists outnumbered the Parliamentarians, as is shown in Table 16 (and the maps, fig. 3).

It is perhaps worth comparing the gentry of Lancashire with those in other counties. In Cheshire the gentry who participated in the Civil War were split almost evenly, 185 supporting the king and 176 aiding Parliament.[12] In Sussex 'the ninety or so leading county families ... were divided roughly equally into royalists, parliamentarians and neutrals'.[13] By contrast, the gentry of Cumberland and Westmorland produced over three Royalists for every one Parliamentarian in both First and Second Civil Wars.[14] It was, however, the gentry of Leicestershire and Yorkshire who most closely resembled those of Lancashire, since they produced two Royalists for every one Parliamentarian.[15]

[Continued on page 46

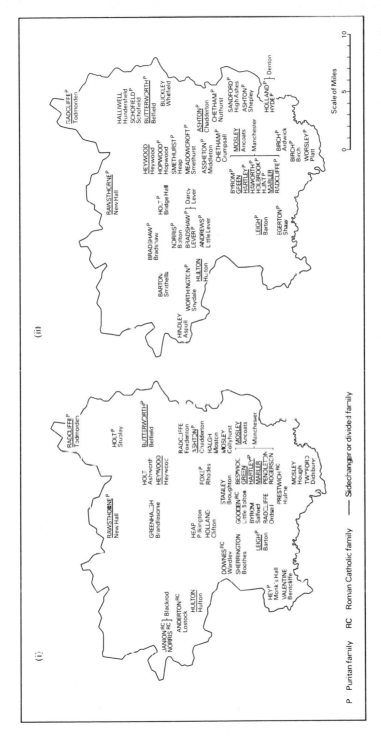

(i)

RADCLIFFE P
Todmorden

HOLT P
Stubley

BUTTERWORTH P
Belfield

RADCLIFFE
Foxdenton

ASHTON P
Chadderton

HALGH
Moston

MOSLEY
Collyhurst

MOSLEY
Ancoats

Manchester

RAWSTHORNE P
New Hall

GREENHALGH
Brandlesome

HOLT
Ashworth

HEYWOOD
Heywood

HEAP
Pilkington

HOLLAND
Clifton

FOX P
Rhodes

STANLEY
Broughton

BESWICK
GREEN
HARTLEY P
MARLER

PENDLETON
ROGERSON

PRESTWICH RC
Hulme

DOWNES RC
Wardley

SHERRINGTON
Boothes

GOODEN RC
Little Bolton

BYROM
Salford

RADCLIFFE
Ordsall

MOSLEY
Hough

TWYFORD
Didsbury

HEY P
Monk's Hall

VALENTINE
Bentcliffe

LEIGH P
Barton

JANION RC
NORRIS RC } Blackrod

ANDERTON RC
Lostock

HULTON
Hulton

P Puritan family   RC Roman Catholic family   —— Sidechanger or divided family

(ii)

RADCLIFFE P
Todmorden

HALLIWELL
Hundersfield
SCHOFIELD P
Schofield

BUTTERWORTH P
Belfield

BUCKLEY
Whitfield

HEYWOOD
Heywood

HOPWOOD P
Hopwood

SMETHURST P
Smethurst

MEADOWCROFT P
Heap

ASSHETON P
Middleton

ASHTON P
Chadderton

CHETHAM P
Nuthurst

CHETHAM P
Crumpsall

SANDFORD P
High Ashes

ASHTON P
Shepley

HOLLAND P
HYDE P   Denton

RAWSTHORNE P
New Hall

BRADSHAW P
Bradshaw

HOLT P
Bridge Hall

BRADSHAW P }
LEVER P   Darcy Lever

ANDREWS P
Little Lever

NORRIS P
Bolton

BARTON
Smithells

WORTHINGTON P
Snydale

HULTON P
Hulton

HINDLEY
Aspull

MOSLEY P
Ancoats

Manchester

BYROM P
GREEN
HARTLEY P
HOLBROOK P
HUNT P
MARLER
RADCLIFFE P

BIRCH P
Ardwick

BIRCH P
Birch

WORSLEY P
Platt

LEIGH P
Barton

EGERTON P
Shaw

Scale of Miles

0   5   10

Fig. 3. Royalist and Parliamentarian gentry families of Lancashire (a) Salford Hundred. (i) Royalist gentry families, (ii) Parliamentarian gentry families.

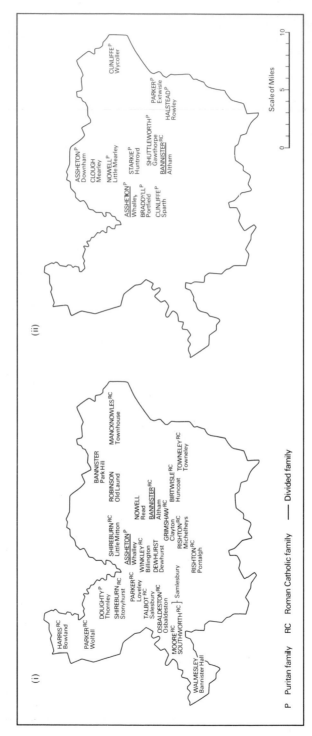

(i)

(ii)

P Puritan family   RC Roman Catholic family   —— Divided family

Fig. 3. Royalist and Parliamentarian gentry families of Lancashire. (b) Blackburn Hundred. (i) Royalist gentry families, (ii) Parliamentarian gentry families.

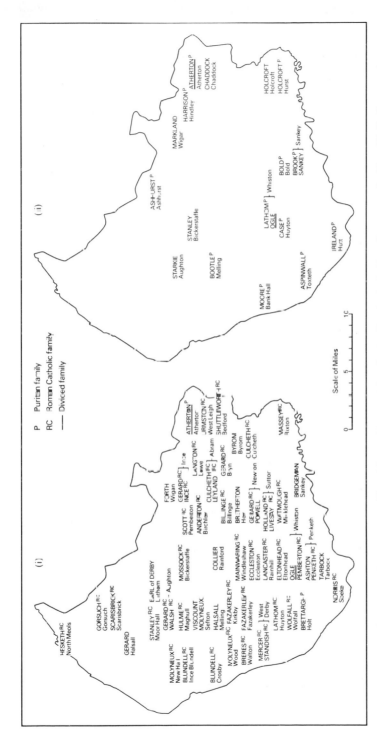

Fig. 3: Royalist and Parliamentarian gentry families of Lancashire. (c) West Derby Hundred. (i) Royalist gentry families, (ii) Parliamentarian gentry families.

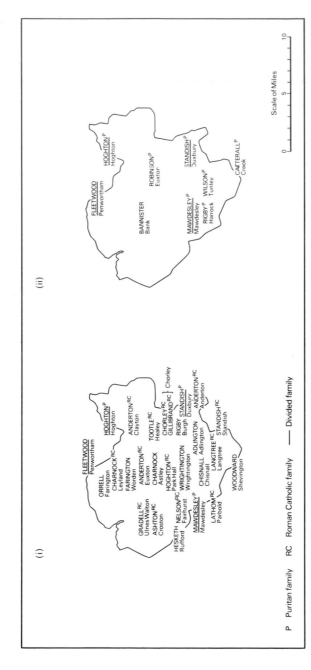

(i)

(ii)

P Puritan family   RC Roman Catholic family   —— Divided family

Fig. 3. Royalist and Parliamentarian gentry families of Lancashire. (*d*) Leyland Hundred. (i) Royalist gentry families, (ii) Parliamentarian gentry families.

Scale of Miles

0   5   10

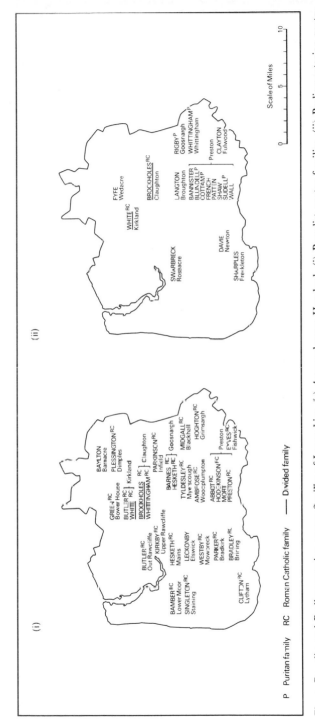

Fig. 3. Royalist and Parliamentarian gentry families of Lancashire. (e) Amounderness Hundred. (i) Royalist gentry families, (ii) Parliamentarian gentry families.

P Puritan family   RC Roman Catholic family   —— Divided family

(i)

BAMBER RC
Lower Moor

SINGLETON RC
Staining

CLIFTON RC
Lytham

BUTLER RC
Out Rawcliffe

KIRKBY RC
Upper Rawcliffe

HESKETH RC
Mains

LECKONBY RC
Elswick

WESTBY RC
Mowbreck

PARKER RC
Bradkirk

BRADLEY RC
Brining

GREY RC
Bower House

BUTLER RC ⎤ Kirkland
WHITE RC ⎦

BROOKHOLES RC
WHITTINGHAM RC ⎤ Claughton

BAYLTON
Barnacre

PLESSINGTON RC
Dimples

PARKINSON RC
Infield

BARNES RC ⎤
HESKETH RC ⎦ Goosnargh

TYLDESLEY RC
Myerscough

AMBROSE RC
Woodplumpton

ABBOT RC
HODGKINSON FC ⎤ Preston
MORT ⎦
PRESTON RC

MIDGALL RC
Blackhall

HOGHTON RC
Grimsargh

EYVES RC
Fishwick

(ii)

WHITE RC
Kirkland

BROCKHOLES RC
Claughton

FYFE
Wedacre

SWARBRECK
Roseacre

DAVIE
Newton

SHARPLES
Freckleton

LANGTON
Broughton

RIGBY P
Goosnargh

WHITTINGHAM P
Whittingham

BANNISTER
BLUNDELL P
COTTAM
FRENCH
PATTEN
SHAW
SUDELL P
WALL ⎦ Preston

CLAYTON
Fulwood

Scale of Miles

0   5   10

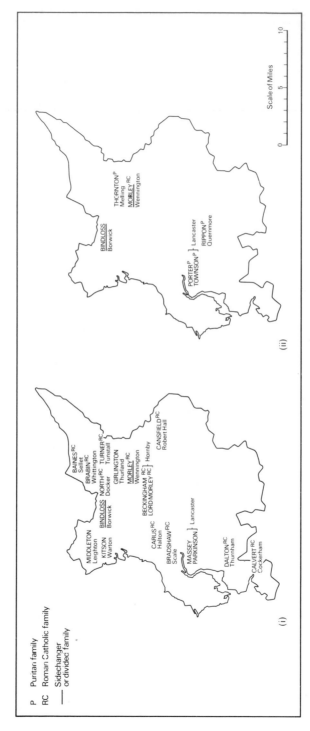

P   Puritan family
RC Roman Catholic family

— Sidechanger
    or divided family

(i)

MIDDLETON
Leighton

KITSON
Warton

BINDLOSS
Borwick

CARUS RC
Halton

BRADSHAW RC
Scale

MASSEY
PARKINSON } Lancaster

DALTON RC
Thurnham

CALVERT RC
Cockerham

BAINES RC
Sellet

BRABIN RC
Whittington

NORTH RC TURNER RC
Docker   Tunstall

GIRLINGTON
Thurland

MORLEY RC
Wennington

BECKINGHAM RC
LORD MORLEY RC } Hornby

CANSFIELD RC
Robert Hall

(ii)

BINDLOSS
Borwick

THORNTON P
Melling

MORLEY RC
Wennington

PORTER P
TOWNSON P } Lancaster

RIPPON P
Quernmore

Scale of Miles

0   5   10

Fig. 3. Royalist and Parliamentarian gentry families of Lancashire. (*f*) South Lonsdale. (i) Royalist gentry families, (ii) Parliamentarian gentry families.

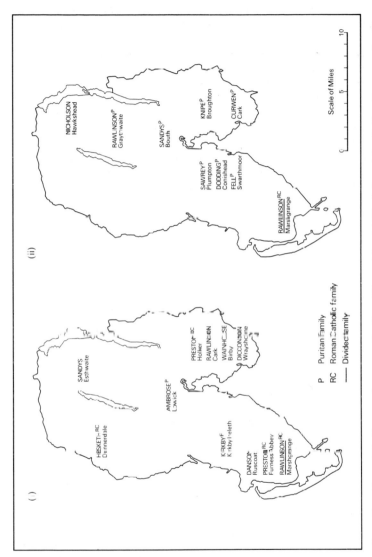

Fig. 3. Royalist and Parliamentarian gentry families of Lancashire. (g) North Lonsdale. (i) Royalist gentry families, (ii) Parliamentarian gentry families.

Continued from page 38]

Dr J. T. Cliffe has shown that in Yorkshire there were not only Royalist and Parliamentarian gentry, but also 69 families who divided or changed sides, a far greater number than in Lancashire.[16] When dealing with the Civil War Dr Cliffe makes it clear that he is dividing the gentry on a family rather than on an individual basis. In view of the supreme importance of the family as a social unit during the seventeenth century,[17] this method seems sensible enough. On the other hand it could present a statistically misleading picture of Civil War allegiances. Some families sent far more of their members into battle than others. William Blundell of Crosby, a Cavalier, was the only one of his family to engage in the Civil War, but among the Royalist Brethertons of Hey both father and son took part, the other three sons apparently remaining neutral. Every male member of the

TABLE 16

CIVIL WAR ALLEGIANCE OF LANCASHIRE GENTRY FAMILIES

Hundred	Royalist families	Parliamentarian families	Sidechangers/ Divided families	Neutral/ Other families	Total No. of families
Salford	26 (13·3%)	31 (15·8%)	11 (5·6%)	128 (65·3%)	196 (100·0%)
Blackburn	22 (20·0%)	10 (9·1%)	2 (1·8%)	76 (69·1%)	110 (100·0%)
West Derby	54 (27·3%)	17 (8·6%)	2 (1·0%)	125 (63·1%)	198 (100·0%)
Leyland	23 (32·4%)	5 (7·1%)	4 (5·6%)	39 (54·9%)	71 (100·0%)
Amounderness	27 (25·2%)	16 (15·0%)	2 (1·9%)	62 (57·9%)	107 (100·0%)
Lonsdale	25 (27·2%)	12 (13·0%)	3 (3·3%)	52 (56·5%)	92 (100·0%)
Total	177 (22·9%)	91 (11·7%)	24 (3·1%)	482 (62·3%)	774 (100·0%)

Rigby family of Goosnargh supported Parliament: Alexander Rigby, the elder, and his two younger brothers, Joseph and George, together with Alexander, the younger, and his brother Edward. The case for classifying the gentry on an individual as well as on a family basis is further strengthened when it is realised that split families did not always divide equally between the two sides. The Butterworths of Belfield certainly did, Edward supporting Parliament and his younger brother, Alexander, the king. But among the Hoghtons of Hoghton Tower there were four Royalists and only one Parliamentarian. The Standishes of Duxbury were noted for their Puritan and Parliamentarian sympathies. Even so, Thomas, the eldest son, fought (and died) for the king in defiance of his father and two younger brothers.[18] If, then, we classify the Lancashire gentry on an individual basis, the following picture emerges of their Civil War loyalties (see Table 17).

Once again it will be noted that, except in Salford hundred, the Royalists greatly outnumbered the Parliamentarians, although their numerical superiority is less marked in Blackburn hundred, largely because of the adherence of all six Shuttleworths to the Parliamentary cause. Also noticeable is the fact that a mere nine (2·1 per cent) of the 419 participants changed sides.[19]

The geographical distribution of the Royalist and Parliamentarian gentry shows that political divisions in Lancashire roughly coincided with religious divisions. The Parliamentary gentry were strongest in Salford hundred, the most puritanical part of Lancashire. Many of the Parliamentarian gentry lived in or near Manchester—'a Goshen, a place of light'[20]—and Bolton—'the Geneva of Lancashire'[21]—and were consequently open to Puritan influences. Altogether 34 (74 per cent) of the 46 individual Parliamentarian gentry in Salford hundred were Puritan. The Royalist gentry, on the other hand, were strongest in the western and northern hundreds, the most pro-Catholic parts of Lancashire. In West Derby Hundred 43 (80 per cent) of the 54

TABLE 17

CIVIL WAR ALLEGIANCE OF INDIVIDUAL LANCASHIRE GENTRY

Hundred	Royalists	Parliamentarians	Sidechangers
Salford	39	46	6
Blackburn	35	21	0
West Derby	75	25	0
Leyland	44	10	0
Amounderness	45	22	0
Lonsdale	34	14	3
Total	272	138	9

Royalist gentry families included one or more participating members who were Papist, and this is a conservative estimate. In Amounderness 24 (89 per cent) of the 27 Royalist families were Catholic and so were 38 (84 per cent) of the 45 individual Royalist gentlemen.

Many Royalist gentry were heavily concentrated near the main residences of the Lancashire Royalist peers, while most Parliamentarian gentry lived at safe distances away from them. The Royalist gentry must have been influenced by the Royalist nobility. The immense power of the seventh Earl of Derby has been generally acknowledged by historians and contemporaries. The author of *Discourse of the Warr in Lancashire* considered that the Stanley family was 'esteemed by most about them with little lesse respect than kings'.[22] Clarendon believed that the Earl of Derby had 'a greater influence' and 'a more absolute command over the people' in Lancashire and Cheshire 'than any subject in England had in any other quarter of the kingdom'.[23] It would have taken great courage to defy so powerful a magnate,[24] and it is difficult to believe that the influence of the Earl of Derby was not at least a partial explanation for the large number of Royalist gentry in West Derby hundred, for it was there that he held over half his Lancashire estates, including Lathom, the Royalist headquarters in north-west England.[25] But the Stanleys were not the only influencial noble family in West Derby. The Molyneuxes of Sefton also had considerable property and power in the region,[26] and a number of the neighbouring Royalist gentry families had been previously in their service, such as Fazakerley of Fazakerley, Fazakerley of Kirkby, Hulme of Maghull, Mercer of West Derby, Molyneux of the Wood and Standish of West Derby.[27] Finally, it can hardly have been an accident that in south Lonsdale several Royalist gentry lived near the Cavalier nobleman, Henry, Lord Morley and Mounteagle.

2 CIVIL WAR ACTIVITIES

Such was the geographical spread of the Royalist and Parliamentarian gentry. What part did they play in the Civil War? First, we must keep a sense of proportion and not exaggerate the part played by the gentry. The Civil War in Lancashire was not a class war,[28] but neither was it just a fratricidal conflict among the ruling classes, even at the outset.[29] Although neutrality was probably the prevailing mood among the common people in Lancashire,[30] many of them nevertheless participated in the struggle.[31] Some did so under compulsion, like the Earl of Derby's Lancashire men who, at Marston Moor, threw down their arms, crying that they were pressed men and did not want to fight.[32] Others joined in of their own accord, like the 'countrie people' of the Kirkham area who 'came with great cheerfulnesse unto' the same earl.[33] In the strongly Parliamentary Manchester region a contemporary spoke of 'ther being noe compulsion but all freely put themselves under such Captains as they Judged most convenient for them'.[34] Moreover, the importance of popular participation is further shown by the fact that in neither the Royalist nor the Parliamentarian forces did the gentry have a monopoly of officers between 1642 and 1648. (See Table 18.)

The social status of the various ranks of Lancashire Royalist and Parliamentarian army officers will be analysed in more detail in the next chapter and in Appendix II. Suffice it to say for the present that some of the bravest and most active Lancashire officers were commoners, such as Captain William Kay of Cobhouse, Yeoman, and Lieutenant Robert Walthew, Yeoman and money lender, both of whom gallantly tried to defend Lathom House for the Countess of Derby.[35]

Despite the important part played by plebeians, it nonetheless remains true that the real drive and leadership during the Civil War in Lancashire came from the gentry. Even so, some of them had at first little desire for war. Among the Lancashire gentry there was of course far less moderation and far more zeal than among the gentry of Cheshire, Kent, Sussex, East Anglia and some other parts of England.[36] Yet even in Lancashire there were moderates on both sides and these tried hard to prevent a conflict. In the autumn of 1642 peace negotiations were opened through the medium of Roger Nowell of Read, a Royalist captain but a relative of the Parliamentarian Colonel Richard Shuttleworth of Gawthorpe. The latter was equally anxious to avert a civil war. Eventually six leaders from each side were to meet, the Parliamentarians being Shuttleworth, John Braddyll of Portfield, John Bradshaw of Bradshaw, Peter Egerton of Shaw, Richard Holland of Denton and John Starkie of Huntroyd, and the

TABLE 18

ARMY OFFICERS' SOCIAL STATUS AND ALLEGIANCE[a]

	Royalists	Parliamentarians
Peers	3 (1·3%)	–
Gentry	126 (52·7%)	79 (50·3%)
Gentry?	26 (10·9%)	17 (10·8%)
Plebeians	84 (35·1%)	61 (38·9%)
Total	239 (100·0%)	157 (100·0%)

[a] For sources see below, p. 66 n. 11, and above, p. 30 n. 35–40. It is impossible to compile a complete list of gentle and plebeian officers on both sides. In addition to the above, there were five Parliamentarian and 52 Royalist gentry soldiers whose rank is unknown, although most of them may have been officers. At least two Royalist gentlemen—Thomas Heap of Pilkington and William Holland of Clifton—appear to have been gentlemen-rankers. See *Roy. Comp. Papers*, iii, 175, 248–9.

Royalists being William Farington of Worden, John Fleetwood of Penwortham, Savile Radcliffe of Todmorden, Alexander Rigby of Burgh and, it was hoped, Sir Thomas Barton of Smithells and Robert Holt of Stubley. But the intended meeting never took place. On 15 October Richard Holland wrote from Manchester saying that Parliament had forbidden any local pacts. Shuttleworth forwarded the letter to the Royalists and the matter was closed.[37] Moderate though he was, Shuttleworth and all his five sons were soon organising the Calder and Pendle Roundheads from Gawthorpe as the military headquarters. The other five Parliamentarians were also active, and so were the Royalist leaders.

However, once the Civil War had broken out, support for either king or Parliament was a shifting rather than a stable condition. Participation was often determined by the course of events. For example, there was apparently much neutralism in the Liverpool area until the approach of Prince Rupert in May 1644. Then 'the country thereabout who formerly lurked as neuters do now show themselves in arms for the Earl of Derby'.[38] It was perhaps also then that Roger Breres of Walton, John Lathom of Huyton, James Pemberton of Whiston and Thomas Wolfall of Wolfall became Royalists.[39] In Leyland hundred some of the gentry—Peter Catterall of Crook, Robert Mawdesley of Mawdesley and Thomas Wilson of Tunley—did not openly declare themselves for Parliament until 1646, by which time the main Royalist garrison in the region, Lathom House, had fallen to the Parliamentary forces.[40]

Having thus reminded ourselves about the important part played by plebeians, the large number of possible neutral gentry, the reluctance of moderates on both sides to prosecute a civil war, and the shifting condition of political allegiances, it remains true that there was a bitter and bloody conflict in Lancashire, that large numbers of the gentry took a leading part in it, and that it is possible to divide these gentry into two sides: the Royalists and the Parliamentarians.

We have seen that the Royalist gentry greatly outnumbered the Parliamentarian gentry. Why, then, were they not able to hold Lancashire for the king, especially during the early years of the First Civil War? There were perhaps three main reasons for this. First, many more Cavaliers than Parliamentarian gentry were busy fighting outside the county and the local Royalist forces were thus short of officers and men. Mr R. N. Dore has partly explained the collapse of the Royalists in Lancashire and Cheshire in 1643 by the fact that three Lancashire and two Cheshire regiments had marched with the king to Edgehill and never returned as units to the north-west.[41] At least 16, and possibly as many as 29, Lancashire Royalist gentlemen fought at Edgehill. A few, like Major Henry Byrom of Byrom, William Radcliffe of Foxdenton, and his son Robert, died on the battlefield. But it was not only at Edgehill that Lancashire Royalist gentry were to be found. Several saw action at the first and second battles of Newbury, Marston Moor, Lichfield and Oxford. A few fought at Naseby and Worcester and in more distant places like Bristol, Cornwall and Ireland. The most ubiquitous of all the Lancashire Royalists, and a well known national figure, was Major-General Charles Gerard of Halsall, who was at Edgehill, Lichfield, Bristol, Aldbourne Chase, the First Battle of Newbury, Oxford, Newark, Beeston Castle, Rowton Moor, Worcester and in South Wales. At least 71 (40 per cent), and possibly as many as 92 (51 per cent), of the 178 Royalist gentry soldiers fought at some time or other outside Lancashire.[42] By contrast, the overwhelming majority of the Parliamentary gentry soldiers were confined to their native soil. Apparently as many as 83 per cent of the Parliamentarians fought only in Lancashire, as compared with 60 per cent of the Cavaliers. Only eight Parliamentarian gentlemen were killed in the Civil War, at least six of them in Lancashire.[43] It is true that

a number of Lancashire Parliamentarian gentry, such as Major-
General Ralph Assheton of Middleton, Colonel George Dodding of
Conishead and Colonel Alexander Rigby of Goosnargh, were fairly
conspicuous at Marston Moor.[44] Assheton also saw service in Westmorland, took part in the siege of Chester and played a prominent
role in the battle of Nantwich.[45] But it is not easy to find examples
of Lancashire Parliamentarian gentlemen fighting outside the adjoining counties of Westmorland, Yorkshire and Cheshire. Indeed, a mere
6 per cent of the Parliamentary gentry soldiers seem to have gone
farther afield, like Colonel John Moore of Bank Hall, who saw service
in distant Ireland as well as in neighbouring Cheshire.[46] In fact there
appears to have been a certain reluctance on the part of the Parliamentarian gentry to move too far away from Lancashire.[47] But this

TABLE 19

MILITARY ACTIVITIES AND ALLEGIANCE

	Royalists	Parliamentarians
(a) Total number of soldiers	178	84
(b) Fought in Lancashire only	107 (60%)	70 (83%)
(c) Fought in neighbouring counties	13 (14½%)	11 (13½%)
(d) Fought in other parts of the British Isles	55 (31%)	5 (6%)
(e) Total fighting outside Lancashire[a]	71 (40%)	14 (17%)

[a] Two Parliamentarians and nine Royalists fought both in neighbouring counties
and in other parts of the British Isles. For a full list of Lancashire gentlemen fighting
outside the palatinate see Blackwood, D.Phil. thesis, App. IV.

seems to have paid dividends and must have been one of the main
reasons why the Lancashire Parliamentarian gentry quickly won control of the palatinate, at a time when their brethren in other counties
were suffering their heaviest defeats. The military activities of the
Lancashire gentry during the First and Second Civil Wars may be
summarised as in Table 19.

A second reason for the military failures of the Lancashire Royalist
gentry was popular opposition to their recruiting drive. When the
Civil War broke out in the provinces in 1642, the armies were officially
raised for the king by local commissioners of array and for Parliament
by its own appointed deputy lieutenants. But in Lancashire it was
perhaps more often as landlords than as officials that the gentry recruited troops. Many of the Royalist and Parliamentarian gentry
seem to have had the obedient military support of their tenantry

during the Civil War. The Parliamentary gentry in south-east Lancashire—Edward Butterworth of Belfield, Thomas Chetham of Nuthurst, Peter Egerton of Shaw, Richard Holland and Robert Hyde, both of Denton—'came with their tenants to assist the Towne' of Manchester when it was besieged in 1642. Also defending Manchester were 'about an hundred and fiftie of the tenants of Master Ashton of Middleton in compleat armies'.[48] Among the Royalists 'most of the Popish affected Gentlemen in Amounderness Hundred' had the assistance of 'there Tenants in Armes',[49] while the Earl of Derby was able to raise three regiments of foot and three troops of horse among his tenants, dependants and friends in Lancashire.[50] But the earl met resistance as well as obedience to his orders. Clarendon said that many Lancastrians engaged 'themselves against the King that they might not be subject to that Lord's commands'.[51] Certainly many of his tenants openly defied him. Sixty of them in Bury and Pilkington apparently not only refused to render him military service but also 'joined with the wel affected in and about Manchester', serving the Parliam' ffaithfully'.[52] The earl's tenants in West Derby and Wavertree also supported Parliament.[53] The Countess of Derby found difficulty in preparing for the defence of Lathom House because of 'the ill will of some of her tenants who inclined to the popular cause'.[54] By contrast the Lancashire Parliamentarian gentry seem to have encountered virtually no opposition to their recruiting campaign, except in Lytham, where 'the people of the pish [parish] would not raise with or follow' Captain George Sharples of Freckleton, 'but some few only'.[55]

A third reason why the Parliamentarian gentry in Lancashire were able to triumph was that, like those in Cheshire,[56] they appear to have played a more active part in the Civil War than the Royalist gentry. Of the 138 Parliamentarians 84 were soldiers, and most of them fairly active too. Seventy-nine undertook civilian work as members of local committees, treasurers, collectors, sequestration agents or other officials. To judge by such sources as the Commonwealth Exchequer Papers, most of those officials were busy men. Only eight Parliamentarians seem to have played a merely nominal role in the conflict. By contrast the Royalists had a high proportion of lukewarm and passive supporters, as they had in Cheshire.[57] Although 178 out of 272 Lancashire Royalist gentry were soldiers, a number of these alleged that they had been 'enforced' or 'commanded' to bear arms against their will.[58] Thomas Heap of Pilkington, Gentleman, told the Committee for Compounding that 'being a tenant under the Earl of Derby he was threatened from his dwelling house into service as a common trooper'.[59] A mere 36 of the Royalist gentry were officials, half of them in name only.[60] Altogether there were at least 64 passive Royalists, and these included gentlemen like Henry Pendleton of Manchester, who simply retreated into a royal garrison for protection, with little intention of doing any fighting themselves.[61] There were also a number of Royalists, like William Ambrose of Lowick and Christopher Anderton of Lostock, who retired early from the struggle.[62] With so many unenthusiastic supporters, it is little wonder that the Royalist gentry failed to hold Lancashire for the king.

3 SIMILARITIES AND DIFFERENCES

So much for the military and political history of the Lancashire gentry during the Civil War. We must now compare the two sides in 1642 from a social, economic and religious standpoint. Did the Royalist and Parliamentarian gentry differ in respect of age, lineage, status, power, wealth, education and religion? Let us deal first with the ages of the two sides. In a recent article on 'Youth as a Force in the Modern World',[63] Herbert Moller has argued that from the Reformation until the twentieth century revolutionaries have generally tended to be younger than conservatives. But in Lancashire there was no correlation between youth and revolutionary fervour. Of the 226 Civil War contestants whose ages are known and who were 15 or over in 1642, the average age of the Royalists was 37 and that of the Parliamentarians 38. The median age of the Royalists was 34 and that of the Parliamentarians 38.[64] These differences were not as great as those among Members of Parliament. The median age of the Royalist members of the Long Parliament was 36 and that of the Parliamentarians 47.[65] Moreover, among officials of the central government a noticeably higher proportion of Royalists than of Parliamentarians were aged 42 or under in 1642.[66] But it would seem that in Lancashire the younger gentry were no more radical nor significantly more conservative than their elders.

Closely linked with age is the problem of younger sons. Professor Lawrence Stone has suggested that the Civil War must have come as a welcome relief to many younger sons living in a hopeless economic situation and that they rushed to enroll as officers in both armies.[67] Certainly in Lancashire some of them played a very active part in the conflict. One need only think of such men as Captain John Ashhurst, second son of Henry Ashhurst, bravely defending Bolton for Parliament, or of Cuthbert, second son of Sir Cuthbert Clifton of Lytham, raising a regiment of soldiers in the Fylde and, as Governor of Liverpool, taking desperate but unpopular measures to provision the garrison for the king.[68] Yet younger sons played a lesser role in Lancashire than in Kent and Sussex, where they were apparently prominent among the more zealous Cavaliers.[69] In Lancashire, however, younger sons formed only a minority on both sides, although Table 20 shows that they were marginally more prominent among the Parliamentarian than among the Royalist gentry.

TABLE 20

PLACE IN THE FAMILY AND ALLEGIANCE[a]

	Royalists	Parliamentarians
First sons	164 (60·3%)	81 (58·7%)
Younger sons	68 (25·0%)	40 (29·0%)
Unknown	40 (14·7%)	17 (12·3%)
Total	272 (100·0%)	138 (100·0%)

a Apart from local and family histories the best sources are the Heraldic Visitations for 1613 and 1664–65. See below, p. 68 n. 64.

As regards median age and proportion of younger sons, the differences between the Royalist and Parliamentarian gentry of Lancashire were statistically negligible. Far more significant were differences in lineage, as Table 21 shows. A somewhat higher proportion of Royalists than of Parliamentarians belonged to families which in the Middle Ages had been gentry. In fact the differences were even greater than appear in the table because 35 (50 per cent) of the Parliamentary gentry of mediaeval stock belonged to cadet branches of the main family,[70] whereas only 50 (30 per cent) of the 'mediaeval' Royalist gentry did so. Professor Everitt remarks that 'it was natural that the more deeply rooted ... gentry should tend to support what seemed, in the 1640s, the more conservative side' and that 'it was equally natural for the brisker, newer and more dynamic gentry to support political innovations'.[71] Certainly in Lancashire a rather higher percentage of Parliamentarians than of Royalists had risen to gentility during the Tudor and early Stuart periods. Nineteen per cent of the Parliamentarians but only 13 per cent of the Royalists

TABLE 21

LINEAGE AND ALLEGIANCE[a]

Gentry origins	Royalists	Parliamentarians
Middle Ages	163 (60%)	69 (50%)
Tudor period	58 (21%)	37 (27%)
Stuart period	35 (13%)	26 (19%)
Uncertain	16 (6%)	6 (4%)
Total	272 (100%)	138 (100%)

a For sources regarding lineage see above, pp. 22 n., 30 n. 35–40.

could be described as Stuart or *parvenu* gentry. In short, a greater proportion of Parliamentarians than of Royalists belonged to families experiencing upward social mobility. This contrasts sharply with Yorkshire, where 14 per cent of the Royalists but only 13 per cent of the Parliamentarians had established themselves among the county gentry since 1603.[72] However, the differences in lineage between the Parliamentarian and Royalist gentry of Lancashire should not be exaggerated. It will be noted that the Stuart gentry were a small minority among both the Royalists and the Parliamentarians, while a large proportion on both sides were of 'ancient stock'. If the Royalists could boast such families as the Cliftons of Lytham, who had provided a sheriff for Lancashire in 1284,[73] and the Hoghtons of Hoghton Tower, who could accurately trace their descent back to the Norman Conquest,[74] the Parliamentarians could muster support from such ancient families as the Chethams of Nuthurst, one of whom was a knight in 1260,[75] and the Asshetons of Middleton, whose ancestor, Sir John de Assheton, had his brave deeds recorded by Froissart.[76] Indeed, such differences in lineage as existed in Lancashire were trifling compared with those to be found in Leicestershire. There 57 per cent of the Royalists as against 33 per cent of Parliamentarians belonged to the older, 'mediaeval' families.[77]

Closely linked with lineage was status, and here too the differences between the two sides in Lancashire were not outstanding. It is not always easy to assess the correct status of individual gentry. The lists of county committeemen tend to overestimate the numbers of Parliamentarians who belonged to the greater gentry, since office-holding was an important status elevator. On the other hand, the Royalist Composition Papers frequently downgrade the Royalists. This was because the latter sometimes deliberately debased themselves so as to escape heavy composition fines. For example, William Forth of Wigan and Ralph Scott of Pemberton, designated yeomen in the Royalist Composition Papers, were described as gentlemen in the 1641 lay subsidy roll for West Derby hundred. Luke Hodgkinson of Preston, a yeoman according to the Royalist Composition Papers, was called a gentleman in the Protestation Returns of 1641. These returns, together with the 1641 Lay Subsidy Rolls, the Knighthood Composition lists 1631–32, the Muster Rolls of 1632, and the Freeholders' lists of 1600 and 1633,[78] are the most reliable indication of status. They show that on the eve of the Civil War the greater gentry were only slightly better represented among the Royalists than among the Parliamentarians and that, excluding plebeians, the lesser gentry formed a large majority on both sides. (See Table 22.)

During the seventeenth century status often determined the exercise of political power. One view of the Civil War is that it was a conflict between the 'ins' and the 'outs', between Court and Country, between office-holders and those excluded from office.[79] But Professor

G. E. Aylmer has noted the very small number of Lancashire men
in the central government between 1625 and 1642.[80] Only two Royalist families had held important offices of state and two others held
minor offices. The father of the second Viscount Molyneux was Re-
ceiver-General of the Duchy of Lancaster until his death in 1636,
while Edward Mosley of Hough's uncle and namesake was Attorney-
General for the Duchy of Lancaster and died in 1638, leaving the
manor of Rolleston in Staffordshire to his nephew. One Parliamentarian—John Bradshaw of Bradshaw—may have been Windsor
Herald from about 1626 to 1633,[81] while another was Serjeant at law
in the Duchy of Lancaster.[82]

A number of Royalists and Parliamentarians, or their fathers, held
such local offices as sheriff, bailiff, master forester, escheator and local

TABLE 22

SOCIAL STATUS AND ALLEGIANCE

	Royalists	Parliamentarians
Peers	3 (1·0%)	–
Baronets	4 (1·5%)	2 (1·4%)
Knights	4 (1·5%)	1 (0·7%)
Esquires	82 (29·8%)	35 (25·4%)
Gentlemen	182 (66·2%)	100 (72·5%)
Total	275 (100·0%)	138 (100·0%)

receiver of the Duchy of Lancaster. There were also a few legal offices,
such as the clerkship of the peace. These offices were by no means
the monopoly of the Cavaliers. If the Royalist Hoghtons of Hoghton
Tower were regularly master foresters of Bleasdale and Amounderness, the Parliamentarian Rigbys of Goosnargh held a tenacious grip
on the clerkship of the peace from 1608 until 1663. Of the sheriffs
between 1625 and 1642, six belonged to families that were to support
the Parliament and 10 to families that were to aid the king.

These offices carried fees, if only small ones. But there were other
offices, such as justice of the peace, deputy lieutenant, commissioner
of sewers, which officially carried no financial reward, although
expenses would normally be paid. Here too Parliamentarians were
no more excluded than were the Royalists. Between 1625 and 1642
36 Royalists, or their fathers, and 24 Parliamentarians were appointed
to the commission of the peace, while 16 Royalists and 10 Parliamentarians were sewers commissioners. Among the lay subsidy commissioners there were 15 Parliamentarians and 13 Royalists. Indeed, if
we take both paid and unpaid public service into account, we find

that the Parliamentarians had, in proportion to their numbers, a slightly greater share of power than their opponents (see Table 23). It must be remembered, of course, that many Royalists, on account of their Roman Catholicism, were legally disqualified from royal service.[83] Yet it was reported in 1626 that a number of Catholic gentry, such as Sir William Norris of Speke, or gentlemen with Catholic wives, such as Richard Shireburn of Stonyhurst, were acting as magistrates.[84] This does not alter the fact that the Parliamentarian gentry had enjoyed a slightly greater share of position and authority in the

TABLE 23

OFFICE-HOLDING AND ALLEGIANCE

		Royalists	Parliamentarians
(a)	Total number of gentry	272	138
(b)	Commissioners for:		
	Knighthood compositions, 1631–32	5 (2%)	2 (1%)
	Lay subsidies, 1626, 1628, 1641	13 (4%)	15 (10%)
	Sewers, 1632	16 (6%)	10 (7%)
(c)	Deputy Lieutenants, 1625–42	8 (3%)	2 (1%)
(d)	Justices of the Peace, 1625–42	36 (13%)	24 (17%)
(e)	Militia officers, 1628, 1634, 1636, 1640	20 (7%)	8 (5%)
(f)	Sheriffs, 1625–42	10 (3%)	6 (4%)
(g)	Other local officials, 1625–42	18 (7%)	13 (9%)
(h)	Central government officials, 1625–42	4 (1·5%)	2 (1%)
(i)	Total number of gentry holding one or more offices	56 (20%)	38 (27%)

For sources see above, pp. 17 n., 32 n., 80.

county than had the Royalist gentry. Furthermore, as in Cheshire, the Parliamentarians took more advantage of their opportunities.[85] Only five (21 per cent) of the 24 Parliamentarian magistrates could be classed as inactive, whereas 14 (39 per cent) of the 36 Royalist justices seldom attended quarter sessions.[86]

Let us now turn our attention to the economic state of the Royalist and Parliamentarian gentry, beginning with incomes. For reasons discussed elsewhere,[87] the 1641 lay subsidy rolls are the only means of comparing the annual landed incomes of the two sides.[88] It would appear from these rolls[89] that the Royalist families commanded considerably more wealth than did the Parliamentarian families. In terms of known aggregate income the former were worth at least £39,780

TABLE 24

INCOME AND ALLEGIANCE

Annual income from land in 1642 £	Royalist families	Parliamentarian families
2,000 and over	4⎫ 8 (4·5%)	0⎫ 5 (5·5%)
1,000–1,999	4⎭	5⎭
750–999	2⎫	1⎫
500–749	15⎬45 (25·4%)	3⎬13 (14·3%)
250–449	28⎭	9⎭
100–249	39⎫67 (37·9%)	23⎫37 (40·6%)
Under 100	28⎭	14⎭
Unknown	57 (32·2%)	36 (39·6%)
Total	177 (100·0%)	91 (100·0%)

and the latter only £14,627. However, in terms of *per capita* income, the Royalists were only slightly richer than the Parliamentarians. Details are given in Table 24.

Excluding the seventh Earl of Derby, whose annual income was at least £6,000,[90] and the second Viscount Molyneux, whose income was £4,080, the wealthiest Royalist was probably Sir William Gerard of Bryn, with estates worth £2,750 per annum.[91] The wealthiest Parliamentarian was Peter Bold of Bold, Esquire, with an annual income of £1,750. Yet the above table shows that the proportion of rich gentry (£1,000 p.a. upwards) was about the same on both sides. So also was the proportion of poor gentry (under £250 p.a.). What really distinguished the Royalists from the Parliamentarians was that 25 per cent of the former belonged to middle-income groups, as against only 14 per cent of the latter. This contrasts with Yorkshire, where 'roughly half the parliamentarian gentry consisted of middling landowners'.[92]

If the Lancashire Cavaliers possessed more economic wealth, the Roundhead gentry enjoyed more economic health. Yet at first sight this does not seem to have been so, for a study of the land market between 1600 and 1642 shows that some of the best examples of rising gentry are to be found on the Royalist side. Francis Sherrington, a gentleman merchant, acquired for £5,450 four manors in south Lancashire and an outlying piece of property in north Lancashire between 1632 and 1634.[93] Robert Blundell of Ince Blundell, Esquire, a prosperous common lawyer, bought five manors in the south-western seaboard, as well as property in Preston and Chipping, at a total cost of £5,454.[94] Sir Edward Mosley of Hough, as well as inheriting his deceased uncle's extensive lands in Leicestershire and Staffordshire, is said to have bought Sir William Gerard's Derbyshire property for

£9,000 in about 1641.[95] By contrast only one Lancashire Parliamentarian gentleman—Humphrey Chetham—spent over £5,000 on land, and he invested a total of £9,800.[96] Yet the spectacular purchases of a few individual Cavaliers should not blind us to the fact that 15 per cent of the Parliamentarian as against only 11 per cent of the Royalist families bought considerable property during the early seventeenth century.[97] However, let us keep a sense of proportion. By any criterion the numbers of rising families among both Parliamentarians and Royalists were extremely small.

A study of debts and land sales suggests that the declining gentry were also a very small minority among both Parliamentarians and Royalists. Only 8 per cent of families on either side seem to have sold on a large scale between 1600 and 1642.[98] However, this figure conceals the fact that sales by the Parliamentarians were far less extensive than those by the Royalists. Among the Parliamentarians only the Sankeys of Sankey lost their patrimonial estate,[99] and only the Holcrofts of Holcroft may have sold land for over £1,000. In 1628 John Holcroft sold property in Manchester for £482 and in 1642 conveyed land in Marton and Burscough for £1,067 to Sir Edward Wrightington of Wrightington, a prerogative lawyer and future Royalist.[100] Yet it is not absolutely clear whether Holcroft's second transaction was a sale or a mortgage. Among the Royalists three families sold their patrimonial lands and a number of others endured heavy losses. Those losing their main estates were the Kirkbys of Rawcliffe, the Penkeths of Penketh and the Tarbocks of Tarbock. The Kirkbys sold out to the Westbys of Mowbeck about 1636.[101] The Penkeths alienated their manor to Thomas Ashton, Esquire, some time between 1613 and 1624.[102] The Tarbocks sold their manor of Tarbock and rectory of Huyton between 1611 and 1614, and henceforth seem to have lived in humble circumstances.[103] Some Royalists who retained their patrimonial estates still lost considerable land. The Charnocks of Astley managed to hold on to Astley Hall and their manor of Charnock Richard, but between 1622 and 1636 they appear to have sold all their other property in Lancashire for a total of £8,040.[104] Heavy debts seem to have been the main reason for such vast sales. The Charnocks were borrowing money on recognisance in 1626,[105] but by 1633 they were outlawed for debt.[106] In 1634 their debts amounted to £1,266,[107] and by 1642 had reached £1,400.[108] This last sum was well over four times their annual income of £300,[109] and even by early seventeenth-century standards was a clear indication of financial insolvency.

The evidence suggests that in Lancashire, as in Cheshire and Yorkshire, the proportion of those in economic straits was higher among the Royalists than among the Parliamentarians.[110] Ignoring family liabilities, as well as debts to the Crown, and relying solely on private debts, it would appear that 28 (16 per cent) of the Royalist but only six (6 per cent) of the Parliamentarian families were in serious financial difficulties in the decade or so before the Civil War.[111] Even these figures do not tell the whole story, for the debts of the Parliamentarians were by no means crippling, except possibly those of the Braddylls of Portfield and the Schofields of Schofield, both of whom were outlawed.[112] But no Parliamentarian family could compare with the Gerards of Halsall, who, with an annual income of about £500 per annum in 1641,[113] were in debt to the tune of £5,168;[114] nor with the Norrises of Speke, who, with an annual income of at most £900 in 1635,[115] owed the large amount of £6,164 in 1631.[116] Table 25, then, sums up the financial state of the Lancashire Parliamentarian and Royalist gentry.

TABLE 25

FINANCIAL STATE AND ALLEGIANCE[a]

	Royalist gentry	Parliamentarian gentry
(a) Total number of families	177	91
(b) Families buying considerable property, 1600–42[b]	20 (11%)	14 (15%)
(c) Families selling considerable property, 1600–42	14 (8%)	7 (8%)
(d) Families in financial difficulties, 1630–42	28 (16%)	6 (6%)

a Figures given in this table are to some extent overlapping since the families which were in financial difficulties in the period 1630–42 included some which were selling or buying property in the early seventeenth century.

b If we added lands acquired by marriage, the total numbers of rising families between 1600 and 1642 would be: Royalist gentry 23 (13 per cent), Parliamentarian gentry 20 (22 per cent).

Thus, although a very small minority on both sides, the economically declining element was more noticeable among the Royalist than among the Parliamentarian gentry. Why was this? Was it, as Dr Christopher Hill has suggested, because the political division between the Royalist gentry and the Parliamentarian gentry might have broadly corresponded with an economic division between 'those who were becoming mere rentiers, and those who were actively engaged in productive activities, whether in agriculture, industry, or trade'?[117] In Lancashire this was most unlikely. However, a comparison of the economic activities of the two sides is made difficult, if not impossible, by a paucity of evidence on the Parliamentarian gentry.[118] Apart from some scattered references to coal mining among the Duchy of Lancaster Pleadings, there seems to be very little evidence about Parlia-

mentarian methods of estate management. The Lancashire Royalists
are much better documented, and this enables us to come to three
main conclusions. The first is that the Royalists seem to have included
almost every kind of landowner: the *rentier*, like John Calvert of Cockerham;[119] the demesne farmer, like John Hoghton of Park Hall;[120]
the wealthy lay impropriator, like Richard Urmston of Westleigh;[121]
the reactionary landlord, like John Brockholes of Lancaster, who re-
introduced boonworks on his estate;[122] the progressive landlord, like
Richard Holt of Ashworth, whose four fulling mills must have helped
the local textile industry;[123] the kindly, paternal squire, like William
Blundell of Crosby;[124] the harsh landlord, like Sir George Middleton
of Leighton;[125] the enterprising landlord, like John Preston of Furness
Abbey, noted, *inter alia*, for his money lending and iron works;[126] and
the 'gambling', coal-mining landlord, like Thomas Gerard of Ince.[127]

The second generalisation is that oppressive landlords seem to be
found entirely on the Royalist side. In south-west Lancashire and the
Fylde the Cavaliers appear to have been kindly, paternal landlords.
But in Lonsdale hundred they seem to have ruthlessly exploited their
tenants.[128] Although the evidence is rather meagre, I have not found
an example of a severe Parliamentarian landlord in the pre-war
period.[129] But I have found a few kindly, considerate Parliamentarian
(and Puritan) landlords, like the younger John Atherton of Atherton
and the younger Sir Ralph Assheton of Whalley.[130] The possible
absence of serious landlord–tenant conflict on the estates of the Parliamentarian gentry may partly explain why they encountered far less
opposition to their recruiting drive than did the Royalist gentry.

The third generalisation is that coal-mining adventurers are to be
found mainly on the Royalist side, and that some of them, like the
Charnocks of Astley and the Gerards of Ince, seem to have been seriously in debt as a result of their enterprise.[131]

As well as, or instead of, agriculture and industry, some of the Lancashire Royalist and Parliamentarian gentry were engaged in trade
or in some professional occupation, such as medicine or the law. There
were a few commercial tycoons on both sides. The Parliamentarians
included in their ranks Humphrey Chetham of Crumpsall, the famous
clothier and money-lender, who was to become Treasurer of the
County Committee in 1643,[132] while the Royalists had the support
of Francis Sherrington of Boothes, who, after making a fortune as a
wine merchant, bought vast quantities of land and helped to defend
Lathom House for the king during the Civil War.[133] The best known
lawyers on the Parliamentarian side were the elder Alexander and
George Rigby of Goosnargh.[134] Among the Royalists Robert Blundell
of Ince Blundell accumulated considerable wealth as a common
lawyer in London,[135] while Sir Edward Wrightington of Wrightington must have acquired both wealth and fame as a prerogative
lawyer in York, where he served on the Council of the North.[136] There

do not seem to have been any physicians among the Parliamentarian gentry, but among the Royalists were two gentlemen doctors: Richard Billing of Billing and Thomas Westby of Mowbreck, 'the Popish Doctor', who lost his life at the siege of Preston in 1643.[137] Business and professional men were, however, a very small minority on both sides, although Table 26 shows that they were more prominent among the Parliamentarian than among the Royalist gentry.

The economic differences between the Parliamentarian gentry and the Royalist gentry may be summarised as follows. The Royalists were wealthier than their opponents, but included a higher proportion of declining gentry. For shortage of evidence, it is difficult to compare

TABLE 26

OCCUPATION AND ALLEGIANCE[a]

	Royalists	Parliamentarians
(a) Total number of gentry	272	138
(b) Merchants or traders	13 (4·8%)	14 (10·1%)[b]
(c) Lawyers[c]	14 (5·1%)	14 (10·1%)
(d) Physicians	2 (0·7%)	–
Total	29 (10·6%)	28 (20·2%)

a For sources regarding occupation see above, p. 17 n.
b One of the Parliamentarian gentry—John Moore of Bankhall—was not only a ship owner but also a lawyer (Liverpool Record Office, Moore Deeds and Papers, 312 (unfoliated); Lotte Glow, 'The Committee-men in the Long Parliament, August 1642–December 1643', Historical Journal, viii, 1965, 11).
c These include counsellors at law, recorders, and those holding Crown appointments. Among the Royalist lawyers were two attorneys: Luke Hodgkinson of Preston and Christopher Towneley of Towneley, both Catholic. Parliamentarian lawyers also included two attorneys: Peter Harrison of Hindley, a Puritan, and George Rigby, younger brother of Alexander of Goosnargh.

the two sides with regard to their estate management, but harsh landlords and coal-mining adventurers were apparently more common among the Royalists than among the Parliamentarians. On the other hand a higher proportion of Parliamentarians than of Royalists seem to have been business or professional men. On the whole the economic differences between the two sides would seem to cancel each other out.

Were there, then, no major differences between the Royalist and Parliamentarian gentry of Lancashire other than the obvious numerical and political differences? There were indeed. One major distinction was that, in proportion to their numbers, the Parliamentary gentry were apparently better educated than the Royalist gentry. Of the 138 Parliamentarians, 34 (24 per cent) had attended either

Oxford or Cambridge, while among the 272 Royalists the number was only 30, a mere 11 per cent. Neither side produced many graduates, but 7 per cent of the Parliamentarians had obtained degrees, as against 3 per cent of the Royalists. Thomas Hobbes referred to the universities as 'the core of rebellion'.[138] There is of course no proof that the Lancashire Parliamentarian gentry had acquired their political or religious beliefs at the universities. But several of the Parliamentary leaders had been undergraduates at puritanically inclined Cambridge colleges. Major-General Ralph Assheton of Middleton had attended Sidney Sussex, Colonel George Dodding Emmanuel and Colonel Alexander Rigby St John's College.

Some of the Lancashire Royalist and Parliamentarian gentry also went to the inns of court. Most of these students attended Gray's Inn, which Sir Charles Ogilvie has called a nursery of discontent with the Stuart regime.[139] But this cannot have been, as he suggests, because it bred many common lawyers, for no systematic legal education was received at the inns of court during the early seventeenth century. On the other hand the inns apparently provided something in the way of a liberal education and this may have encouraged a critical outlook among their students.[140] At any rate it is significant that a higher percentage of the Parliamentarian than of the Royalist gentry had attended an inn of court: 21 per cent of the former and 13 per cent of the latter.[141] An even higher proportion of Parliamentarians than of Royalists had been educated at both an inn and a university: 15 per cent of the former and only 5 per cent of the latter.

The fact that the Parliamentarians were somewhat better educated than the Royalists may be partly explained by attempts to exclude Catholics—who formed a very high proportion of the Lancashire Royalist gentry—from centres of higher learning. Only 15 of the 157 Catholic Royalists managed to obtain an advanced education in England. But some of the Catholic gentry sent their sons to seminaries abroad, such as Douai or the English College of Rome, and the academic education received there was probably more rigorous than that obtained at the universities and the inns of court. However, only four of the Catholic Royalist gentry had attended continental seminaries, and two of these—Christopher Anderton of Lostock and Thomas Grimshaw of Clayton—apparently idled their time away.[142] In short, a detailed examination as well as a cursory glance shows that the Parliamentarian gentry were better educated than the Royalist gentry (see Table 27).

The second major distinction between the Royalist and Parliamentary gentry was a religious one. Two-thirds of the Royalist families were Catholic and almost three-quarters of the Parliamentarian families were Puritan.[143] This would seem to endorse the view that 'the chief cause of the division in Lancashire was the religious question, and especially the mutual hostility of the Puritans and the

Roman Catholics'.[144] Indeed, Catholics probably gave more support to the king's cause in Lancashire than in any other county, despite the fact that anything up to 100 recusant gentry families may have been neutral.[145] But 157 individual Catholic gentry took the royal side and these formed 57 per cent of the 272 Royalists. Despite the large passive element among them,[146] Catholics provided most of the more vigorous Lancashire Royalists. This is partly suggested by the heavy casualties they suffered. Forty-two Royalist gentlemen lost their lives in the Civil Wars and of these 30 (71 per cent) were Catholic. Among those killed were such leading Catholics as Major-

TABLE 27

HIGHER EDUCATION AND ALLEGIANCE[a]

		Royalists	Parliamentarians
(a)	Total number of gentry	272	138
(b)	Attending Catholic seminary	4 (1%)	–
(c)	Attending university only	16 (6%)	13 (9%)
(d)	Attending inn of court only	21 (8%)	8 (6%)
(e)	Attending university and inn of court	14 (5%)	21 (15%)
(f)	Receiving university degree	9 (3%)	11 (7%)
(g)	Total receiving higher education	55 (20%)	42 (30%)

a For sources regarding higher education see above, p. 24 n.

General Thomas Tyldesley at Wigan Lane in 1651 and Colonel Charles Towneley of Towneley at Marston Moor, while Captain William Blundell of Crosby was maimed for life.[147]

If Catholics were the real driving force among the Cavaliers, Puritans were the most numerous and dedicated among the revolutionaries. The Puritan author of *Discourse of the Warr in Lancashire*, himself a Parliamentarian officer, observed that 'of those that first put themselves into Armes [for Parliament] were men of the best affection to Religion'.[148] Almost all the leading Lancashire Parliamentarians were Puritans, and these included such gentlemen as Major-General Ralph Assheton of Middleton, commander-in-chief of the Lancashire Roundhead forces and patron of the Reverend Thomas Pyke, the 'godly preachinge Minister' of Radcliffe;[149] Lieutenant-Colonel John Bradshaw of Bradshaw, rebuilder of a Puritan chapel in 1640;[150] Robert Hyde of Denton, active as both a county committeeman and Presbyterian elder;[151] and Major Joseph Rigby, author of *The Drunkard's Prospective* (1655).[152] In few counties can Puritans have formed such a large proportion of the Parliamentarian gentry. Of the 138 individual Parliamentarian gentry, 88 (63 per cent) were Puritan. Of the 84 soldiers only 47 were Puritan, but among the 79 officials as many as 65 were of this faith. Twenty-nine of the Parliamentarians served as both soldiers and officials and of these all save three were Puritan. That religion was a major issue among both the Royalist and Parliamentarian gentry is perhaps also suggested by the very

TABLE 28

RELIGION AND ALLEGIANCE[a]

	Royalist families	Parliamentarian families	Sidechangers/ Divided families	Neutral/ Other families
Roman Catholic	116 (65·5%)	–	5 (20·8%)	100 (20·8%)
Puritan	7 (4·0%)	67 (73·6%)	11 (45·9%)	29 (6·0%)[b]
Anglican or indifferent	54 (30·5%)	24 (26·4%)	8 (33·3%)	353 (73·2%)
Total	177 (100·0%)	91 (100·0%)	24 (100·0%)	482 (100·0%)

a For sources regarding religion see above, p. 36 n. 196–7.
b Seventeen of these Puritan families supported the Republic at some time or other between 1649 and 1660.

small number of divided families and side-changers. Where ideological differences are sharp, we are less likely to find people changing sides or experiencing deep family divisions. It is significant that in Yorkshire, where somewhat fewer of the Parliamentarian gentry were Puritan and considerably fewer of the Royalists were Catholic, the proportion of divided families and side-changing gentlemen was much higher.[153] In Yorkshire religion was, of course, a vital issue, as Dr Cliffe has shown. Nevertheless, religious divisions often cut across political divisions. Although 64 Puritan families supported Parliament, a surprisingly large number—24—joined the king. Eighty-six Catholic families were Royalist, but 10 supported Parliament.[154] In Lancashire, on the other hand, religion and politics were more closely intertwined. Sixty-seven Puritan families aided Parliament, but only seven helped the king. One hundred and sixteen Catholic families were Royalist, while none was Parliamentarian.[155] (See Table 28.)

CONCLUSION

Among the minority of Lancashire gentry who took sides during the Civil War, the Royalists had a two-to-one majority. Nevertheless, they failed to win Lancashire for the king, for three main reasons. First, many more Royalist than Parliamentarian gentry were busy fighting outside the county and the local Royalist forces were thus short of officers and men. Secondly, there was much popular opposition to the Royalist recruiting drive. Thirdly, the Royalist gentry included a large passive and reluctant element, whereas most Parliamentarian gentry appear to have actively and willingly supported their cause. Socially and economically no great gulf separated the Royalist and Parliamentarian gentry. Neither in terms of age, younger sons, lineage, status, office-holding or even of economic state does there seem to be any marked distinction between the two groups. Two significant differences alone stand out. First, the Parliamentarians appear to have been better educated than the Royalists—an interesting fact in view of Hobbes's remark about the universities as 'the core of rebellion'. Secondly, most Parliamentarian families were Puritan and most Royalist families were Papist. There seems little doubt that religion was the issue which principally divided the two sides in the Civil War.

NOTES

[1] Richard Baxter, *Reliquiae Baxteriana*, ed. M. Sylvester (1696), i, 30.
[2] *Rebellion*, iii, 80.
[3] Cliffe, chapter XV.
[4] Blackwood, B.Litt. thesis, 11–32.
[5] B. Manning, *The English People and the English Revolution, 1640–1649* (1976), 186, 209–10, 215, 217–19, 226, 239.
[6] In his definitive military history of *The Great Civil War in Lancashire*, Broxap provided interesting accounts of the exploits of many individual Lancashire gentlemen, but made no attempt at a statistical analysis of the part played by the Royalist and Parliamentarian gentry inside or outside the palatinate. Nor did he make a serious attempt to distinguish between the active and the passive, the willing and the reluctant gentlemen on either side.
[7] For details see below Chapter III, section 1.
[8] This figure includes 26 families who supported the Republic at some time or other between 1649 and 1660 but whose Civil War allegiance is unknown. Also included are seven families who fought for the Stuarts in the Third Civil War (1651) but not in the earlier wars.
[9] For comparative purposes the income is based on the lay subsidy rolls, 1641. The 292 families participating in the First or Second Civil Wars were vastly superior in income and status. One hundred and twenty-one belonged to the greater gentry, and of the 197 families whose landed income is given in the lay subsidy rolls, the average was £326 per annum. For references to those rolls see above, p. 30 n. 39.
[10] With Lancashire perhaps in mind, John Seacome, a historian of the Stanleys, said that 'many gentlemen in the north . . . remained neuter'. See *Hist. of the House of Stanley* (Preston, 1793), 193. However, neutralism—at least among non-Catholics—is extremely difficult to prove.
[11] On the whole Royalists are easier to discover than Parliamentarians. Names of Parliamentarians may be gleaned from A. & O., i–iii; L.R.O., QSR 40–42 (1646–

48); P.R.O., SP16; SP19; SP23; SP28; E121. The last source is the nearest thing to a muster roll of the Parliamentarian army in 1648, although many of the soldiers are difficult to identify. Volumes particularly relevant to Lancashire are E121/3/1; 4/6; 4/8; 5/5; 5/7. For soldiers on both sides E. Peacock's *Army Lists of the Cavaliers and Roundheads* (2nd edn., 1874) is of little use, since many of those named are impossible to identify, and the student must rely on the following records published by the Chetham Society: G. Ormerod, ed., *Civil War Tracts*, O.S., Vol. 2, 1844; S. M. ffarington, ed., *The Farington Papers*, O.S., Vol. 39, 1856; J. Harland, ed., *The Lancs. Lieutenancy*, O.S., Vol. 50, 1859; W. Beamont, ed., *Discourse*, O.S., Vol. 62, 1864. Also useful is G. Chandler, *Liverpool under Charles I*, which has lists of Parliamentarian and Royalist soldiers stationed in Liverpool during the Civil War, although it is not always easy to distinguish between Lancastrians and outsiders. The papers of the Committee for Compounding (P.R.O., SP23) give a lengthy, if incomplete, list of those who supported the king. Thomas Dring's *Catalogue of the Lords, Knights and Gentlemen who have compounded for their Estates* (1655) and the three Acts of Sale, 1651–52 (A. & O., ii, 520–1, 591, 623–35), together with the Commonwealth Exchequer Papers (P.R.O., SP28) and the papers of the Committee for Advance of Money (P.R.O., SP19), also give the names of Royalist supporters. A valuable, if critically used, Royalist source is *A List of Officers claiming to the Sixty Thousand Pounds, etc.* (1663). Brigadier Peter Young kindly drew my attention to this *List*.

[12] Morrill, *Cheshire*, 69.

[13] Fletcher, 276.

[14] Phillips, thesis, 298, 305.

[15] Everitt, *Local Community*, 18; Cliffe, 336.

[16] Cliffe, 336–7. The 69 families formed 15 per cent of the participants and 10 per cent of all the 679 Yorkshire gentry families. In Lancashire the 24 divided families and Sidechangers formed 8 per cent of the participants and a mere 3 per cent of the total number of gentry families.

[17] P. Laslett, *The World we have lost* (2nd edn., 1971), passim.

[18] For evidence of the Civil War activities of the above persons and other combatants in this chapter, see sources listed above, n. 11, and Blackwood, D.Phil. thesis, App. IV, V.

[19] In Lancashire, unlike Cheshire, no gentleman apparently tried to opt out of the conflict by giving financial aid to both sides. See Morrill and Dore, 54–5.

[20] R. Heyrick, *Queen Esther's Resolve* (1646), 24.

[21] *Mercurius Belgicus*, 28 May 1644, B.L., E.1099(3).

[22] *Discourse*, 63.

[23] *Rebellion*, ii, 469.

[24] But see above, p. 52.

[25] Fourteen of the Earl's 26 Lancashire manors were in West Derby hundred. See below, Chapter IV, for details of his estates.

[26] The family papers show that the Molyneuxes also held much land in Leyland hundred, another Royalist stronghold.

[27] L.R.O., DDM 11/15: A note of all ... psons ... in the Lyvery of Sr Richard Molyneux, Knight (c. 1620?).

[28] As suggested by Manning, op. cit., 186, 208–10, 217–19, 221, 233, 235. For contrary arguments see Blackwood, B.Litt. thesis, chapter IV, Section I.

[29] For the fratricidal interpretation of the English Civil War see especially C. Wilson, *England's Apprenticeship* (1965), 110.

[30] See F. Peck, *Desiderata Curiosa* (1777), iii, 430; Seacome, *Hist. House of Stanley*, 195.

[31] See Manning, op. cit., 179, 186, 206–10, 217–19, 221, 226, 239, 241, 246–7.

[32] C. V. Wedgwood, 'The Common Man in the Civil War', *Truth and Opinion: Historical Essays* (1960), 235.

[33] C.W.T., 84.

[34] *Discourse*, 10.

[35] C.W.T., 169, 177. For Kay of Cobhouse see W. Hewitson, 'Capt. Kay, Royalist', *Bury and Rossendale Historical Review* (Bury, 1910–11), ii, 35–8. For Walthew see intro. by J. J. Bagley to his Will, Inventory and Accounts in R. Sharpe France, ed., *A Lancs. Miscellany*, L. & C. Rec. Soc., Vol. 109 (1965), 49–61.

[36] Morrill, *Cheshire*, Chapter II; Morrill and Dore, 47–62; Everitt, *Kent*, passim; Fletcher, 276–89; Holmes, esp. Chapter III; Morrill, *The Revolt of the Provinces* (1976), esp. 36–46, 93–6, 111–13.

[37] Broxap, 55–6. Radcliffe later supported Parliament, serving on the County Committee. Robert Holt of Stubley was to support the Royalist cause, but Sir Thomas Barton did not. Instead, he served as a Parliamentary magistrate in July 1646 (L.R.O., QSR 40).

[38] C.S.P.D., 1644, p. 176.

[39] None of these individuals was an active Royalist at any time. The other Royalist gentry in the Liverpool area—Brettargh of Holt, Fazakerley of Fazakerley, Mercer of West Derby, Norris of Speke, Tarbock of Tarbock, and Standish of West Derby—had declared for the king long before Prince Rupert's arrival.

[40] We know nothing about any Civil War activities of Catterall, Mawdesley and Wilson until January 1646, when all three appear as members of the Lancashire Accounts Sub-committee (P.R.O., SP16/513/18).

[41] *The Civil Wars in Cheshire* (Chester, 1966), 29.

[42] The three Lancashire peers also fought outside, as well as inside, Lancashire. For their activities, together with lists of gentry soldiers fighting outside the palatinate, see Blackwood, D.Phil. thesis, App. IV.

[43] See lists of casualties in ibid., App. V.

[44] P. Young, *Marston Moor* (Kineton, 1970), 66.

[45] For Assheton's role in the Battle of Nantwich see Dore, *The Civil Wars in Cheshire*, 36.

[46] For his activity in Cheshire see P.R.O., E121/5/7/68. For his activities in Ireland see Firth and Davies, *Regimental Hist. of Cromwell's Army* (Oxford, 1940), ii, 650–1.

[47] For example, in 1645, Richard Holland of Denton was the only colonel whom the Lancashire commanders at Ormskirk would spare from the second siege of Lathom (Dore, *The Great Civil War (1642–46) in the Manchester Area* (B.B.C. Radio Manchester publication, 1971), p. 26).

[48] C.W.T., 51–2.

[49] *Discourse*, 21.

[50] C. Hill, *Change and Continuity in seventeenth century England* (1974), 24.

[51] *Rebellion*, ii, 471.

[52] L.R.O., DDK 12/7: Copy of Petition to House of Commons (1653?).

[53] Manning, op. cit., 186.

[54] Henrietta Guizot de Witt, *The Lady of Lathom* (1869), 78.

[55] *Discourse*, 42.

[56] Morrill and Dore, 49–50.

[57] Ibid., 49–51, 54, 61–2.

[58] See, for example, *Roy. Comp. Papers*, ii. 368–9, iii. 27–8, iv. 126.

[59] Ibid., iii, 175. We need not necessarily dismiss such statements as special pleading. Even a highly unpopular landlord like Sir George Middleton of Leighton obtained the support of his tenants for the king (P.R.O., SP19/22/97; SP19/145/18).

[60] Some named in 1642 as commissioners of array never seem to have served, like Richard Shireburn of Stonyhurst, Ralph Standish of Standish and Peter Bold of Bold, a mere boy of 15.

[61] *Roy. Comp. Papers*, v, 48.

[62] Ibid., i, 35; V.C.H., v, 297.

[63] *Comparative Studies in Society and History*, x, 1968, 237–60.

[64] Sources for ages include the admissions registers of the universities and colleges listed above, p. 24 n. F. R. Raines, ed., *Visitation 1613 by St. George*, Chet. Soc., O.S., Vol. 82 (1871); F. R. Raines, ed., *Visitation 1664–65 by Dugdale*, Chet. Soc., O.S., Vols. 84, 85, 88 (1872–73); J. P. Rylands, ed., *Lancs. Inquisitions, 1603–25*, L. & C. Rec. Soc., Vols. 3, 16, 17 (1880, 1887–88); P.R.O., DL7/25–30 (1625–42); Chet. Lib., Towneley MS.C.8, 13 (Towneley Deeds).

[65] D. Brunton and D. H. Pennington, *Members of the Long Parliament* (1954), 16.

[66] G. E. Aylmer, *The King's Servants* (2nd edn., 1974), 393–4.

[67] *Causes*, 112.

[68] C.W.T., 77–8, 81–3; *Discourse*, 52–3.

[69] Everitt, *Kent*, 100 1; Fletcher, 278–9.

[70] Such as the Parliamentarian Blundells of Preston, an offshoot of the Royalist Blundells of Ince Blundell (Fishwick, *Hist. of Preston*, 355).

[71] *Local Community*, 19.

[72] Cliffe, 357.

[73] P.R.O., *List of Sheriffs*, ix, 72.

[74] L. G. Pine, *They came with the Conqueror* (1966), 71.

[75] V.C.H., iv, 265.
[76] W. M. Bowman, *England in Ashton-under-Lyne* (Altrincham, 1960), 9.
[77] Everitt, *Local Community*, 18–19.
[78] For references see above, p. 30 n. 35–40.
[79] H. R. Trevor-Roper, *The Gentry*, 1540–1640, Ec.H.R., Supplement I (1953), 22, 26–7, 32–4, 42, 52–3.
[80] *King's Servants*, 268.
[81] Information kindly supplied by Professor Aylmer.
[82] This and the two subsequent paragraphs are based on sources named above, pp. 17 n., 32 n. 80.
[83] See above, p. 11.
[84] John Rushworth, *Historical Collections* (1659), 398.
[85] In Cheshire two-thirds of the Bench were Royalist, though the Parliamentarians were supported by almost all the most active Justices (Morrill, *Cheshire*, 70).
[86] For sources concerning the nominated and active J.P.s, see above, p. 32 n. 80.
[87] Blackwood, 'Economic State', pp. 55–7; 'Cavalier and Roundhead Gentry', 84–5; D.Phil. thesis, 166–7.
[88] No comparison is possible which relies solely on private estate papers. As will be seen in the Bibliography, a fairly large amount of material belonging to 27 Royalist families has survived, but largely fragmentary estate papers are extant for only seven Parliamentarian families.
[89] See above, p. 30 n. 39.
[90] This was according to the papers of the Committee for Compounding. See Trevor-Roper, op. cit., 54. Cf. Stone, *Crisis*, 761.
[91] It is not absolutely certain whether Gerard was wealthier than Henry, Lord Morley and Mounteagle, or Sir Edward Mosley of Hough. Lord Morley had a gross rental of between £2,200 and £4,399 (ibid.). Mosley's income was anything from £1,500 to over £3,000 (C.A.M., i, 58; Long, thesis, 175).
[92] Cliffe, 361.
[93] For references see above, p. 33 n. 130.
[94] For references see above, p. 33 n. 118.
[95] Long, thesis, 148–9, 207.
[96] Raines and Sutton, *Life of Humphrey Chetham*, Chet. Soc., N.S., Vol. 49, 19, 30–1.
[97] See above, Table 25. For details of purchases see Blackwood, D.Phil. thesis, App. I.
[98] For details of their sales see ibid., App. II.
[99] L.R.O., QDD 19/4.
[100] L.R.O., QDD 36/9d; Wigan Cen. Lib., Wrightington–Dicconson Deeds, Burscough, 615.
[101] *Roy. Comp. Papers*, vi. pt. i., 287.
[102] V.C.H., iii, 413; Rylands, ed., *Lancs. Inquisitions*, L. & C. Rec. Soc., Vol. 17, 303.
[103] V.C.H., iii, 181. In 1664 a George Tarbock of Tarbock, Gentleman, apparently possessed only two hearths (P.R.O., E179/250/11).
[104] Hart-Davis, *Wardley Hall*, 86; P.R.O., C54/2930/5, PL17/129/12; L.R.O., QDD 29/3; 34/13; 35/3; Wigan Cen. Lib., Wrightington–Dicconson Deeds, Penwortham, 68, 80.
[105] P.R.O., LC4/200, f. 198.
[106] P.R.O., E379/73, f. 7.
[107] P.R.O., DL1/340.
[108] P.R.O., SP23/212/853–4.
[109] P.R.O., E179/131/335.
[110] See Morrill, *Cheshire*, 71; Cliffe, 354. Figures given by Cliffe are not strictly comparable with mine. My statistics deal with the period 1630–42 whereas Cliffe's only cover the years 1638–42. Morrill refers to the 1620s and 1630s but gives no statistics.
[111] If family debts are added to private debts, the total number of financially unstable Royalist families rises to 35 (19 per cent). The Parliamentarian total is unaffected. For main sources concerning debts see above, p. 19 n. Evidence of Royalist debts is also to be found among the papers of the Committee for Compounding. To escape heavy composition fines, Royalists would often overstate their debts as well as understate their income to the committee. But even if we ignore these papers, the number of Royalist families in serious financial difficulties falls only from 28 (16 per cent) to 25 (14 per cent).
[112] For the Braddylls see above, p. 16. For the Schofields see P.R.O., DL1/355; 373.

[113] P.R.O., E179/132/340.
[114] *Roy. Comp. Papers*, iii, 17.
[115] P.R.O., DL5/32, f. 107.
[116] B.L., Add. MS. 36926, f. 138.
[117] *Puritanism and Revolution* (1958), 8.
[118] See Bibliography. Unfortunately the valuable *House and Farm Accounts of the Shuttleworths of Gawthorpe Hall*, ed. J. Harland, Chet. Soc., Vols. 35, 41, 43, 46 (1856–58) cover the period 1582 to 1621 and are too early for our purposes.
[119] See above, p. 14.
[120] See above, p. 15.
[121] See above, p. 15.
[122] See above, p. 15.
[123] Richard inherited these mills from his father in 1624 (P.R.O., Wards 5/22). In that year his uncle, William, entered into possession, probably as guardian (V.C.H., v, 179).
[124] Blackwood, 'Lancs. Cavaliers', 20–1.
[125] Ibid., 24–7.
[126] Long, thesis, 103, 218, 223.
[127] See above, p. 16.
[128] Blackwood, op. cit., 20–31.
[129] But see below, p. 145, for a post-war example.
[130] See above, p. 15.
[131] See above, pp. 16, 59. On the Parliamentary side the only coal-mining adventurer seems to have been John Braddyll of Portfield, who, like Charnock and Gerard, was apparently seriously in debt. See above, p. 16.
[132] Raines and Sutton, op. cit., 137.
[133] *Roy Comp. Papers*, i, 265. For his land purchases see above, p. 33 n. 130.
[134] For references see above, p. 33 n. 19–23.
[135] See above, p. 16.
[136] P.R.O., C181/4; L.R.O., QSC 33–6. For details of Wrightington's purchases see Blackwood, D.Phil. thesis, App. I.
[137] C.W.T., 75.
[138] F. Tönnies, ed., *Behemoth*, 58.
[139] *The King's Government and the Common Law, 1471–1641* (Oxford, 1958), 151. Referring to the Cheshire gentry, Dr Morrill writes: 'There was a considerable majority of Parliamentarians among those who had attended Gray's Inn' (*Cheshire*, 71).
[140] Prest, *Inns of Court*, esp. Chapter VII.
[141] Dr Prest found that among the benchers of the inns of court Parliamentarians greatly outnumbered Royalists (ibid., 237).
[142] Burton and Williams, eds., *Douay College Diaries*, C.R.S., Vol. 10, 208, 221.
[143] For details see above, Table 28.
[144] G. H. Tupling, 'The Causes of the Civil War in Lancashire', Trans. L. & C. Antiq. Soc., Vol. 65 (1955), 31. For similar views see J. J. Bagley, *A History of Lancashire* (5th edn., Henley-on-Thames, 1970), 34; Broxap, 3–4; Walker, *Hist. Geog. of S.W. Lancs.*, 82 seq.; V.C.H., ii, 236.
[145] On Catholic neutralism in Lancashire and elsewhere see Keith Lindley, 'The Part Played by the Catholics', in B. Manning, ed., *Politics, Religion and the English Civil War* (1973), 127–76. For reasons stated in my D.Phil. thesis, pp. 183–4, I cannot agree with Dr Lindley that among the Lancashire Royalist gentry Protestants outnumbered Catholics.
[146] For details see Blackwood, 'Cavalier and Roundhead Gentry', 90.
[147] For a list of Royalist casualties see Blackwood, D.Phil. thesis, App. V.
[148] *Discourse*, 10.
[149] Fishwick, ed., *Commonwealth Church Surveys*, 29.
[150] Jordan, *Social Institutions of Lancs.*, 87.
[151] P.R.O., SP28/211 (loose papers); SP28/236 (unfoliated); Shaw, ed., *Manchester Presbyterian Classis*, vols. i–iii, passim. Hyde attended 68 meetings of the Manchester Classis between 1647 and 1660.
[152] For an account of Rigby's strict Puritanism see Blackwood, 'Catholic and Protestant Gentry', p. 14.
[153] In Yorkshire 64 (50 per cent) of the 128 Parliamentarian families were Puritan, while 86 (35 per cent) out of 242 Royalist families had Catholic sympathies. Sixty-nine families divided or changed sides (Cliffe, 336, 344).

[154] Ibid., 343–8, 360–2.

[155] Even if we concentrate on the individual rather than on the family, the total number of Puritan Royalists would only amount to nine. Two Catholics—Thomas Brockholes of Heaton and Francis Morley of Wennington—began as Royalists and ended as Parliamentarians. But not a single Lancashire Catholic gentleman seems to have supported Parliament alone.

CHAPTER III
THE ROUNDHEADS IN POWER

INTRODUCTION

Contemporaries portrayed the period from 1646 to 1660 as one when 'new men' of lower social status seized political power, confiscated the estates of the Crown, Church and Royalists, and established a new landed class. Clarendon declared that after the Civil War local power passed from the county elite to men of lower social status.

A more inferior sort of the common people ... who were not above the condition of ordinary inferior constables six or seven years before, were now the justices of the peace, sequestrators and commissioners.[1]

To the victors went also the spoils, and the Levellers lamented that 'Parliament men, Committee men, and their kinsfolkes were the only buyers' of episcopal lands.[2] Thomas Fuller noted with disapproval that a new gentry had emerged, that 'many up-starts in our late civil wars' had 'injuriously invaded the arms of ancient families'.[3]

How far do these arguments apply to Lancashire? To what extent did the greater gentry lose their monopoly of local government to lower social groups after the Civil War? How much Crown, Church and Royalist land did the Lancashire Parliamentarian gentry acquire? How many new landed families emerged from the ranks of the Roundheads?

Before any of these questions can be satisfactorily answered it is necessary to examine briefly the political situation in Lancashire from the end of the First Civil War to the Restoration.

I POLITICAL ALLEGIANCES DURING THE POST-WAR PERIOD

Several historians have linked the social changes and divisions in local administration with the political conflicts among the Parliamentarians. Thus Mr D. H. Pennington, referring to the county committees of Kent and Staffordshire, writes:

... in general there were significantly more from the old ruling groups and the richer families on the side of peace than on the side of war, and more of the 'new men' among the militants and later Cromwellians.[4]

But in Lancashire it is not possible to relate political to socio-economic divisions. This is because we know so little about the political sympathies of most of the Parliamentarian gentry. During the Civil War in Lancashire there were few signs of any serious division among the king's opponents. There is no evidence of any contest between a win-the-war group and a compromise–peace group. Undoubtedly some Lancashire gentlemen supported the Parliamentary cause more enthusiastically than others. Few could have been as dedicated as the elder Alexander Rigby of Goosnargh, who led the attack on Lathom House in 1644.[5] By contrast, Colonel Richard Holland of Denton was sometimes a rather lukewarm commander, although this may have been due as much to cowardice as to any pro-Royalist sympathies.[6] In spite of these differences, however, Holland and Rigby were not leaders of opposing factions within the Lancashire Parliamentary party. Nor did the Lancashire Parliamentarians split at the end of the First Civil War. Between 1646 and 1648 the palatinate was not racked by serious feuds between political Presbyterians and political Independents, largely because there were so few Independents.[7] The execution of Charles I in 1649 was, however, a turning point in the history of Lancashire, and it was then that serious political divisions seem to have occurred among the Parliamentarians. Between 1643 and 1648–49 Lancastrians served for long or short periods on the commission of the peace or on the county committee,[8] but 22 of them ceased to act after the king's death. At least five were strongly opposed to the trial of Charles I and/or the English Republic. These gentlemen were Ralph Assheton of Middleton, Sir Robert Bindloss of Borwick, Sir Richard Hoghton of Hoghton Tower, Richard Holland of Denton and William Langton of Broughton.[9] On the other hand, there is no positive proof that most of the remaining 17 were politically conservative,[10] although it is quite likely. Only one—the elder Alexander Rigby of Goosnargh—seems to have been a radical.[11]

Twenty-seven of the 49 Lancastrians continued to serve Parliament after the king's execution, either on the Bench or on the county committee. One of the 27—John Holcroft of Holcroft—attended only five quarter sessions after the death of Charles I,[12] and was dropped from the commission of the peace after 1650.[13] He must clearly be ranked as a conservative, since he had been secluded from Parliament by Colonel Pride in 1648.[14] Three of the other 27 officials—Edward Butterworth of Belfield, Peter Egerton of Shaw and Sir Thomas Stanley of Bickerstaffe—had a reputation for leniency towards Royalists[15] and were obviously moderate men. But two others—Thomas Birch of Birch, 'a bitter enemy to the king',[16] and John Moore of Bank Hall, the sole Lancashire regicide—were undoubtedly radicals, since their loyalty to the republican ideal was never in doubt.[17] As to the political opinions of the remaining 21 officials, we are completely ignorant.

During the Interregnum another 35 Lancastrians joined the Bench or the county committee. Three of them—Edward Robinson of Euxton, John Sawrey of Plumpton and William West of Middleton—were definitely radicals,[18] and three Preston aldermen—Edward French,

William Patten and Edmund Werden—may also have been.[19] The political outlook of the remaining 29 officials is unknown, but it would be facile to suppose that they were all radicals just because they happened to serve the Republic.

Of the 62 Lancastrians who acted as magistrates or county committeemen during the Interregnum, only a handful can be confidently called radicals. A majority appear to have been moderate, practical men, who were prepared to co-operate with the Republic—at least for a time.[20] Why was this? It is very difficult to say. Perhaps some were just time-servers with no serious political convictions. The elder Richard Shuttleworth of Gawthorpe served almost continuously as a magistrate from 1625 to 1665[21] and one suspects that he occasionally acquiesced in order to remain in power. On the other hand, he may have been merely one of many country gentlemen seeking any kind of permanent political settlement. Other moderates may have supported the Commonwealth and Protectorate for religious reasons, because the new regime gave them, as magistrates, the opportunity to reform the religion and morals of the people.[22] But perhaps the main reason why so many Lancashire gentlemen supported the Republic was a strong fear of Royalism.

Lancashire was gripped by a Catholic Fear in 1640–42,[23] a Quaker Fear in 1659,[24] and a Royalist Fear in 1648 and the years that followed. In Kent and Westmorland many members of the county committee supported Charles I in the Second Civil War.[25] But in Lancashire not a single Parliamentarian gentleman can be found joining the king's forces in 1648. Much as they detested the sectaries, the Lancashire Parliamentarians hated the Royalists, Papists and their Scottish allies even more, a fact made plain by the *Declaration of the Officers and Soldiers of the County Palatine of Lancaster* (19 May 1648).[26] Hence Major-General Ralph Assheton of Middleton and his 'Presbyterian' troops fought alongside Cromwell's forces at the battle of Preston.[27] In July 1649 fear of Royalism reached panic proportions when in Manchester and Wigan a bold but peaceful proclamation of Charles II as king by 'severall Gentlemen ... of quality' was referred to as 'a new rising in Lancashire'.[28] Anti-Royalist feeling ran so high that in 1651 only a handful of ex-Parliamentarian gentry joined the seventh Earl of Derby's rising in support of Charles II.[29] In 1655 the Royalist menace was still taken very seriously in Lancashire, and Major-General Charles Worsley drew up a list of just over 1,000 suspected delinquents.[30] Perhaps the best testimony, however, to the fear of Royalists is the fact that during the period 1643–59 only three of our 84 senior Lancashire Parliamentarian officials[31] came from former Cavalier families. These were John Foxe of Rhodes, Robert Hesketh of Rufford and William Hulton of Hulton, all of whom served as magistrates. But only Foxe was really active,[32] perhaps because, unlike the other two, he was a Puritan[33] and religiously motivated. The situation in Lancashire contrasts sharply with that in some Welsh counties, where several ex-Royalists were on the county committees soon after the First Civil War.[34] But in Wales anti-Royalist feelings did not run as deeply as they did in Lancashire.

So long as the fear of Royalists persisted, a large number of Lancashire committeemen and magistrates gave the Republic their active support. But in 1659 it was no longer the Royalists but the sectaries who posed a threat to the Parliamentarian gentry. To make matters worse, the restored Rump and the army appeared to be supporting the sects, hence Sir George Booth's uprising in August 1659. Booth hoped for widespread support, but it was largely in the Presbyterian heartlands of Lancashire and Cheshire that the revolt made much headway. It was said that 'the gentry and ministry of Cheshire and Lancashire appeare much in this insurrection'.[35] Unfortunately, we do not know the exact numbers of Lancashire gentlemen directly involved. Apart from the eighth Earl of Derby, two irreconcilable opponents of the Republic took part in the uprising: the younger Ralph Assheton of Middleton and Sir Richard Hoghton of Hoghton.[36] Far more significant was the fact that Gilbert Ireland of Hutt was one of the Lancashire leaders of the rebellion. One of the leading county gentry,[37] Gilbert Ireland is a classic example of a moderate man, and his political career seems little different from that of other Lancashire moderates. During the Civil War Ireland had been a Captain of Horse[38] and in 1646 and 1647 he served as a magistrate and sequestration commissioner.[39] In December 1647 he was appointed High Sheriff of Lancashire.[40] Although not a radical, Ireland supported the Republic, again serving on the county committee.[41] Under both the Commonwealth and Protectorate he was moderately active on the Bench,[42] and in 1655 was made Governor of Liverpool, promising Cromwell his diligent support.[43] In 1657, as Member for Liverpool, Ireland voted that Cromwell should take the crown.[44] In August 1659 he declared for Booth in Liverpool.[45] At the Restoration he was knighted.[46]

Why did Gilbert Ireland, and doubtless many other moderate Lancashire Parliamentarians, join Booth's uprising? It was because social and religious revolution seemed imminent. In his much-quoted letter of 2 August 1659 Sir George Booth spoke of 'a mean and schismatical party depressing the Nobility and understanding Commons'.[47] A week earlier the militia committees throughout the kingdom had been put into the hands of those whom Clarendon called 'persons of no degree or quality'.[48] In Lancashire it really did seem as if such persons were in control, for only 30 per cent of those nominated to the 1659 militia committee belonged to the greater gentry.[49] Never before had the county committee included such a small proportion of the county elite.[50] The Lancashire gentry were also well aware of a threat from what Booth called 'a schismaticall party'. In the palatinate most of

the schismatics or sectaries were Quakers, whose support came largely
from the lower middle classes.[51] Just before Booth's rising of 1659 it
was spread abroad that the Quakers were up in arms, and men were
called upon to join Booth in suppressing their 'rebellion' in Manchester and Warrington.[52] This was an absurd rumour, for in general
even the early Quakers were not violent men, nor were they social
or political radicals.[53] Nevertheless, they gave the impression that they
were, by their boisterous behaviour[54] and by their opposition to oath-
taking and hat-honour. The fact that in Lonsdale some of the early
Friends or their relatives had been strong opponents of tithes and
heavy entry fines[55] may have strengthened their (quite unjustified)
revolutionary image, and struck fear into the hearts of the Lancashire
gentry and clergy.

Memories of what the Reverend Henry Newcome wildly called the
'Munsterian anarchy' of 1659[56] caused the Lancashire gentry to close
ranks. As in Kent and Sussex,[57] both ex-Royalists and ex-Parliamentarians welcomed the restored monarch in 1660.[58] The Restoration
in Lancashire was accomplished peacefully.[59] Although it meant the
return of the Royalist gentry to positions of power, many former Parliamentarians or their heirs shared in the government of the county

TABLE 29

SELECTION OF POST-RESTORATION OFFICIALS
(BY CIVIL WAR LOYALTIES)[a]

Ref.[b]	Position	Date	Roy	Parl	SC	Rep	Neut/Others	Totals
					Civil War Allegiances			
a	M.P.s	1660	3	6	1	1	1	12
		1661	3	3	0	0	2	8
b	J.P.s	1665	17	15	3	7	10	52
c	Dep. Lieuts.	1661	6	1	1	0	4	12
d	Sheriffs	1660–70	5	0	0	0	4	9
	Commissioners:							
e	Army and Navy	1661	26	24	3	4	19	76
f	Voluntary Gift	1661	12	15	2	1	14	44
g	Lay Subsidies	1663	18	9	2	2	11	42

a Sons are classed with the same party as the father. Where the family was divided
the allegiance of the appointee has been counted. The abbreviations are mostly self-
explanatory, but 'SC' denotes a side-changer and 'Rep' applies to an individual who
served the Republic but apparently not Parliament during the Civil War. Among
M.P.s 'carpetbaggers' are excluded. Among J.P.s, peers, 'foreigners' and ex-officio
members of the Bench are ignored.

b References are: (a) Pink and Beavan, Parliamentary Representation of Lancs., passim;
(b) P.R.O., SP29/94/63; (c) P.R.O., SP29/60/66; (d) P.R.O., List of Sheriffs, ix, 73;
(e) Statutes of the Realm, 12 Car. II, cap. 9, 12 Car. II, cap. 27, 13 Car. II, Stat. ii,
cap. 3; (f) P.R.O., E179/250/5; (g) Statutes of the Realm, 15 Car. II, cap. 9; P.R.O.,
E179/132/349; 132/350; L.R.O., DDX 3/96; 3/97.

during the early 1660s, as Table 29 shows. The number of Parliamentarians is particularly striking when it is remembered that during the Civil War in Lancashire the Royalist gentry had had an almost two-to-one majority over their opponents.[60] It should be noted, however, that 16 of the Parliamentarians in Table 29 had not served on Interregnum committees of any kind, and that a majority of those who had were excluded from local government after 1660.[61] Nevertheless, at least 18 who had served the Republic were in local positions of trust and responsibility in the early 1660s, 12 of them being magistrates. There was apparently a fair degree of political and administrative continuity between the pre- and post-Restoration periods. Here Lancashire resembled Cheshire and Glamorgan,[62] but differed from Sussex, Wiltshire and the Lake Counties.[63]

2 COUNTY GOVERNMENT AND SOCIAL CHANGE

After the Civil War Lancashire witnessed a minor social revolution in government. Prior to the Great Rebellion county government had been dominated by the greater gentry, who were regarded as the 'natural' rulers of county society. Between 1625 and 1642 no one below the rank of esquire held the post of magistrate, deputy lieutenant, sheriff or militia officer, while 89 per cent of those who acted as commissioners for sewers, lay subsidies or knighthood compositions belonged to the upper gentry.[64] The post-war period, or more accurately the Interregnum, saw this monopoly broken and, as happened in England after the Great Reform Act of 1832, the greater gentry had to share their power with socially inferior groups. This is evident in the Lancashire magistracy, the county committee, the accounts sub-committee, the shrievalty and the militia.

(a) *The Justices of the Peace.* Eighty Lancastrians were nominated to the Bench at some time or other between the end of the First Civil War and the Restoration.[65] Twenty-six of these never appeared at quarter sessions and so need not concern us. A study of the 54 acting justices suggests that the social composition of the magistracy varied considerably from year to year. Nevertheless, Table 30 shows that between 1646 and 1648 the greater gentry dominated the magistracy almost as much as they had done in pre-war days, but that during the Interregnum they lost not only their near-monopoly of the Bench but, often, their majority on it.

Eighteen of the 32 magistrates who had acted between 1646 and 1648 continued to serve after the execution of Charles I. Nevertheless, despite this continuity, the Lancashire Bench was somewhat different after the king's death from what it had been before. The distinctions between the pre- and post-1649 magistracy are outlined in Appendix III. They show that under the Republic a slightly higher proportion

TABLE 30

THE SOCIAL COMPOSITION OF THE ACTING LANCASHIRE MAGISTRACY, 1646–59[a]

Year	Greater gentry	Lesser gentry	Plebeians	Total
1646	19 (90%)	2 (10%)	–	21 (100%)
1647	21 (87·5%)	3 (12·5%)	–	24 (100%)
1648	21 (87·5%)	3 (12·5%)	–	24 (100%)
1649	12 (71%)	5 (29%)	–	17 (100%)
1650	15 (65%)	7 (30%)	1 (5%)	23 (100%)
1651	15 (68%)	6 (27%)	1 (5%)	22 (100%)
1652	13 (50%)	11 (42%)	2 (8%)	26 (100%)
1653	10 (42%)	10 (42%)	4 (16%)	24 (100%)
1654	9 (43%)	9 (43%)	3 (14%)	21 (100%)
1655	9 (45%)	8 (40%)	3 (15%)	20 (100%)
1656	6 (43%)	5 (36%)	3 (21%)	14 (100%)
1657	8 (50%)	6 (37·5%)	2 (12·5%)	16 (100%)
1658	7 (47%)	6 (40%)	2 (13%)	15 (100%)
1659	5 (42%)	6 (50%)	1 (8%)	12 (100%)

a The names of the active magistrates are in L.R.O., QSR 40–53. In this table, and also in Tables 31, 34 and 35, status is that held on nomination to the office concerned and does not always correspond with the 1642 social position. When William Langton of Broughton was appointed to the Bench in 1647 he was a gentleman, a rank which he also held in 1642. On the other hand, James Ashton of Chadderton, a gentleman in 1642, has been classified as an esquire because, just before joining the magistracy in 1650, he had acquired the status of his recently deceased father.

TABLE 31

SOCIAL STATUS OF ACTING MAGISTRATES, 1625–59

Status	The Lancashire Magistracy		
	1625–42	1646–48	1649–59
Baronets	4 (5·0%)	3 (9·4%)	1 (2·5%)
Knights	12 (15·0%)	1 (3·1%)	–
Esquires	64 (80·0%)	24 (75·0%)	21 (52·5%)
Gentlemen	–	4 (12·5%)	14 (35·0%)
Plebeians	–	–	4 (10·0%)
Totals	80 (100·0%)	32 (100·0%)	40 (100·0%)[a]

a The 18 magistrates who served before and after 1649 comprised one baronet—Sir Thomas Stanley of Bickerstaffe—15 esquires and two gentlemen.

of magistrates were Puritans, urban dwellers, merchants and of recent gentry origins. On the other hand, a slightly smaller proportion of Interregnum justices were younger sons, ex-soldiers, lawyers, pre-war office-holders and debtors. However, none of these differences was statistically significant. What really distinguished the justices of the Interregnum from those of the preceding period was their greatly inferior status, education and wealth.

Table 31 shows the changing social composition of the Lancashire Bench between 1625 and 1659. It will be seen that the greater gentry had a monopoly of the Bench before 1642, a near-monopoly in the late 1640s and a bare majority in the 1650s. Those who gained most from the social changes of the Interregnum were the lesser gentry. On the other hand contemporaries might have attached even more social significance to the unprecedented appointment of four plebeians to the commanding heights of local government.[66]

Lancashire was not the only county whose Bench deteriorated socially during the Interregnum. In Somerset 'most of the new J.P.s were landowners, but their status was far less impressive than that of the magnates of the old days'.[67] In Cheshire power passed from the leading county families to the middling and parochial gentry.[68] In Sussex the magnates, though still in control of the Bench, were outnumbered by the lesser gentry and merchants during the late 1650s.[69]

In Sussex the educational standards of the Bench also declined during the 1650s.[70] This happened in Lancashire too. In the period 1625–42 the justices in Lancashire, compared with those elsewhere,[71] had been a poorly educated lot. The magistrates of the late 1640s were marginally better educated, despite their slightly lower social status.

TABLE 32

THE EDUCATIONAL EXPERIENCE OF ACTING MAGISTRATES,
1625–59[a]

	The Lancashire Magistracy		
	1625–42	*1646–48*	*1649–59*
(a) Total number of justices	80	32	40
(b) Attending university only	10 (12·5%)	4 (12·5%)	7 (17·5%)
(c) Attending inn of court only	12 (15·0%)	3 (9·4%)	4 (10%)
(d) Attending university and inn of court	18 (22·5%)	10 (31·2%)	4 (10%)
(e) Total receiving higher education	40 (50·0%)	17 (53·1%)	15 (37·5%)

a For sources in this and Table 36 see above, p. 24 n.

However, during the 1650s the educational level of the Lancashire Bench fell far below that of the pre-war period. (See Table 32.)

As regards *per capita* income, Table 33 shows the main distinctions between the pre-war justices, the immediate post-war justices and the Interregnum justices.[72] It will be noticed that there were far greater differences between the last two groups than between the first two, and that during the Interregnum there was a marked fall in the proportion of rich and middle-income magistrates. It is most likely that after the Restoration the magistrates were considerably wealthier than those who had served during the Interregnum, although detailed research is needed to confirm this supposition. However, there is abundant evidence that the post-Restoration justices were socially

TABLE 33

THE INCOMES OF ACTING MAGISTRATES, 1625–59

Annual income from land in 1642	The Lancashire Magistracy		
	1625–42	*1646–48*	*1649–59*
2,000 and over	4 } 15 (18·7%)	1 } 5 (15·6%)	1 } 4 (10·0%)
1,000–1,999	11	4	3
750–999	5 } 42 (52·5%)	2 } 16 (50·0%)	1 } 15 (37·5%)
500–749	13	3	3
250–499	24	11	11
100–249	10 } 12 (15·0%)	8 } 8 (25·0%)	7 } 10 (25·0%)
Under 100	2	–	3
Unknown	11 (13·8%)	3 (9·4%)	11 (27·5%)
Total	80 (100·0%)	32 (100·0%)	40 (100·0%)

and educationally superior to their predecessors. Twenty-eight of the 31 Lancashire justices who attended quarter sessions in 1661 held the rank of esquire or above,[73] while 45 (86·5 per cent) of the 52 magistrates who appeared at the Lancaster assizes in March 1665 were members of the greater gentry.[74] Socially this was a return to the pre-1649, though not quite to the pre-1642, position. Educationally the justices had never been of higher calibre, for 31 (59·6 per cent) of the 52 gentry who appeared at the 1665 assizes had received some form of advanced education.[75] High status and higher education had seldom been so closely linked.

(b) *The county committeemen.* Parliament could hardly have won the Civil War and afterwards held the obedience of a hostile or bewildered population if it had relied solely on existing local institutions, such

as the commission of the peace and the shrievalty. For financial, political and military reasons new organs of government had to be created
in the provinces. From 1643 onwards various county committees were
set up by Parliamentary ordinances: committees for assessment, for
the sequestration of delinquents, for the militia and for various other
purposes.[76] In theory, these committees were separate institutions; in
practice, since membership was often the same, they were collectively
known as the 'county committee'. It is important to stress that this
committee was a supplement to, not a substitute for, the older local
institutions. Whatever may have been the case elsewhere, in Lancashire the county committee maintained amicable relations with the
commission of the peace. Indeed, prior to the king's execution, 61
per cent of the committeemen were also magistrates, and even during
the Interregnum nearly half of them served on the Bench.[77]

TABLE 34

SOCIAL STATUS OF THE NOMINATED LANCASHIRE COMMITTEEMEN,
1643–60[a]

Date of committee	Greater gentry	Lesser gentry	Plebeians	Total
1643 March	14 (70%)	6 (30%)	–	20 (100%)
1648 February	18 (64%)	10 (36%)	–	28 (100%)
1649 April	10 (42%)	14 (58%)	–	24 (100%)
1652 December	14 (33%)	23 (55%)	5 (12%)	42 (100%)
1657 June	17 (36%)	24 (51%)	6 (13%)	47 (100%)
1659 July	9 (30%)	16 (53%)	5 (17%)	30 (100%)
1660 January	17 (55%)	13 (42%)	1 (3%)	31 (100%)

a For names of committeemen see below, p. 104 n. 81.

A hundred and thirty-seven Lancastrians were members of the
county committee at one time or another between 1643 and 1660.[78]
But only 69 of them can be shown to have served. This is largely
because virtually no records exist of the committee's activities after
1653.[79] Hence it does not necessarily follow that the other 68 members
were merely nominal, at least not if they were appointed in the late
1650s.[80] At any rate it seems worth analysing the nominated lists of
committeemen from 1643 to 1660 to see whether changes in the personnel of local government corresponded to similar changes in the
personnel of the national government in London.[81]

The social composition of the Lancashire committee, like that of
the Kentish, varied considerably from year to year. But whereas in
Kent the upper gentry easily maintained their majority on the committee throughout the period from 1643 to 1660,[82] in Lancashire they
lost it after the king's execution in 1649. A particularly black month

for the Lancashire elite was July 1659, when minor gentry and plebeians comprised 70 per cent of the committee—hence Booth's uprising.[83] But even in 1657, when Oliver Cromwell's government was at
its least radical, only 36 per cent of those nominated to the committee
belonged to the esquire class. Not until January 1660, after the second
restoration of the Rump, was the county committee again dominated
by the country gentry. (See Table 34.)

If we concentrate—as we should—on the working members of the
county committee, we find that 17 of the 41 who acted between 1643
and 1648 continued to serve after the execution of Charles I. Nevertheless, the Lancashire committee was somewhat different after the
king's death from what it had been before. The distinctions between

TABLE 35

SOCIAL STATUS OF ACTING COMMITTEEMEN, 1643–53

Status	The Lancashire Committeemen	
	1643–48	*1649–53*
Baronets	3 (7·3%)	1 (2·2%)
Esquires	23 (56·1%)	17 (37·8%)
Gentlemen	15 (36·6%)	20 (44·4%)
Plebeians	—	7 (15·6%)
Totals	41 (100·0%)	45 (100·0%)[a]

a The 17 persons who served on the committee before and after 1649 comprised
one Baronet—Sir Thomas Stanley of Bickerstaffe—11 esquires and five gentlemen.

the pre- and post-1649 committee are outlined in Appendix IV. They
show that under the Republic a slightly higher proportion of committeemen were Puritans, urban dwellers, merchants and of recent gentry
origins. On the other hand a slightly smaller proportion of the Interregnum committeemen were younger sons, ex-soldiers, lawyers, pre-
war office-holders and debtors. But these differences were not statistically significant. What really distinguished the committeemen of the
Interregnum from those of the preceding period was their greatly inferior status, education and wealth. Table 35 shows the social composition of the Lancashire committee before and after 1649. It will
be seen that the greater gentry formed a clear majority of committeemen in the earlier period and a clear minority in the later period.
Those who gained at their expense were the lesser gentry and plebeians.

However, social changes in the Lancashire committee must be kept in perspective. In some other county committees changes seem to have occurred earlier and on a somewhat larger scale. In Kent most of the really active committeemen were parochial gentry even before 1649.[84] In Somerset minor gentry and plebeians seem to have dominated various local committees between 1645 and 1657.[85] In Staffordshire a majority of the active committee members between 1643 and 1645 were from outside the ruling elite.[86] In Cumberland, and even more in Westmorland, the greater gentry formed a distinct minority on the county committee before and after 1649. Indeed, the Westmorland committee was not even dominated by the lesser gentry but by yeomen, lawyers, merchants and minor office-holders.[87]

We do not know what were the educational standards of the committeemen in the aforementioned counties. But in Lancashire there was a marked drop in the educational level of the county committee after 1649 (see Table 36.)

TABLE 36

THE EDUCATIONAL EXPERIENCE OF ACTING COUNTY COMMITTEEMEN, 1643-53

	The Lancashire committeemen	
	1643-48	1649-53
(a) Total number of committeemen	41	45
(b) Attending university only	6 (14·6%)	7 (15·6%)
(c) Attending inn of court only	4 (9·8%)	3 (6·6%)
(d) Attending university and inn of court	11 (26·8%)	6 (13·3%)
(e) Total receiving higher education	21 (51·2%)	16 (35·5%)

Finally, it would appear that the county committeemen after 1649 were much poorer than those of the preceding period. The known aggregate income of the pre-1649 committeemen was £12,812, while that of the post-1649 committeemen was only £9,150. Table 37 shows that in the earlier period men of high and middling incomes were prominent on the county committee, while in the later period men of low incomes were conspicuous.[88]

The social and economic differences between the pre- and post-1649 county committee become even more pronounced when we concentrate on the most active among the working members. The three most vigorous men on the committee between 1643 and 1648 were John Bradshaw of Bradshaw, Richard Holland of Denton and Sir Thomas Stanley of Bickerstaffe.[89] The latter was a baronet, worth

£1,000 a year.[90] Richard Holland was an esquire with an annual income of at least £600. He was also a well educated man, having matriculated at Brasenose College, Oxford, in 1615 and gained admission to Gray's Inn three years later.[91] John Bradshaw, also an esquire, was worth only £200 per annum in 1641. But his good education perhaps compensated for his low income: he matriculated at Christ's college, Cambridge, in 1602 and was admitted to Gray's Inn in 1605.[92]

In complete contrast to Bradshaw, Holland and Stanley were Robert Cunliffe of Sparth, Peter Holt of Bridge Hall and George Pigott of Preston, three very active committeemen in 1650 and 1651.[93]

TABLE 37

THE INCOMES OF ACTING COUNTY COMMITTEEMEN, 1643-53

Annual income from land in 1642 (£)	The Lancashire committeemen	
	1643-48	1649-53
2,000 and over	1 ⎫ 4 (9·8%)	0 ⎫ 3 (6·7%)
1,000–1,999	3 ⎭	3 ⎭
750–999	2 ⎫	1 ⎫
500–749	3 ⎬ 13 (31·7%)	2 ⎬ 9 (20·0%)
250–499	8 ⎭	6 ⎭
100–249	9 ⎫ 11 (26·8%)	11 ⎫ 17 (37·8%)
Under 100	2 ⎭	6 ⎭
Unknown	13 (31·7%)	16 (35·5%)
Total	41 (100·0%)	45 (100·0%)

Apparently not one of them had received a higher education. Holt was the only esquire of the three, but his annual income was a mere £100 in 1641.[94] Cunliffe was by rank a gentleman and evidently lived in genteel poverty. He inherited only 72 acres from his father in 1614,[95] and 'in his life tyme' had land worth only £35 per annum.[96] George Pigott was a Puritan lawyer[97] and almost certainly a gentleman. Nothing is known about his income or education, but even if these had been impressive he could hardly have commanded the respect of the greater Lancashire gentry. Pigott was the son and heir of Thomas Pigott of Bonishall, Cheshire, and apparently settled in Preston only after the Civil War.[98] To the county elite, a stranger who crashed his way into local power was just as suspect as a native upstart.[99]

(c) *Other local officials.* We must now very briefly examine the social composition of three other organs of local government: the accounts sub-committee, the shrievalty and the militia.

In 1645 the Committee for Taking the Accounts of the Kingdom set up sub-committees in each shire to audit the accounts of the county committee. These sub-committees functioned from 1645 to 1648.[100] They were generally distinct in membership from the county committee and were directly responsible to London for their actions. A study of the Lancashire sub-committee shows that the county elite did not control every branch of administration during the 1640s. While they dominated the magistracy and the county committee, they were virtually unrepresented on the accounts sub-committee. Only one of the 17 members—Richard Assheton of Downham—was an esquire,[101] the others consisting of 11 gentlemen and five plebeians.[102] But perhaps the most interesting fact about the Lancashire accounts sub-committee was that seven of its 17 members were townsmen, while two others—William Langton of Broughton, a gentleman lawyer, and Ralph Worsley of Platt, a gentleman merchant—had close urban connections. Here the accounts sub-committee differed considerably from the magistracy and the county committee, whose members were overwhelmingly rural.[103] The Lancashire sub-committee was not, of course, unique. Accounts sub-committees in several other counties had many town members.[104] Indeed, it would have been surprising if this had not been so, for many townsfolk were lawyers or merchants and well qualified to audit accounts. Moreover, since the towns in Lancashire had been mainly Parliamentarian during the Civil War,[105] it was perhaps inevitable that many of their leading citizens should have attained positions of local power after the king's defeat.

Finally, a brief word about two older institutions: the militia and the shrievalty. During the periods 1625–42 and 1660–85 the Lancashire shrievalty was the preserve of the greater gentry. In the earlier period two of the 17 sheriffs were baronets and the rest were esquires. In the later period the 18 sheriffs comprised three baronets, three knights and 12 esquires. However, during the Interregnum the county gentry lost their monopoly of the shrievalty. To be sure, two of the 12 Interregnum sheriffs were baronets and another six were esquires of ancient lineage. But two of the remaining sheriffs—Hugh Cooper of Ormskirk and John Hartley of Manchester—had only recently attained the rank of gentleman,[106] while the other two—Henry Wrigley and George Chetham—were just merchants.[107]

Perhaps the greatest social change in Lancashire after the Civil War occurred in the county militia. Under Charles I it was almost an axiom that the militia officers should be recruited from the county elite. Thus between 1628 and 1642 all 29 Lancashire militia officers held the status of esquire or above.[108] But when the Council of State reorganised the Lancashire militia in 1650 and appointed 27 officers, only two of them belonged to the greater gentry.[109] Among the other 25 officers, 10 were not even plain gentlemen. The situation in Lancashire seems to have been similar to that obtaining in Somerset, where several low-born persons were also granted commissions in the new militia, though, as in Lancashire, most officers were minor gentry.[110]

(d) *General comments*. There is abundant evidence, then, to suggest that important social changes occurred in the government of Lancashire after the Civil War, and especially during the Interregnum. To deny this would be not only over-cautious but intellectually dishonest. Yet it is also necessary to keep a sense of proportion and not over-dramatise the situation. It would be wrong, for example, to assume that the lesser gentry as a whole supported the Republic just because during the Interregnum the county committee, the militia and at times the magistracy were dominated by the lesser gentry. In 1642 there were 621 minor gentry families in Lancashire. At most, 54 of them supported the Republic—a mere 8 per cent—and only 33 were at all active.[111] Thus while most 'republicans' were perhaps lesser gentry, most lesser gentry were certainly not 'republicans'.

It should also be noted that in Lancashire, as to a lesser extent in the national administration,[112] power shifted not from one class to another—from the gentry to 'the middle sort'—but *within* a class: from the greater to the lesser gentry. The overwhelming majority of those who ruled the palatinate during the Interregnum were still gentry. Moreover, the few plebeians employed in the more responsible positions in local government were not always accepted with a good grace by their betters. The case of Robert Massey illustrates this point. In 1650 the sequestration committees throughout the kingdom were drastically reduced in size and brought more directly under central government control. Robert Cunliffe of Sparth, Robert Holt of Bridge Hall and George Pigott of Preston were appointed commissioners for Lancashire.[113] In 1651 the London committee stirred up the determined resistance of the new Lancashire committee by forcing upon them as fellow commissioner one Robert Massey, a mercer of Warrington. Holt died shortly afterwards, but Cunliffe and Pigott both refused to act with Massey and were discharged. Their places were taken by Edward Aspinwall of Toxteth and John Sawrey of Plumpton, although Aspinwall consented to act only after much hesitation. While Massey may well have been a mere seeker of personal advantage, it seems clear that it was his status rather than his character that aroused resentment. Although Aspinwall, Cunliffe and Pigott were themselves only minor gentry, they evidently considered that a wide gulf existed between them and 'a Tradesman', who 'hath not anie estate' sufficient for his office.[114] To the twentieth-century mind this may seem a classic example of social snobbery, but in the seventeenth century it was widely believed that power should depend on property and prestige.[115]

The case of Robert Massey would seem to suggest that the social changes in the government of Lancashire were due not so much to the triumph of any radical ideology as to the exigencies of war and revolution. War is sometimes an agent of social change,[116] and revolutions almost always lead to an increase in bureaucracy.[117] As more men were needed in the government of Lancashire during and after the Civil War, the balance of power inevitably shifted towards those families who normally took little part in county affairs.[118] Indeed, similar social changes might possibly have occurred if the Royalists had won the Civil War. This is suggested by the social status of many of the Lancashire Royalist army officers.

We have observed that before the Civil War the militia officers in Lancashire were all drawn from the ranks of the county elite. After the Restoration and indeed until the end of the nineteenth century a majority of British army officers belonged to the aristocracy and gentry.[119] But during the English Revolution officers in the army of the Eastern Association were 'chosen for their military ability and politico-religious zeal rather than their local prestige',[120] while in the New Model Army 'a good many [junior officers] were drawn from the trading classes in London and elsewhere'.[121] It is interesting therefore to find that in the Lancashire Parliamentary forces only 50 per cent of the officers were gentry. What is even more interesting is that only 54 per cent of the Lancashire Royalist officers were of upper-class status and that the remainder were either plebeians or men of doubtful gentility.[122] Dr Ian Roy discovered that in the main Royalist army at Oxford many officers in the infantry, though not apparently in the socially superior cavalry, were tradesmen or professional men.[123] But the Lancashire Royalist forces employed plebeian officers not only in the Foot but even more in the Horse, the queen of the battlefield.[124] Lancashire Royalist cavalry officers included yeomen, like Lieutenant Richard Waring of Whittingham,[125] and even a few husbandmen, like Quartermaster Robert Tickle of Lowton.[126] The large numbers of plebeian officers in the Lancashire Royalist regiments during the Civil War should not really surprise us. After all, Charles I had not been averse to employing low-born persons in high places if it suited him. As Professor Robert Ashton reminds us, social snobbery played an important role in the building up of the county opposition to the Stuarts, and one of the main objections to Archbishop Laud had been that he was 'a fellow of mean extraction'.[127] However, let us not overstate our case. Among the Lancashire Parliamentarians were some plebeian colonels, like George Kay.[128] But among the Lancashire Royalist forces no plebeian seems to have risen above the rank of captain.[129] This would perhaps suggest that if Charles I had won the Civil War, social changes in the government of Lancashire might not have gone quite as far as they did under Cromwell.

3 THE POST-WAR LAND PURCHASES OF THE PARLIAMEN-
TARIAN GENTRY

After the Civil War many of the Lancashire Parliamentarian gentry obtained power, several for the first time. Far fewer obtained property. At first sight this seems strange, for the post-war period in England saw the greatest transfer of land since the Dissolution of the Monasteries. The victorious Parliament sold off most of the property it had confiscated in a vain attempt to achieve solvency and settle its mounting debts. Episcopal lands were ordered to be sold in 1646, dean and chapter lands in April 1649, Crown lands in July 1649, and fee-farm rents in 1650. Finally three Acts in 1651 and 1652 ordered the sale of lands of those remaining Cavaliers who had refused to compound or who, on account of their Roman Catholicism or high position in the Royalist party, were not permitted to do so.[130] Also from October 1650 delinquents (i.e. Royalists) were allowed to sell land in order to pay their composition fines.[131] Except in the case of fee-farm rents and privately sold land, payment was by doubled bills or debentures; only small balances were paid in cash. Purchasers of confiscated land were in fact frequently creditors—or their assigns—collecting debts on terms, none too favourable to them, set by the government.[132] An army officer owed arrears or a civilian creditor of the State might buy confiscated land simply because he could see no other way of obtaining payment. Nevertheless, the purchase might still be a profitable transaction, adding considerably to his income.

Lancashire contained a vast amount of Royalist land, including the extensive estates of the Earl of Derby, and also a fair portion of Crown property, especially in Blackburn and Lonsdale hundreds. In theory the Lancashire Parliamentarian gentry had ample opportunities for personal aggrandisement. In practice only 21 (11·4 per cent) out of 183 Parliamentarian gentlemen[133] seem to have made first hand purchases of land in the palatinate.

The Parliamentary gentry do not seem to have acquired any episcopal property in Lancashire.[134] Not that very much was sold. On 19 March 1652 the lands of Hadley Hall, part of Blackburn rectory and formerly the property of the archbishopric of Canterbury, were sold to three Londoners for £3,399 16s. 2d.[135] On 13 August 1652 Ribchester Parsonage House, once the property of the bishopric of Chester, was purchased for £1,353 19s. 4d. by Thomas Salmon, a Hackney haberdasher.[136]

During the Interregnum 12 parcels of capitular land in Lancashire were sold, all but one of which had belonged to the Warden and Fellows of the Collegiate Church of Manchester.[137] Only two of these properties were obtained by Lancashire Parliamentarian gentlemen. Richard Haworth, a prosperous Manchester lawyer, obtained for £221 8s. od. some property in Deansgate, which he had previously rented,[138] and Ralph Worsley of Platt, also a tenant, bought a messuage called 'Yieldhouses' for £209 13s. 2d.[139] Four other properties were obtained by two local merchants, a Manchester clergyman and John Whitworth of Newton—all tenants of the Collegiate Church—at a total cost of £1,712 10s. 8d.[140] The other six parcels of land were bought by one London gentleman and six City merchants at a total cost of £3,908 11s. 4d.[141] Clearly London merchants were the main beneficiaries of the sales of capitular land. By contrast the Lancashire Parliamentary gentry acquired a mere 7 per cent.[142]

The Lancashire Parliamentary gentry obtained an even smaller share of Crown land in Lancashire—barely 3 per cent. The Parliamentarian gentlemen buying from the Sales Trustees were Colonel Thomas Birch of Birch and Captain Thomas Rippon of Quernmore, and together they spent only £1,166 14s. 10d.[143] Moreover, there are signs, but no proof, that Birch, in conjunction with Jeremy Whitworth, was not buying for himself but on behalf of another officer— Major Joseph Rigby and ten ordinary troopers.[144] In any case Birch and Rippon bought less Crown land than two Lancashire plebeians— a certain Lieutenant Samuel Hoghton and Captain Jeremy Whitworth of Cripplegate—who spent a total of £5,172 19s. 1d.[145] However, 85 per cent of the royal estates in Lancashire were apparently purchased by outsiders. Ten non-Lancastrians (including eight Londoners) spent £12,517 1s. 6d.,[146] and eight regimental trustees paid a total of £24,428 7s. 8d.[147]

The Lancashire Parliamentary gentry were rather more successful in purchasing fee-farm rents. Two of them—Thomas Birch and Thomas Fell of Swarthmoor—paid a total of £1,394 6s. 8d.,[148] which was considerably more than the £224 6s. 8d. spent by two Lancashire plebeians—John Webster of Clitheroe and Jeremy Whitworth of Cripplegate.[149] Nevertheless, the lion's share of Lancashire fee-farm rents was not obtained by the Parliamentary gentry but by seven non-Lancastrians (six Londoners and one Cheshire gentleman), who paid a total of £4,257 15s. od.[150]

The Lancashire Parliamentary gentry obtained 22 per cent of the fee-farm rents that were sold. By contrast they acquired from the Sales Trustees only 9 per cent of the forfeited Lancashire lands of the Earl of Derby. Nevertheless, they seem to have spent more on Derby land than on any other kind of property.[151] This was partly because several of them had been the earl's tenants. The Confiscation Act of 1651— in which the earl's name appeared—assisted tenants to buy their lands by guaranteeing them pre-emptive rights for 30 days after the announcement of each sale. At the Restoration the king's commissioners, investigating the sale of Crown and Church lands during the

TABLE 38

PURCHASERS OF LAND IN LANCASHIRE, 1644–59, SHOWING NUMBERS OF PROPERTIES ACQUIRED

| Purchasers | Nos. | Church property | | | | | | Crown property | | | | | | Forfeited Royalist property | | | | | | Privately sold property | | | | | | All categories of property | | |
| | | Episcopal land | | | Capitular land | | | Crown land | | | Fee-farm rents | | | Earl of Derby's lands | | | Royalist gentry land | | | Royalist gentry land | | | Non-Royalist gentry land | | | | | |
		T	M	N–M	T	M	N–M	T	M	N–M	T	M	N–M	T	M	N–M	T	M	N–M	T	M	N–M	T	M	N–M	T	M	N–M
Lancs. Parl. gentry	21 (7·4%)	Nil?			2	0	2	2	0	2	3	0	3	13	3	10	3	0	3	3	0	3	5	1	4	31 (10·4%)	4	27
Other Lancastrians	102 (36·3%)	Nil?			4	0	4	4	0	4	2	0	2	40	0	40	9	0	9	23	1	22	12	1	11	94 (31·4%)	2	92
Non-Lancastrians	57 (20·3%)	2	0	2	6	1	5	14	8	6	4	0	4	4	1	3	17	10	7	2	1	1	2	1	1	51 (17·1%)	22	29
Agents or possible agents[a]	101 (36·0%)	Nil?			Nil?			6	5	1	Nil?			40	17	23	77	33	44	Nil?			Nil?			123 (41·1%)	55	68
Totals	281 (100·0%)	2	0	2	12	1	11	26	13	13	9	0	9	97	21	76	106	43	63	28	2	26	19	3	16	299 (100·0%)	83	216

Abbreviations: *T* Total number of properties, *M* Manors, *N–M* Non-manors.
a Agents include both Lancastrians and non-Lancastrians.

TABLE 39

PURCHASERS OF LAND IN LANCASHIRE, 1644–59, SHOWING AMOUNTS PAID[a]

Purchasers	Nos.	Church property				Crown property						Forfeited Royalist property						Privately sold property						All categories of property		
		Episcopal land			Capitular land			Crown land			Fee-farm rents			Earl of Derby's lands			Royalist gentry land			Royalist gentry land			Non-Royalist gentry land					
		£	s.	d.	£	s.	d.	£	s.	d.	£	s.	d.	£	s.	d.	£	s.	d.	£	s.	d.	£	s.	d.	£	s.	d.
Lancs. Parl. gentry	21 (7·4%)	Nil?			431	1	2	1,166	14	10	1,394	5	8	3,544	16	5	1,973	16	7	500	0	0	510	0	0	250 15 8 (6·0%)		
Other Lancastrians	102 (36·3%)	Nil?			1,712	10	8	5,172	19	1	224	6	8	5,823	16	5	1,168	1	2	3,883	0	0	5,352	0	0	27,336 14 0 (14·9%)		
Non-Lancastrians	57 (20·3%)	4,753	15	6	3,908	11	4	12,517	1	6	4,227	15	0	371	4	9	5,475	19	0	1,300	0	0	2,330	0	0	3,914 7 1 (22·1%)		
Agents or possible agents[b]	101 (36·0%)	Nil?			Nil?			24,428	7	8	Nil?			29,105	0	9	36,282	12	0	Nil?			Nil?			8,816 0 5 (57·0%)		
Totals	281 (100·0%)	4,753	15	6	6,052	3	2	43,285	3	1	5,846	8	4	38,844	18	4	14,900	8	9	5,683	0	0	8,192	0	0	15,587 17 2 100·0%		

a Transactions totalled 259. We are ignorant of the purchase price in 5[c] of the 170 forfeited Royalist, six of the 28 private Royalist and four of the 19 private non-Royalist transactions.
b Agents include both Lancastrians and non-Lancastrians.

Interregnum, regarded tenants, who had bought 'to preserve their houses... lands ... from waste or injury', more favourably than those who had bought 'for gain and advantage'.[152] It is interesting therefore to find that eight of the 10 Parliamentary gentry who purchased Derby property did so because they already rented it or because it lay near their existing holdings.[153] The exceptions were Thomas Birch of Birch and Charles Worsley of Platt, but even they can hardly be said to have bought 'for gain and advantage'. Colonel Birch, although he had an eye to the main chance,[154] seems to have purchased property in Chetham in 1653 in *lieu* of arrears of pay.[155] Charles Worsley, then a lieutenant-colonel, may have bought the manors of Bolton and Bury in 1653 and 1654 for similar reasons.[156]

The Parliamentary gentry obtained an extremely small share of other forfeited Royalist land. Three Parliamentarian gentlemen— John Braddyll of Portfield, Robert Cunliffe of Sparth and Edward Robinson of Euxton—acquired only three of the 106 parcels of Lancashire land sold by the Treason Trustees. John Braddyll seems to have made a modest purchase for an unknown sum. On the other hand, Robert Cunliffe and Edward Robinson appear to have obtained a fairly substantial amount of land at a total cost of £1,973 16s. 7d.[157] However, this was a mere 4·4 per cent of the total sum paid by the 87 purchasers of forfeited Royalist gentry land.[158]

The Parliamentary gentry seem to have been no more successful at the private than at the public sales of land. Between 1644 and 1659 21 Royalist gentry sold 28 parcels of land in Lancashire.[159] This was mainly due to the financial costs of sequestration, composition fines[160] and repurchasing forfeited land. But only three Parliamentarian gentlemen were able or willing to take advantage of their enemies' misfortune. John Starkie of Huntroyd bought a tenement in Simonstone from Roger Nowell of Read for an unknown sum.[161] Edward Rigby of Goosnargh purchased some of the outlying lands of the elder William Farington of Worden for £100.[162] Thomas Birch bought Carleton Hall from Alexander Rigby of Burgh for £400.[163] In monetary terms the Parliamentary gentry bought a mere 8 per cent of land sold privately by the Cavaliers.[164]

In addition to the Cavaliers, 17 non-Royalist gentry sold 19 parcels of land between 1646 and 1659. Only five Parliamentarian gentry seem to have bought from them,[165] and only one of these—Sir Robert Bindloss of Borwick—made a possibly substantial purchase. About 1650 Bindloss apparently acquired the manor of Capernwray for an unknown sum from Robert Blackburn, a Catholic squire. In financial terms the Parliamentarian gentry bought only 6 per cent of the lands sold by the non-Royalist gentry.[166]

To sum up: between 1644 and 1659 299 properties in Lancashire were sold publicly or privately to 281 purchasers. Only 21 of these purchasers—a mere 7·4 per cent—were Lancashire Parliamentarian gentry. The other buyers consisted of 102 Lancastrians (36·3 per cent), 57 non-Lancastrians (20·3 per cent) and 101 agents (36·0 per cent). Not only did the Lancashire Parliamentary gentry form a tiny minority of the purchasers, they also acquired a tiny proportion of the Lancashire land: only 10·4 per cent of the number, and a mere 6·0 per cent of the value, of the properties sold.[167] Tables 38 and 39 show that other Lancastrians and non-Lancastrians obtained much more land and that, in monetary terms, agents purchased the bulk of the property that was sold.[168]

We have so far concentrated on the *first* sales of forfeited Church, Crown and delinquent land in *Lancashire*, and on sales made privately

TABLE 40

LAND PURCHASED BY LANCASHIRE PARLIAMENTARIAN GENTRY,
1647–59[a]

Type of property	Number of properties sold	Amount paid £ s. d.
Irish land[b]	1	600 0 0
Episcopal land	10	2,773 19 11
Capitular land	2	431 1 2
Crown land	8	2,124 2 0
Fee-farm rents	3	1,991 6 8
Earl of Derby's forfeited Lancashire estates	16	4,098 9 9
Other forfeited Royalist estates	5	2,317 14 7
Royalist land sold privately	4	500 0 0
Non-Royalist land sold privately	9	1,566 6 8
Total	58	15,746 0 9

a Except for Irish land; see Blackwood, D.Phil. thesis, App. VIII, for details.
b Only one Lancashire gentleman was a recipient of Irish land. The elder Richard Shuttleworth of Gawthorpe adventured £600 and drew 617 acres in county Westmeath (Karl S. Bottigheimer, *English Money and Irish Land* (Oxford, 1971), 209).

by Royalist and non-Royalist *gentry*. But if we added sales of non-Lancashire (including Irish) land, second-hand Crown and Royalist estates,[169] and property belonging to Lancashire plebeians, then the amount of land obtained by the Lancashire Parliamentary gentry would rise considerably: from 31 to 58 properties, and in monetary terms from £9,520 15s. 8d. to £15,746 0s. 9d. The number of individual purchasers would also rise from 21 to 33. The number and value of the various properties obtained by the Lancashire Parliamentarian gentry are set out in Table 40.

We do not know what eight of the 33 Parliamentarian buyers paid for their purchases. The other 25 spent a total of £15,746, of which £9,446 7s. 0d. was paid by only six individuals: John Birch of Ardwick, Thomas Birch of Birch, Robert Cunliffe of Sparth, Thomas Fell of Swarthmoor, Edward Robinson of Euxton and Sir Thomas Stanley of Bickerstaffe.[170] These are the only Parliamentary gentlemen known to have spent over £1,000 on land.[171] At least four of these six purchasers—Birch of Ardwick, Birch of Birch, Cunliffe of Sparth and Fell of Swarthmoor—were men of very small landed incomes before the Civil War.[172] John Birch had an annual landed income of only £50, Thomas Birch had £250 and Thomas Fell £150,[173] while Robert Cunliffe had 'in his life tyme' a mere £35 per annum.[174] Why, then, were they able to buy more property than other, sometimes wealthier, landed gentry? It is extremely hard to say. Perhaps they may have had better opportunities. It has been suggested that John Birch's governorship of Hereford enabled him to speculate in episcopal lands.[175] A man like Thomas Fell may have been helped by a successful post-war legal career; in 1649 he became vice-chancellor of the duchy and attorney for the county palatine of Lancaster, and in 1650 was an assize judge.[176] But perhaps most significant of all was that shortly before, or at the time of, making their purchases the two Birches, Cunliffe and Fell were all Members of Parliament.[177] As such they were well placed to obtain land. Although not guilty of corruption, they must have had valuable inside information about the land market which was denied to outsiders. However, at least two of the gentry may have enriched themselves by dishonest means. Thomas Birch and Thomas Fell were said to have bought confiscated property with forged debentures, amounting to £1,816 12s. 6d. and £4,738 19s. 4½d. respectively.[178]

It would have been very surprising indeed if the Great Rebellion had not produced some war profiteers like Birch and Fell. At the same time it is important to stress that such persons were not common among the Lancashire Parliamentary gentry. Birch and Fell were a minority among the six substantial purchasers of land. The substantial purchasers were a minority among the total number of Parliamentary gentry purchasers. These 33 purchasers in turn formed only 18 per cent of the 183 Parliamentarian gentry.

Why did so few Lancashire Parliamentarian gentlemen acquire land after the Civil War? It is impossible to give a positive answer to such a question and only the most tentative suggestions can be made. However, the low incomes of most of the Lancashire Parliamentarian gentry would seem to be a partial explanation.[179] This must have made it difficult for them to compete against the rich Londoners who, for themselves or for others, bought up most of the confiscated property in the palatinate.[180]

Another possible reason may have been that many civilian supporters of Parliament during the Civil War and Interregnum had few opportunities to enrich themselves. Despite the fulminations of the Levellers and others against 'Committeemen' who bought land, such officials were, in fact, generally unpaid.[181] In Lancashire, at any rate, it was not the county committeemen but the sequestration agents who were accused of making great profits,[182] and these agents were predominantly plebeians, not gentry.[183]

If the leading civilian Parliamentarians in Lancashire had little opportunity to acquire land, the military Parliamentarians had little need to do so. Lancashire seems to have been one of the few shires whose county committee leased sequestered Royalist estates to leading Parliamentary officers.[184] Gentlemen such as Major Henry Porter, Major Joseph Rigby, Major Barton Shuttleworth, Captain Edward Shuttleworth, Lieutenant-Colonel Alexander Standish and Colonel Richard Standish perhaps did not obtain land in *lieu* of arrears because they farmed sequestered property instead.[185] Colonel Nicholas Shuttleworth had even less need to acquire land, because he not only farmed the sequestered estates of eight prominent Lancashire Royalists,[186] but obtained £3,287 12s. 6d. in cash by selling debentures.[187]

Lack of financial wealth, opportunity or need would therefore seem to have been a major reason for the small amount of land obtained by the Lancashire Parliamentarian gentry after the Civil War. But perhaps there may also be a deeper explanation. Would it be too facile to suggest that since the Civil War in Lancashire had been primarily a religious conflict, the victorious Parliamentarians were more concerned to establish a godly society[188] than to feather their own nests? This is not to deny that for some Lancashire gentlemen, such as Birch of Ardwick, Birch of Birch and Fell of Swarthmoor, puritanism and profit, godliness and gain, conveniently coincided.[189]

4   THE RISING AND DECLINING PARLIAMENTARIAN GENTRY,
1642–1700

How much did the Parliamentarian gentry gain or lose in the long run? To what extent did the 33 gentlemen who bought lands after the Civil War lose them at the Restoration? This last question is difficult, and sometimes impossible, to answer because the evidence is not always sufficient. However, it would appear that Richard Shuttleworth of Gawthorpe was allowed by Charles II to keep his Irish land.[190] On the other hand, John Birch of Ardwick saw his purchased lands restored to the Bishopric of Hereford.[191] In a debate in the House of Commons early in 1678 Birch lamented that 'I had bought some [church lands], but now I have none'.[192] Richard Haworth and Ralph Worsley also had to surrender their Manchester Church property to the Warden and Fellows, but were apparently allowed to remain as tenants.[193]

The Parliamentarian gentry seem to have lost most of the Crown lands they had bought. Humphrey Chetham had acquired second-hand the manor of Accrington in 1653, while Birch of Birch and Fell of Swarthmoor had obtained the resold manor of Haslingden in 1650.[194] Accrington and Haslingden both formed part of the vast honor of Clitheroe. So when in 1661 Charles II granted the honor to General George Monck,[195] Chetham, Birch and Fell must have been deprived of their manors. Clement Townson of Lancaster must also have lost his purchased property in Bowland Chase, since it too formed part of Clitheroe honor.[196] Captain Thomas Rippon of Quernmore can no longer have received the rents in Slyne after the Restoration, for it would seem that this manor returned to the monarch.[197] Captain Edward French of Preston was apparently dispossessed of the manor of Chertsey in Surrey.[198] Furthermore, there is no evidence that any of the above families were granted compensatory leases after the Restoration.[199]

Parliamentarian families who had bought fee-farm rents were probably, though not certainly, as unlucky as those who had acquired episcopal or crown land. There are signs that George Fell of Swarthmoor returned to the king the fee-farm rents that his father had bought during the Interregnum.[200] It is also likely that Thomas Birch of Birch lost possession of the fee-farm rents in the manor of West Derby.[201]

Those Parliamentarian gentry who had purchased non-manorial property confiscated from the Earl of Derby almost certainly continued as owners after the Restoration,[202] while the Sawrey family retained possession of the manor of Broughton until the twentieth century.[203] But at some date in the late seventeenth century the Worsleys of Platt apparently had to return the manors of Bolton and Bury to the earl. Likewise John Cliffe of Bretherton would seem to have restored the manor of Bretherton.[204]

Some of the Parliamentarian purchasers of other forfeited Royalist property also seem to have been unfortunate. We do not know whether John Braddyll of Portfield, Richard Shuttleworth of Gawthorpe or Clement Townson of Lancaster kept their purchases.[205] But Edward Robinson of Euxton soon lost his. In 1653 Robinson bought the life estate of Richard Chorley of Chorley,[206] but lost it a year later when Richard died and was succeeded by his son William.[207] The Cunliffes also kept their purchase of Towneley property for a very short time. Robert Cunliffe died in 1653 and as his 'male issue [was] extinct, his estate [was] to fall to a Papist', namely his son-in-law, John Grimshaw of Clayton.[208]

The ten Parliamentarian gentry who had bought land privately, both from Royalists and non-Royalists, must have kept their purchases, since the land settlement at the Restoration did not interfere with private sales made during the Interregnum. However, these Parliamentarians had acquired only one manor and 12 other, mostly small, estates.[209]

At least 23 of the 58 properties (16 manors and seven non-manors), which the Lancashire Parliamentary gentry had purchased after the Civil War, were eventually returned to their original owners. The capital value of these lands amounted to £7,248 16s. 7d.[210] In monetary terms the Parliamentarian gentry lost 46 per cent of their purchases. Altogether 12[211] out of 33 Parliamentarian gentlemen lost all or some of the lands they had bought.

The post-Restoration period was not economically harmful to all the ex-Parliamentarian gentry families, however. Some continued to prosper up to and beyond the end of the seventeenth century. John Birch of Ardwick, although forced to surrender his bishops' lands, was able to buy Ordsall from the Radcliffe family in 1662. Thomas Braddyll of Portfield bought the manor of Samlesbury from Edward Southworth for £3,150 in 1678. Edward Byrom of Manchester purchased Kersall Cell from a kinsman for £1,050 in 1692. Richard Bold of Bold obtained the manor of Sutton from Edward Holland in 1700. These purchases were all at the expense of former Royalist families.[212]

Nevertheless, the post-Restoration period saw far more Parliamentarian families declining than rising. A total of 117 gentry families in Lancashire supported Parliament during the Civil War or the Republic afterwards.[213] Such sources as the Schedule of Contributors to the 'Free and Voluntary Gift', 1661,[214] the Lay Subsidy Rolls, 1663-64,[215] the Hearth Tax Assessments, Ladyday 1664 and Ladyday 1666,[216] Blome's List of Gentry, 1673,[217] and the List of Lancashire Freeholders, 1695,[218] show that 66 (56 per cent) of these 117 families were no longer officially regarded as members of the Lancashire gentry by the end of the seventeenth century. This was an enormous proportion. Even if we exclude 19 families who died out in the male line,[219] we are still left with a very large number of declining gentry. The social eclipse of so many families is very surprising and also difficult to explain. Indeed, one might well ask why they should have declined at all. After all, these families had actually supported the *winning* side during or after the Civil War. Unlike the defeated Royalists, they had not been victims of sequestrations, composition fines and confiscations, to say nothing of discriminatory taxation. It might, however, be suggested that victory itself entailed financial sacrifices. It is well known that John Moore of Bank Hall, the regicide, sustained heavy losses in the service of Parliament.[220] Yet his son Edward, by a judicious marriage,[221] a 'commercial' attitude towards his tenants[222] and considerable luck,[223] was able to restore the family fortunes and achieve a baronetcy in 1675.[224] In fact there does not seem to have been a single Parliamentarian gentry family in Lancashire whose decline was entirely due to participation in the Civil War.

Were the seeds of the decay of the Parliamentary gentry perhaps sown in the pre-war period? This was most unlikely for, as we have seen, very few of the Roundhead gentry were in serious financial straits before the Civil War.[225] But slightly more Parliamentarian families—about thirteen—apparently fell into debt after the Restoration. In some cases the consequences were serious. The estate of the Chethams of Nuthurst became so encumbered that they sold it to a relative in 1692.[226] The Holts of Bury, in debt since 1665, sold Bridge Hall in 1697 for £1,950 to their cousins, the Gaskells of Manchester.[227] After the Restoration the Egertons of Shaw apparently became so impoverished that their lands were gradually sold, although they did not actually part with their family seat until 1722.[228] However, debt does not seem to have permanently ruined many Parliamentarian families and only ten of them apparently sold out completely before the end of the seventeenth century.

The loss of their Interregnum purchases at the Restoration might be thought to have ruined some Parliamentarian families. It is certainly difficult to believe that Edward French's loss of gentility by 1661 was not caused by his forfeiture of Chertsey manor in 1660. Birch of Birch, Cliffe of Bretherton and Rippon of Quernmore may also have declined because all or some of their purchased lands were restored to their original owners. But it is hard to see how the misfortunes of an obscure younger son like Clement Townson—who was almost certainly deprived of land in Bowland Chase—could have harmed the rest of the family. There must have been other reasons for the social eclipse of the Townsons.

Debt and forfeiture together seem to have ruined no more than about fourteen ex-Parliamentarian families. The main reasons for the fall of the Lancashire Parliamentary gentry during the late seventeenth century would seem to have been political rather than financial. It is significant that as many as 30 of the 47 declining families had held some kind of office during the late 1640s and 1650s, and had been excluded from local government after the Restoration. As in Cumberland and Westmorland, loss of power led to loss of status.[229] In fact 27 of these 30 ex-office-holding families had disappeared from the ranks of the Lancashire gentry by 1673. One such family was Green of Wigan and Aspull. The Greens had been gentry since the beginning of the seventeenth century,[230] and in July 1659 Richard Green was appointed to the militia committee by the restored Rump.[231] But Richard was given no office after the Restoration and was one of the 20 Lancastrians disclaimed at the Lancaster Assizes in 1667.[232] Four years later he made his will as a chapman.[233] George Townson of Lancaster was called a gentleman in the lay subsidy roll of 1641.[234] He was a fairly active magistrate during the 1650s[235] but after the Restoration he was excluded from local power. By 1673 the Townson family had disappeared from the ranks of the gentry.[236] Occasionally an ex-Parliamentarian family lost status even when it increased its wealth. The Aspinwalls of Toxteth and Scarisbrick had been gentry since 1600.[237] In 1650 and 1651 Jerehiah Aspinwall served on the militia committee.[238] Edward Aspinwall acted as an assessment commissioner in 1651[239] and a sequestration commissioner between 1652 and 1655.[240] Both Edward and Jerehiah were active magistrates under the Commonwealth and early Protectorate.[241] But the Aspinwalls apparently held no local office after the Restoration and were not recognised as gentry in the 1695 Freeholders List, despite the fact that Edward had vastly increased the family estates by marrying Eleanor, sister and heiress of Gilbert Ireland of Hutt.[242] The case of the Aspinwalls would seem to strengthen the argument that it was the loss of power rather than the loss of property which caused the loss of prestige of so many Parliamentarian families.

Had a new Parliamentarian gentry arisen during the 1640s and 1650s to compensate for the decline of the old? The answer is in the negative. Only 15 plebeian families who had supported Parliament or the Republic had apparently established themselves in the ranks of the gentry by the mid-1660s.[243] This is not really surprising. If the Restoration meant the social ostracism of many ex-Parliamentary gentry, few plebeian Parliamentarians could expect social advancement. Not only political but economic factors were against the establishment of a new Parliamentary gentry. The dominance of the post-war land market in Lancashire by agents, Londoners and other wealthy outsiders[244] meant that few plebeian Parliamentarians were able to 'buy' their way into the gentry. Among those who succeeded were Richard Whitehead of Garstang, William West of Middleton, James Smith of Kirkham, Henry Wrigley of Salford and Richard King of Preston. Captain Richard Whitehead, 'a poore capp maker and a sequestratour' was said '... by abuse of sequestracions [to have] gotten a very faire Estate'.[245] William West, a radical lawyer, magistrate and county committeeman, bought several parcels of land, including the manors of Gressingham and Middleton, for a total of £539 16s. 8d.[246] James Smith, a sequestration agent in Amounderness in 1650 and 1651,[247] bought confiscated Derby property in his own locality in 1653 for £749 3s. 6d.[248] Henry Wrigley, a prosperous merchant,[249] who was High Sheriff of Lancashire in 1651[250] and a nominal magistrate in 1655,[251] bought Chamber Hall, Werneth, in 1646,[252] a messuage in Heaton in 1652[253] and second hand capitular property in Newton for £354 in 1654.[254] Finally, Richard King, an auditor of the accounts of the county committee in 1652,[255] bought Ribbleton Hall and adjoining land in 1656 for £1,500.[256] In view of their moderately substantial purchases, it is perhaps not surprising that Whitehead, West, Smith and King were all officially recognised as gentlemen for the first time in 1661,[257] and that Wrigley was acknowledged as one in the 1664 (Ladyday) Hearth Tax Assessment.[258]

The other ten Parliamentary plebeian families seem to have attained their gentility without buying land, [259] perhaps by enriching themselves as officials, merchants, farmers or landlords. But whether the 15 Parliamentarian families had acquired their gentility by purchasing land or by other means is really immaterial. What matters is that they formed less than 9 per cent of the 171 new gentry families who arose between the outbreak of the Civil War and the mid-1660s.[260] Thomas Fuller was right when he said that a new gentry had emerged after the Civil War. But in Lancashire they seem to have belonged mostly to those who may have 'sate still' during the Great Rebellion.

However, before attaching too much importance to the emergence of any new gentry class in Lancashire, two points should be made. First, the gentility of nearly all the 171 new families seems to have been shortlived; only 19 of them appear as gentry in the Lancashire Freeholders list in 1695.[261] Secondly, the new gentry were greatly outnumbered by the 'disappearing' gentry. As many as 318 families seem to have lost their gentle status between 1642 and 1664. This is hardly surprising. A civil war is generally a time of great social and economic upheaval, and the late 1640s witnessed 'what was probably the worst economic crisis of the [seventeenth] century'.[262] Lancashire suffered especially badly from the effects of the Civil War,[263] and falling rents, bad harvests and loss of markets must have been particularly harmful to the smaller gentry. Among the 318 families who lost their gentility between 1642 and 1664 over 80 per cent had apparently played no part in the Civil War. Evidently neutrality was not always socially and economically advantageous and indeed far more 'neutral' families left than entered the Lancashire gentry during the English Revolution.[264] On the other hand there appear to have been fewer social casualties among the politically committed. Although 66 Parliamentarian families had disappeared from the Lancashire gentry by the end of the seventeenth century, only 17 of them apparently declined between 1642 and 1664.[265] Among the Royalists 38 families ceased to be gentry between 1642 and 1664, but these formed only a small proportion of the total number of Cavaliers. The reasons why so many Royalist families survived the revolutionary decades will be considered in the next chapter. Meanwhile, the main social changes in Lancashire between the outbreak of the Civil War and the Restoration may be summarised as in Table 41.

CONCLUSION

During and after the Civil War the Parliamentarian gentry appear to have been less politically divided in Lancashire than in some other counties. Among a selected number of Lancashire magistrates and county committeemen, extremists of the left or right were few. A majority appear to have been moderate men who were prepared to co-operate with the central government, largely, it would seem, because of a strong fear of Royalism, a fear that remained until the

TABLE 41

THE NEW AND DISAPPEARING LANCASHIRE GENTRY, 1642-64[a]

Political groups	Families entering the gentry between 1642 and 1664	Families disappearing from the gentry between 1642 and 1664
Parliamentarians/supporters		
of the Republic	15 (8·8%)	17 (5·3%)
Royalists	4 (2·3%)[b]	38 (12·0%)
Sidechangers/Divided families	–	3 (0·9%)
Neutrals/Others	152 (88·9%)	260 (81·8%)
Totals	171 (100·0%)	318 (100·0%)

a For sources see below, p. 108 n. 214–16. For further details and comments see below, Chapter V and Appendix I.
b The new Royalist gentry families were Kellett of Fishwick, Parkinson of Swainshead, Potter of Manchester and Stanley of Maghull.

late 1650s. Then an equally strong fear of social and religious anarchy drove them to support Booth's uprising in 1659 and to welcome the Restoration in 1660.

When the Roundheads held power in Lancashire a minor social revolution in government occurred. During the Interregnum the greater gentry lost their monopoly of the Bench and their majority on the county committee. The most active and dedicated officials were the lesser gentry. However, the changes in local government lose some of their social significance when one notes the large number of non-gentry officers among the Lancashire Royalist forces and realises that similar changes in government might have occurred if the Cavaliers had won the Civil War.

When the Roundheads held power in Lancashire their gentry supporters apparently bought only a tiny proportion of confiscated and privately sold land in the palatinate. Even if we added other categories of property, the number of Parliamentary gentry purchasers would still be statistically insignificant. Few Parliamentarian gentlemen gained in the short run. Many suffered in the long run. After the Restoration the Parliamentary gentry apparently lost at least 46 per cent of their Interregnum purchases to their original owners. Moreover, by the end of the seventeenth century 56 per cent of those families who had supported Parliament or the Republic had apparently lost their gentility. Failure of the male line, debt and loss of their Interregnum acquisitions explain the decline of some families. But the largest single group of falling gentry comprised those who had held office after the Civil War and been denied it after the Restoration.

Finally, it should be noted that the Civil War and Interregnum saw the disappearance of 318 old and the appearance of only 171 new gentry families, and that among the newcomers fewer than 20 had apparently supported Parliament or the Republic.

NOTES

[1] *Rebellion*, iv, 287.

[2] W. Haller and G. Davies, eds., *The Leveller Tracts* (New York, 1944), 79.

[3] P. Austin Nuttall, ed., *The Hist. of the Worthies of England* (1840), i, 70.

[4] 'The County Community at War', in E. W. Ives, ed., *The English Revolution, 1600–1660* (1968), 74. See also D. H. Pennington and I. A. Roots, eds., *The Committee at Stafford, 1643–1645*, Staffordshire Record Society, 4th Ser., Vol. i, 1957, p. lxxiv; Everitt, *Kent*, 151–2.

[5] Broxap, 104 seq.

[6] Ibid., 79 n. 1, 119. Cf. Manning, *The English People and the English Revolution*, 208. Holland was certainly active as a magistrate and county committeeman until the execution of Charles I. See L.R.O., QSR 42, and above, pp. 83–4.

[7] On the other hand between 1645 and 1648 fierce religious disputes occurred between the leading Lancashire Presbyterian divines and the Independent clergy of north-east Cheshire (V.C.H., ii, 65; R. Halley, *Lancashire: its Puritanism and Nonconformity*, i, 433–6, 466–72).

[8] This chapter is concerned with serving officials only. Nominated magistrates, county committeemen and other officials who cannot be shown to have served at any time are largely ignored. A majority of the serving officials were active men, activity being defined in terms of attending at least one quarter session per annum or of signing at least five documents as members of various county committees. For the serving magistrates between 1646 and 1659 see L.R.O., QSR 40–53; for working members of the county committee from 1643 to 1653 see P.R.O., SP28/211; 218; 236; 332; also B.L., Harl. MS. 2112, fos. 51–5.

[9] For details see Blackwood, D.Phil. thesis, 197–8.

[10] Three of these no longer served in 1649 because of death, old age or illness.

[11] Rigby was a revolutionary but not a regicide (D. Underdown, *Pride's Purge* (Oxford, 1971), 187). He also had Leveller connections (B. Worden, *The Rump Parliament 1648–1653* (Cambridge, 1974), 39, 198–9). Rigby's career as a county committeeman finally ended, not because he opposed the Republic, but because of his promotion to the post of Baron of the Exchequer in 1649.

[12] L.R.O., QSR 43–44.

[13] No nominated lists of J.P.s exist for 1651. But Holcroft was not nominated to any commission between 1652 and 1656, the year of his death.

[14] Underdown, op. cit., 376.

[15] See below, pp. 114–15.

[16] P.R.O., SP29/26/93.

[17] For details of Birch and Moore see Blackwood, op. cit., 198.

[18] See ibid., 198–200.

[19] M. Mullett, ' "To dwell together in Unity"; the search for Agreement in Preston Politics, 1660–1690', *Trans, Hist. Soc.*, L. & C., Vol. 125 (1974), 62–3, 66–8.

[20] The change from Commonwealth to Protectorate in December 1653 does not seem to have been considered a political turning point by most Lancashire Parliamentarian gentry.

[21] L.R.O., QSR 22–37, 40, 42, 45–52; P.R.O., SP29/94/63.

[22] On the reforming efforts of the Lancashire Puritan magistrates after the Civil War see K. E. Wrightson, 'The Puritan Reformation of Manners, with special reference to the counties of Lancashire and Essex, 1640–1660', Cambridge Univ. Ph.D. thesis, 1974, esp. pp. 165–7.

[23] For details see R. Clifton, 'The Fear of Catholics in England, 1637–1645', Oxford Univ. D.Phil. thesis, 1967, pp. 115, 142, 195, 241–2, 323, 335, 337 and maps I–III; K. J. Lindley, 'The impact of the 1641 rebellion upon England and Wales, 1641–5', *Irish Historical Studies*, xviii, 1972, 147, 154, 156.

[24] See above, p. 76.

[25] Everitt, *Kent*, 244, 246; C. B. Phillips, 'County Committees and Local Government in Cumberland and Westmorland', 1642–1660', North. Hist., v, 1970, 55.

[26] Printed in C.W.T., 248–51.

[27] For details see Broxap, 167; A. Woolrych, *Battles of the English Civil War* (1961), 169; P. Young and R. Holmes, *The English Civil War* (1974), 285–6.

[28] *A new rising in Lancashire for Charles the Second* (1649), 1–2, B.L., E.564(8).

[29] Only two ex-Parliamentarian gentlemen—John Ashhurst of Ashhurst and Sir Richard Hoghton of Hoghton Tower—definitely supported Charles II in 1651 (Broxap, 34; C.A.M., iii, 1473). Six others—Sir Robert Bindloss of Borwick, Samuel Birch of Ardwick, Peter Harrison of Hindley and his three sons—may have done (V.C.H., viii, 171 n. 24; *Roy. Comp. Papers*, vi, pt. ii, 390; C.A.M., iii, 1445–6, 1472; C.C.C., iv, 2955–6).

[30] B.L., Add. MS. 34013, fos. 2 55. Only one of these Lancastrians was an ex-Parliamentarian gentleman: Alexander Norris of Bolton (ibid., f. 35).

[31] I.e. the acting magistrates and county committeemen.

[32] He attended 28 quarter sessions between 1650 and 1659 (L.R.O., QSR 44, 46–53). By contrast Hesketh attended one meeting in 1652 (L.R.O., QSR 46), although he had been nominated to the commission of the peace in 1649 and 1650 (L.R.O., QSC 51–52; P.R.O. C193/13/3). William Hulton attended one meeting in 1658 (L.R.O., QSR 52), although he was thrice nominated to the Bench in that year (L.R.O., QSC 59–61).

[33] Halley, op. cit., i, 193–4; C.W.T., 343.

[34] A. H. Dodd, *Studies in Stuart Wales* (Cardiff, 1952), 124, 128, 130–2, 137.

[35] C. H. Firth, ed., *The Clarke Papers* (repr. 1965), iv, 38. Quoted in Morrill, *Cheshire*, 314.

[36] C.C.C., v, 3253; C.S.P.D., 1659–60, pp. 145, 171.

[37] Professor David Underdown wrongly implies that Ireland was of obscure social origins ('Settlement in the Counties', in G. E. Aylmer, ed., *The Interregnum: the Quest for Settlement, 1646–1660* (1972), 180). In fact one of his ancestors had been a knight under Henry IV (W. Beamont, *Hale and Orford* (Warrington, 1886), 25). Ireland also seems to have been wealthy: his annual income in 1641 was £1,000, judging by the lay subsidy rolls (P.R.O., E179/132/340).

[38] P.R.O., E101/4/8/43.

[39] L.R.O., QSR 40–41; *Roy. Comp. Papers*, vi. pt. i, 135, 153.

[40] P.R.O., *List of Sheriffs*, ix, 73.

[41] P.R.O., SP28/211 (loose papers).

[42] L.R.O., QSR 43–46, 48–49, 51–52.

[43] G. V. Chivers, 'The Members for the Northern Counties in Richard Cromwell's Parliament', Manchester Univ. M.A. thesis, 1954, ii, 276 and n. 6.

[44] Ibid., 277.

[45] Sir Richard Baxter, Knight, *A Chronicle of the Kings of England*, ed. Edward Phillips (1670), 672. I have to thank Professor Austin Woolrych for this reference.

[46] W. A. Shaw, *The Knights of England* (1906), ii, 220.

[47] J. A. Atkinson, ed., *Tracts relating to the Civil War in Cheshire, 1641–59*, Chet. Soc., N.S., Vol. 65, 1909, 186.

[48] *Rebellion*, vi, 176.

[49] The names are given in A. & O., ii, 1326. How many of the commissioners were active is unknown.

[50] See above, p. 81.

[51] A. Cole, 'The Social Origins of the Early Friends', J.F.H.S., xlviii, 1957, 102–6.

[52] Morrill, op. cit., 322–3.

[53] Dr Christopher Hill makes a strong case for the existence of militant and radical tendencies among the early Quakers. See *The World Turned Upside Down* (1972), chapter X. But I consider that Professor Hugh Barbour gives a more balanced account of this sect. See *The Quakers in Puritan England* (New Haven, 1964), esp. chapters VI-IX.

[54] See Major-General Worsley's complaints about Quakers in Lancashire, Cheshire and Staffordshire in T. Birch, ed., *A Collection of the State Papers of John Thurloe, Esq., 1638–1660* (1742), iv, 333.

[55] Blackwood, 'Agrarian Unrest', 72–6.

[56] R. Parkinson, ed., *The Autobiography of Henry Newcome*, Chet. Soc., O.S., Vol. 26, 1852, 119.

[57] Everitt, *Kent*, 312–18; Fletcher, 320–2.

[58] Former Parliamentarians who joined in the loyal addresses to Charles II included Bindloss of Borwick, Clayton of Fulwood, Fyfe of Wedacre, Ireland of Hutt and Porter of Lancaster (P.R.O., SP29/1/34, 35).

[59] Although in the mid-1660s various plots and risings were alleged to have been discovered. See V.C.H., ii, 241. For a similar situation in Cheshire see Morrill, op. cit., 327–8.

[60] See above, pp. 38–47.

[61] For the consequences see above, pp. 98–9.

[62] Morrill, op. cit., 327–8; A. M. Johnson in *Glamorgan County Hist.*, iv, 308–9.

[63] Fletcher, 134, 321–2; J. Hurstfield, *Freedom, Corruption and Government in Elizabethan England* (1973), 292–3; Phillips, art. cit., 60–6.

[64] See above, p. 11.

[65] In addition there were six 'foreign' justices: the elder and younger George Booth, and also John Booth, of Dunham Massey, Cheshire, Major-General Tobias Bridges of London, George Pigott of Bonishall, Cheshire, and Philip Wenman, son and heir of the 2nd viscount. Of these only Wenman was active. See L.R.O., QSR 40–42.

[66] We know virtually nothing about two of them: John Gilliam of Droylsden and Randle Sharples of Blackburn. The other two—William Halsall of Harleton and William West of Middleton—were lawyers (P.R.O., SP18/101/123; Gibson, *Lydiate Hall*, 120).

[67] Underdown, *Somerset*, 158.

[68] Morrill, *Cheshire*, 223–5, 233–4, 256–8.

[69] Fletcher, 133, 355. See also pp. 295, 316.

[70] Ibid., 133–4, 356.

[71] See J. H. Gleason, *The Justices of the Peace in England, 1558–1640* (Oxford, 1969), 87–8; Fletcher, loc. cit.

[72] Their known aggregate incomes were £43,192, £15,150 and £12,950 respectively. For comparative purposes income is based on the 1641 lay subsidy rolls. See above, p. 30 n. 39.

[73] L.R.O., QSR 55. The status of members of the post-Restoration Bench is derived from P.R.O., E179/250/9; Hearth Tax Assessment, Ladyday 1666, and sources cited above, p. 30 n. 43.

[74] See P.R.O., SP29/94/63 for list of magistrates present. Twenty-two persons, comprising peers, ex-officio members of the Bench and 'foreign' justices, are excluded from our discussion.

[75] For sources regarding education see above, p. 24 n.

[76] This chapter is not concerned with county committees whose functions were religious, such as those for the Survey of Church Livings, 1650, or for Ejecting Scandalous Ministers, 1654.

[77] The J.P.s are generally considered to have been more politically conservative than the committeemen as well as socially superior to them.

[78] In addition there were 12 'foreigners', mostly Cheshire men. Only three of these—Colonel John Booth, Sir John Meldrum and George Pigott—can be shown to have served.

[79] This is largely because of the virtual disappearance of the sequestration committee.

[80] Eighty-three Lancastrians were nominated to various committees in the late 1650s. We do not know whether they ever served, but 29 of them were certainly acting committeemen in an earlier period.

[81] For *nominations* to the Lancashire Committee see A. & O., i, 92, 114, 149, 232, 546, 642, 707, 758–9, 968, 1085, 1142, 1238; ii, 37, 301, 469, 666, 1071–2, 1326, 1371, 1433–4. No Lancashire names appear in the *Lords* or *Commons Journals* which are not also in A. & O. For *activity* on the committee see references above, p. 102 n. 8. In the case of the militia commissioners from 1650 to 1652, records exist of their activities but not of their nominations. See P.R.O., SP28/211; B.L., Harl. MS. 2112, f. 51.

[82] Plain gentlemen never rose above 22 per cent on the Kentish committee. See Everitt, *Kent*, 329, Table IV. Everitt is here referring to the general body of committeemen and not to the active core, for which see above, p. 83. Our comparison with Kent is somewhat vitiated by the fact that Everitt accepts uncritically the status accorded the committeemen in the nominated lists.

[83] See above, pp. 75–6.

[84] Everitt, op. cit., 151–2.

[85] Underdown, *Somerset*, 124–5, 152, 168–9, 186. Underdown's account of the social

changes in the government of Somerset suffers from vagueness and lack of quantification.

[86] Pennington and Roots, eds., *The Committee at Stafford*, pp. xxii-iii.

[87] Phillips, art. cit., 40, 47, 56, 59.

[88] Income is again based on the 1641 lay subsidy rolls.

[89] Between 1643 and 1648 Bradshaw and Stanley signed at least 10, and Holland at least 16, documents (P.R.O., SP28/211 (loose papers); SP28/236 (unfoliated)).

[90] Estimates of income in this paragraph are based on the 1641 lay subsidy rolls. See P.R.O., E179/131/334; 132/340.

[91] *Brasenose College Register, 1509–1909*, 126; *Gl. Adm. Reg.*, 150.

[92] Peile, ed., *A Biographical Register of Christ's College*, i, 242; *Gl. Adm. Reg.*, 109.

[93] During those years Cunliffe signed at least 26 documents, Holt 20 and Pigott 25 (P.R.O., SP28/211 (loose papers)). Cunliffe was also fairly active on the county committee before 1649 (ibid.; SP28/236 (unfoliated)).

[94] According to the 1641 lay subsidy roll. See P.R.O., E179/131/334.

[95] J. P. Rylands, ed., *Lancs. Inquisitions, 1603–25*, L. & C. Rec. Soc., Vol. 16 (1887), 24–5.

[96] L.R.O., DDLx 7/2, f. 5.

[97] Fishwick, ed., *Commonwealth Church Surveys*, 1; P.R.O., SP18/101/123.

[98] Information kindly supplied by Mr R. N. Dore.

[99] Pigott was one of the very few 'foreigners' involved in the work of the Lancashire Committee. Such men were more prominent on other county committees, such as the Kentish (Everitt, *Kent*, 143–4).

[100] The Lancashire sub-committee functioned from 1646 to 1648.

[101] He had acquired the title as recently as 1643, when his elder brother died (V.C.H., vi, 554).

[102] Names are in P.R.O., SP28/253B; 256; 257. See also P.R.O., SP16/513/18. Unfortunately some of the Commonwealth Exchequer Papers (P.R.O., SP28/255; 259; 260) are 'unfit for production'.

[103] See Appendices III and IV.

[104] See D. H. Pennington, 'The Accounts of the Kingdom, 1642–1649', in F. J. Fisher, ed., *Essays in the Economic and Social History of Tudor and Stuart England* (Cambridge, 1961), 193. Mr Pennington does not include the Lancashire sub-committee in his study.

[105] See Blackwood, B.Litt., thesis, 11–32.

[106] They first appear as gentry in the Knighthood composition lists, 1631–32 (J. P. Earwaker, ed., *Miscellanies*, I, L. & C. Rec. Soc., Vol. 12 (1885), 213, 215).

[107] For sheriffs see P.R.O., *List*, ix, 73. The only Lancashire sheriffs nominated during the Civil War period—John Bradshaw of Bradshaw in 1644 and Gilbert Ireland of Hutt in 1647—were both esquires of mediaeval gentle stock.

[108] Names are in L.R.O., DDN 64, fos. 47–9, 112, 164; P.R.O., SP16/337/81.

[109] Names are in C.S.P.D., 1650, pp. 505–11.

[110] Underdown, *Pride's Purge*, 313; id., *Somerset*, 168.

[111] Twenty-five served as magistrates or on the county committee, five were paid officials of that committee and two were militia officers. Two of the committeemen were also sheriffs. The other 21 were nominated to the Bench or the county committee, but no evidence exists that they served. The most active official of all was, of course, Major-General Charles Worsley of Platt.

[112] Aylmer, *The State's Servants*, 178, 198, 279.

[113] *Roy. Comp. Papers*, vi. pt. i, 6–7, 26–7.

[114] For a full account of the Massey affair see ibid., vi. pt. i, 29–30; vi. pt. ii, 379–89.

[115] Such values were of course being challenged by Levellers, Diggers and other radicals.

[116] See 'War and Society, 1300–1600', *Past & Present*, No. 22 (1962), 11, 14, 16–17.

[117] See 'Social Mobility', ibid., No. 32 (1965), 8–10.

[118] The reduction in the size of the sequestration committee in 1650 and the decline in the number of acting J.P.s in the late 1650s do not invalidate our argument that the number of officials in Lancashire increased during the English Revolution.

[119] J. Childs, *The Army of Charles II* (1976), 31, 37–8; C. B. Otley, 'The Social Origins of British Army Officers', *Sociological Review*, N.S., xviii, 1970, 217.

[120] Holmes, 178.

[121] C. H. Firth, *Cromwell's Army* (4th edn., 1962), 46–7.

[122] For sources concerning Lancashire Royalist and Parliamentarian officers, see above, p. 66 n. 11. For a detailed comparison of the social status of cavalry, infantry and other officers, see Appendix II.

[123] 'The Royalist Army in the First Civil War', Oxford Univ. D.Phil. thesis, 1963, 209.

[124] For details see Appendix II.

[125] For his military rank see *A List of Officers claiming to the Sixty Thousand Pounds, etc.* (1663), col. 129; for his civilian status see *Roy. Comp. Papers*, vi, pt. i, 282.

[126] *List of Officers*, col. 19; *Roy. Comp. Papers*, vi. pt. ii, 417. For financial reasons Tickle may have deliberately lied about his status to the Lancashire sequestration committee. But there is no evidence that either he or Richard Waring was a gentleman.

[127] Lucy Hutchinson, *Memoirs of the Life of Colonel Hutchinson*, ed. J. Sutherland (1973), 48. Quoted in R. Ashton, 'The Aristocracy in Transition', Ec.H.R., 2nd Ser., xxii, 1969, 317.

[128] C.W.T., 250; G. Chandler, *Liverpool under Charles I*, 329. Apart from being a Lancastrian nothing is known about him.

[129] See Appendix II.

[130] For details of the Acts of Sale see A. & O., i, 887–905; ii, 81–104; 168–91; 358–62; 520–45; 591–8; 623–52.

[131] C.J., vi, 476.

[132] H. J. Habakkuk, 'Public Finance and the Sale of Confiscated Property during the Interregnum', Ec.H.R., 2nd Ser., xv, 1962, 70–88.

[133] In this and the next section of the chapter the term 'Parliamentarian' embraces the 147 participants in the Civil War (including nine Side-changers) and 36 individual gentlemen (including three ex-Royalists) who supported the Republic only.

[134] Professor I. G. Gentles, who is currently engaged on a detailed study of the sales of bishops' lands during the English Revolution, 1646–60, agrees with this conclusion.

[135] P.R.O., C54/3668/27.

[136] P.R.O., C54/3670/31.

[137] The exception was the prebend of Flixton, which belonged to Lichfield Cathedral. See P.R.O., C54/3636/1.

[138] P.R.O., C54/3638/21.

[139] P.R.O., C54/3666/23. For Worsley's tenancy see Manch. Cen. Ref. Lib., Carill Worsley Papers, M35/2/31.

[140] P.R.O., C54/3636/7; 3637/8, 16; 3638/22.

[141] P.R.O., C54/3636/1, 11, 14; 3666/26; 3675/14; 3876/46.

[142] Here and in the following paragraphs percentages, unless otherwise stated, refer to the value, not the number, of the properties sold.

[143] For details see Blackwood, D.Phil. thesis, Appendix VIII.

[144] See P.R.O., E121/3/1/124. On the subject of collective purchases of crown lands see H. J. Habakkuk, 'The Parliamentary Army and the Crown Lands', *The Welsh History Review*, iii, 1967, 403–26; M. Kishlansky, 'The Sales of Crown Lands and the Spirit of the Revolution', Ec.H.R., 2nd Ser., xxix, 1976, 125–30. Cf. Ian Gentles, 'The Sales of Crown Lands during the English Revolution', ibid., 2nd Ser., xxvi, 1973, 627–9; id., 'The Sales of Crown Lands: a Rejoinder', ibid., 2nd Ser., xxix, 1976, 131–5.

[145] Hoghton paid only £33 10s. od., while Whitworth spent as much as £5,139 9s. 1d. on his purchases. See I. J. Gentles, 'The Debentures Market and Military Purchases of Crown Land, 1649–60', London Univ. Ph.D. thesis, 1969, 175 and n. 4; also Appendix III, pp. 299, 353. Professor Gentles mistakenly describes Hoghton and Whitworth as gentlemen.

[146] This sum is derived from Professor Gentles' thesis. For the prices paid by individual non-Lancastrians see his Appendix III, pp. 253, 270, 280, 304, 329, 335, 338, 348.

[147] For details see ibid., App. III, pp. 251, 256, 295, 302, 316, 330, 333, 342. Five of the agents—Adam Baynes, John Northend, Edward Salmon, Adam Sheppardson and Thomas Talbot—were apparently attorneys for the Northern Brigade, and the other three agents—Nathanial Bonich, Daniel Henchman and Humphrey Jones, all of London—seem to have bought the manor of Widnes on behalf of Colonel Hewson's regiment (ibid., App. III, pp. 251, 256, 342; S. J. Madge, *The Domesday of Crown Lands* (1938), 223 n. 7). Whether in reality these regimental trustees bought for a small number of officers rather than for entire regiments, does not concern us.

[148] For details see Blackwood, op. cit., App. VIII.

[149] P.R.O., C54/3761/6; 3718/2.

150 P.R.O., C54/3667/3; 3670/18; 3674/1; 3689/3.
151 See Table 39 above.
152 J. Somers, *Tracts*, revised Walter Scott (2nd edn., 1812), vii, 468.
153 For details see Blackwood, App. VIII.
154 See above, p. 94.
155 P.R.O., C54/3766/6. Birch was awarded £1,805 13s. 8d. arrears of pay by the House of Commons on 3 December 1650 (C.J., vi, 504). But in January 1652 it was still owing and was about to be allowed to him 'as so much doubled Monies' in the 'purchase of any Lands of Delinquents'. See ibid., vii, 78. I have to thank Dr Joan Thirsk for this information.
156 For details of his purchases see Blackwood, App. VIII.
157 For details of their purchases see ibid.
158 See Table 39 above for details. The purchase and sale of forfeited Royalist lands, including those of the Earl of Derby, receive detailed treatment in the next chapter.
159 For details see Blackwood, D.Phil. thesis, App. X, 1.
160 Including fines paid on the third Act of Sale, 1652.
161 V.C.H., vi, 498 n. 22.
162 P.R.O., PL17/156/126. In reality Rigby may have paid much more. 'Considerations' cited in the feet of fines seldom represent the full payment.
163 L.R.O., QDD 51/16.
164 For the amount spent by other purchasers, see Table 39 above, p. 91 and Blackwood, App. X, 1.
165 For details see Blackwood, App. VIII.
166 For the amount spent by other purchasers see Table 39 above and Blackwood, D.Phil. thesis, App. IX.
167 See Tables 38 and 39 above.
168 It might be objected that I have underestimated the amount of property bought by the Lancashire Parliamentary gentry and that many of the other purchasers may have been agents acting on their behalf. Agents were certainly very prominent among the purchasers of forfeited Royalist land in Lancashire (see tables 38 and 39 and Chapter IV, sections 2 and 3), although only Peter Legay of London and Edward Lee of Sunderland may have bought on behalf of Lancashire Parliamentarian gentlemen. For details see Blackwood, App. VIII. A number of agents appear to have bought Crown land in the palatinate but apparently not for the local Parliamentary gentry or any other Lancastrians. See above, p. 106 n. 147. It is, of course, quite possible that several of the London purchasers of church lands, fee-farm rents and privately sold property in Lancashire may have been agents, but I have found no clear proof.
169 Only one piece of Church land in Lancashire seems to have been resold—to Henry Wrigley of Salford, Merchant. See above, p. 99. The few resales of fee-farm rents in the palatinate do not seem to have gone to any Lancashire gentlemen.
170 For details of their purchases see Blackwood, loc. cit.
171 Edward French of Preston, Roger Sawrey of Broughton and Sir Robert Bindloss of Borwick, who respectively bought the Crown manor of Chertsey, the Earl of Derby's manor of Broughton and the non-Royalist manor of Capernwray, may also have spent over £1,000, but there is no evidence to prove it.
172 We do not know the income of Edward Robinson. For Sir Thomas Stanley's income see above, pp. 83–4.
173 According to the 1641 lay subsidy roll. See P.R.O., E179/131/334; 132/337.
174 See above, p. 105 n. 96.
175 D.N.B., ii, 525–6.
176 Ibid., vi, 1163.
177 For their dates as M.P.s and as purchasers see Blackwood, App. VIII.
178 P.R.O., SP29/390/40, 47.
179 See Table 24, and below, p. 000.
180 For fuller details of these London purchasers see below, Chapter IV.
181 Pennington in Fisher, ed., *Essays in the Economic and Social Hist. of Tudor and Stuart England*, 193.
182 See *Roy. Comp. Papers*, vi, pt. i, 25.
183 Only two gentleman agents are known to have enriched themselves. For details see Blackwood, D.Phil. thesis, 236 n. 3.
184 Information kindly supplied by Dr J. S. Morrill.
185 For the leases of these gentry, see P.R.O., SP28/211: Half-year accounts ending 24 June 1650, fos. 10, 18, 30, 31, 33, 34, 37, 43, 53–5; SP28/211: Account Book 1651,

f. 64; SP28/211: Account Book 1652, f. 20. Not all gentry officers were satisfied, however. Captain Edward French of Preston and Major Edward Robinson of Euxton farmed sequestered estates (Half year accounts ending 24 June 1650, fos. 16, 23, 36; Account Book 1651, fos. 2, 8, 13; Account Book 1652, fos. 18, 19). Yet they also made substantial purchases of land. See Blackwood, D.Phil. thesis, App. VIII.

[186] P.R.O., SP28/211: Half-year accounts ending 24 June 1650, fos. 9, 16, 26–8, 31; SP28/211: Account Book 1651, f. 60.

[187] Gentles, thesis, 170.

[188] For attempts to do so see Wrightson, thesis, esp. pp. 165–7.

[189] Thomas Fell was the well known protector of George Fox and the Lonsdale Quakers.

[190] *Report from the Commissioners on the Public Records of Ireland*, 15th Report (1821–25), 428.

[191] D.N.B., ii, 526.

[192] W. Cobbett, ed., *The Parliamentary History of England . . . to the year 1803* (1808), iv, 946.

[193] For Worsley's lease of 1661 see Manch. Cen. Ref. Lib., M35/6/1/15. For Haworth's tenancy see *Calendar of Manchester Cathedral Deeds, 1558–1787*, Nos. 226, 335.

[194] For details see Blackwood, App. VIII.

[195] V.C.H., vi, 233 and n. 26.

[196] Ibid., vi, 333 n. 26, 379.

[197] Ibid., viii, 138.

[198] *V.C.H. Surrey* (1911), iii, 406.

[199] A thorough search of the following documents yielded no relevant information: P.R.O., CRES 6/2; LR2/56; LR2/266; B.L., Add. MS. 30208. For details see Bibliography.

[200] P.R.O., SP29/4/21. See the endorsement on the back of George Fell's petition.

[201] P.R.O., SP29/26/93.

[202] For a discussion of this point see below, p. 131 seq.

[203] H. V. Koop, *Broughton in Furness* (N.P., 1955), 61. See also below, p. 133.

[204] V.C.H., iii, 165 n. 8, v, 131–2, 247, vi, 104.

[205] Shuttleworth was more likely than Braddyll and Townson to have kept his purchase, since he had bought at second hand. See Blackwood, App. VIII.

[206] P.R.O., C54/3761/8.

[207] T. Wilson, *The Chorleys of Chorley Hall* (Manchester, 1907), 69–70.

[208] Fishwick, *Jolly's Note Book*, 129; R. Trappes-Lomax, *A Hist. of Clayton-le-Moors*, Chet. Soc., N.S., Vol. 85, 1926, 30.

[209] For details see Blackwood, App. VIII.

[210] For the sale prices of the restored properties see ibid.

[211] This figure excludes Cunliffe of Sparth, who was a special case.

[212] For details of purchases by ex-Parliamentarians from ex-Royalists between 1660 and 1700 see Blackwood, App. X, 2.

[213] Divided families and side-changers are excluded from these calculations.

[214] P.R.O., E179/250/5.

[215] P.R.O., E179/132/349; 132/350; L.R.O., DDX 3/96; 3/97; *Statutes of the Realm*, 15 Car. II, cap. 9.

[216] P.R.O., E179/250/11; 250/9.

[217] Richard Blome, *Britannia* (1673), 388–91.

[218] L.R.O., DDK 1740/2.

[219] Evidence for failure of the male line is to be found in *V.C.H. Lancs.*, iii-viii, and various parish and family histories.

[220] Moore was claiming arrears of £2,368 16s. 4d. in 1649 (Liverpool Record Office, Moore Deeds and Papers, 847 (unfoliated): statement of account with Colonel Moore, 1649).

[221] His wife, an heir of Sir William Fenwick, a Royalist baronet of Northumberland, brought him land worth £700 per annum. This enabled him to pay off his inherited debts of £10,000 (Gibson, *Lydiate Hall*, 162).

[222] See below, p. 145.

[223] The commercial expansion of Liverpool from 1665 to 1675 reacted favourably on Moore's property (W. F. Irvine, *Liverpool in King Charles the Second's Time* (1899), pp. xxiv, xxvii).

[224] G. E. Cokayne, ed., *Complete Baronetage* (Exeter, 1904), iv, 70.

[225] See above, pp. 59–60.

226 V.C.H., vi, 266; E. Axon, *Chetham Genealogies*, Chet. Soc., N.S. Vol. 50, 1903, 27–30.
227 Chet. Lib., Raines MS. XXX, fos. 283–5.
228 J. P. Earwaker, ed., *Local Gleanings* (Manchester, 1875–78), i, 276; ii, 3, 20–21; D. J. Leech, 'Flixton and its Church', Trans. L. & C. Antiq. Soc., Vol. 4 (1886), 191–2.
229 Phillips, art. cit., 61.
230 Earwaker, ed., *Miscellanies*, I, 243.
231 A. & O., ii, 1326.
232 J. P. Rylands, 'Disclaimers at the Heralds' Visitations', Trans. Hist. Soc. L. & C., Vols. 43–44 (1891–92), 76.
233 L.R.O., Will of Richard Green of Aspull, Chapman, 7 November 1671.
234 P.R.O., E179/132/337.
235 L.R.O., QSR 44–9.
236 They are not in Richard Blome's List of Lancashire gentry.
237 Earwaker, op. cit., 240.
238 P.R.O., SP28/211 (loose papers); B.L., Harl. MS. 2112, f. 51.
239 Ibid., f. 54.
240 P.R.O., SP28/211 (loose papers).
241 L.R.O., QSR 43–50.
242 H. O. Aspinall, *The Aspinwall and Aspinall Families of Lancashire* (Exeter, 1923), 21. Nor were the Aspinwalls recognised as gentry by Richard Blome in 1673, although that was two years before they entered into possession of the rich Ireland estates (ibid., 18).
243 Main sources for gentry numbers in this and the next two paragraphs are given above, p. 108 n. 214–16.
244 See Tables 38 and 39 above; also below, chapter IV, sections 2 and 3.
245 *Roy. Comp. Papers*, vi. pt. i, 22. I cannot find that Whitehead spent more than a modest £390 on land (L.R.O., QDD 63/7d, 14). But perhaps some of his purchases went unrecorded.
246 L.R.O., QDD 49/4d; 50/15; P.R.O., PL17/169/176; 164/96.
247 *Roy. Comp. Papers*, vi. pt. i, 27, 192–3; vi. pt. ii, 368, 392. See also idid., ii, 274.
248 P.R.O., C54/9757/9.
249 Wadsworth and Mann, *The Cotton Trade and Industrial Lancs.*, 35.
250 P.R.O., List of Sheriffs, ix, 73.
251 P.R.O., SP18/101/123.
252 G. Shaw, *Annals of Oldham* (Oldham, 1904), i, 102.
253 L.R.O., DDHp 13/1.
254 P.R.O., C54/3832/25.
255 P.R.O., SP28/218 (unfoliated).
256 L.R.O., DX 805.
257 P.R.O., E179/250/5.
258 P.R.O., E179/250/11.
259 These ten families were Boardman of Bolton, Briggs of Broughton-in-Furness, Gilliam of Droylsden, Hammond of Colne, Jackson of Cuerden, Lightbourne of Manchester, Werden of Preston, Westmore of Middleton, White of Claughton and Yates of Mellor.
260 Even if we added two families of 'foreign' gentry origins—Pigott of Preston and Warren of Tockholes—Parliamentarians would comprise barely 10 per cent of the new gentry in Lancashire.
261 L.R.O., DDK 1740/2. Moreover, only eight of the 171 families are mentioned in Richard Blome's List of Gentry, 1673 (*Britannia*, 300–91). In Kent the new gentry of the seventeenth century also seem to have had a low survival rate (Everitt, *Kent*, 324–5, 330, Table VI).
262 J. P. Cooper, 'Social and Economic Policies under the Commonwealth', in Aylmer, ed., *The Interregnum*, 123. Dr Margaret James said that between 1640 and 1650 'the country was to experience a period of economic dislocation which was, for modern England, unique in kind' (*Social Problems and Policy during the Puritan Revolution, 1640–1660* (1930), 35).
263 For details see ibid., 54–6, 244–5; J. Walker and K. Wrightson, 'Dearth and the Social Order in Early Modern England', *Past & Present*, No. 71 (1976), 38–40.
264 Little is known about most of the declining 'neutral' families, but it is hardly conceivable that all, or even a majority, of them failed in the male line or were killed

by the soldiery or the plague. The possible reasons for the decline of the 'neutral' gentry are discussed in the concluding chapter.

[265] Four of these 17 families failed in the male line during the Interregnum. The other 13 families seem to have lost their gentility almost immediately after the Restoration, and in eight cases loss of local power would appear to have been the main reason. See above, pp. 98–9.

CHAPTER IV

THE FATE OF THE CAVALIERS

INTRODUCTION

Let us now turn our attention to those who lost the Civil War. If the Lancashire Roundhead gentry made few material gains during the post-war period, does this mean that the Lancashire Cavaliers endured few material losses? Historical analogy might suggest otherwise. Revolutions and wars have often produced great social changes as well as political and military upheavals. The Norman Conquest, the Reformation, the Cromwellian conquest of Ireland, the American and French Revolutions all led to the expropriation of the vanquished. The Anglo-Saxon thegns, the monks and friars, the Irish Catholic proprietors, the American loyalist landowners and the French *noblesse* all lost their lands and wealth.[1] Did the English Royalists suffer a similar fate after their defeat in the Civil War?

In the post-war period the Royalists were the victims of sequestrations, composition fines and confiscations. How far were they seriously harmed by them? On this question national historians are divided. At one extreme it has been argued that wealth was transferred from one class to another, from debt-ridden Royalist aristocrats and gentry to the commercial class.[2] At the other extreme it has been said that

... in terms of the spread of wealth between social groups, and even between individual families, England at the end of the revolution in 1660 was barely distinguishable from England at the beginning of 1640.[3]

The truth can be discovered only by detailed research at a local level. A start has been made by Dr Joan Thirsk, Dr P. G. Holiday and Sir John Habakkuk. Dr Thirsk has examined the public sales of confiscated Royalist land in 12 south-eastern counties and shown that 70 per cent of the properties sold under the Commonwealth were recovered before or after the Restoration.[4] Dr Holiday has found that in Yorkshire 129 (82 per cent) out of 156 forfeited properties were regained by the Royalist gentry or their heirs.[5] In both Yorkshire and in south-east England most Royalists not only regained but retained the bulk of their estates until well into the 1680s, partly by adopting more efficient methods of estate management.[6] Sir John Habakkuk has investigated the private sales of Royalist property in Northamptonshire and Bedfordshire, and concluded that these were not caused primarily by composition fines but mainly by pre-war debts.[7]

What was the social and economic fate of the Royalist aristocracy and gentry in Lancashire after the Civil War? Were they as fortunate as their brethren in Yorkshire, the Midlands and the South-east? Or did many of them permanently lose their land to their Parliamentarian enemies and to other ranks of society? Five specific questions need answering before any conclusions can be drawn. First, how many of the Lancashire Royalist gentry sold land privately or suffered a serious decline in income as a result of sequestrations and composition fines? Secondly, how much forfeited property did the Royalist gentry recover before and after 1660? Thirdly, what exactly happened to the confiscated Lancashire estates of the seventh Earl of Derby? Fourthly, how many Royalists or their descendants sold land or lost status between 1660 and 1700, and how far was this due to their earlier sufferings? Fifthly, how far was any Royalist recovery due to more efficient methods of estate management? To assess the full significance of the economic state of the Cavaliers in the post-war period, we also need to study the social status and political affiliations of the purchasers of Royalist land.

I SEQUESTRATIONS, COMPOSITION FINES AND PRIVATE SALES, 1644-59

A total of 312 members of the Lancashire upper classes helped the Royalist cause in one or more of the three Civil Wars (1642–46, 1648, 1651).[8] Apart from the 42 (13 per cent) who lost their lives fighting for Charles I or the Earl of Derby,[9] the Royalist gentry seem to have suffered less in Lancashire than in many other parts of England. It was not simply that sequestrations, composition fines and confiscations had few permanently damaging effects. It was also because a fair minority of Royalist gentlemen—66 (21 per cent)—appear to have escaped these punishments altogether.[10] At first sight this seems strange. In a county where the Civil War had been extremely bitter, bloody and ideological, 'where Catholic met Puritan and the furies of Alva were unloosed in the streets of Bolton',[11] one would expect the post-war period to have been marked by vindictiveness on the one side and suffering on the other. Why was this not the case? Why did several Lancashire Royalists escape with either little or no harm to their persons and property? There were perhaps two main reasons. First, many of the Lancashire county committeemen were noted for their political moderation,[12] and their aim was to reconcile the defeated Royalists to the new regime by leniency rather than to alienate them by harshness.[13] But a more important reason for the fair treatment of the Lancashire Royalist gentry would seem to have been their great numbers. Support for the Stuarts was so strong in Lancashire that the Parliamentarian authorities dared not make an example of every Royalist. Indeed, the Lancashire Commissioners frankly admitted this when they wrote in July 1645 that:

... the Ordinance of Sequestration is fully executed when the people are well-affected, but in Colonel Rigby's division, most of the people were sequestrable but few sequestered because the condition of the county would not admit it in safety.[14]

After the Third Civil War the Lancashire Parliamentarians were even more cautious, for almost half the 45 Royalists who had participated were not sequestered.[15] The county committeemen knew that the government was even more unpopular in 1651 than it had been in 1648, for although only a small number of Lancashire gentlemen had taken up arms for Charles II, they had included not only veteran Royalists like Thomas Tyldesley of Myerscough but some former Parliamentarians like brave John Ashhurst of Ashhurst.[16]

This fear of Royalism forms the political background to the sequestrations, composition fines and confiscations and helps to explain the lenient treatment of the Lancashire Cavaliers.

However, let us not underestimate the tribulations of the Lancashire Royalist gentry. The fact remains that the majority—221 (71 per cent)—were at some time or other severely penalised for their 'delinquency', i.e. Royalism. Sequestration was the most common fate which befell the Royalists. When an estate was sequestered the revenue from it was no longer paid to the Royalist but to the sequestration officials appointed by the county committee. The Royalist's wife and children were allowed a mere fifth of his income. As well as his lands and rents, the delinquent had his money, goods and chattels sequestered. Some Lancashire Royalists complained of heavy losses. In 1660 Thomas Norris of Speke alleged that the sequestrators had taken from his father goods to the value of £1,600.[17] When Thomas Ashton of Penketh came forward to compound in 1646 he complained that 'for psonall estate he hathe nothinge but the cloths to his backe'.[18] Ashton and Norris may, of course, have exaggerated their losses. Yet some Royalists should have been harmed by sequestration, since it not only affected their personal possessions but involved a loss of income and sometimes the mismanagement of their estates. Even after their lands were discharged from sequestration, restoring them to their former prosperity was often a slow, difficult or impossible task. Hence some Royalists who endured sequestration suffered a serious decline in their landed wealth. According to the lay subsidy rolls, the annual income of the Girlingtons of Thurland fell from £200 in 1641 to £100 in 1663.[19] There is no evidence that the Girlingtons were in serious financial difficulties under Charles I, so the Parliamentary sequestrations may well have been mainly responsible for their losses. Six other sequestered Royalists also seem to have had their incomes seriously reduced between the outbreak of the Civil War and the

Restoration. These were Bannister of Altham, Byrom of Salford, Holt of Ashworth, Kirkby of Kirkby, Middleton of Leighton and Southworth of Samlesbury.[20] Not all these families could blame sequestration entirely for their predicament in 1663, however. The Byroms, the Middletons and the Southworths were in a delicate economic position before the Civil War.[21] In any case the number of sequestered Lancashire Royalists whose income seriously declined is remarkably small.

An even smaller number of Lancashire delinquents who were sequestered, but not apparently fined,[22] sold land. These were the Bambers of Lower Moor, the Hollands of Clifton, the Radcliffes of Ordsall and the Wolfalls of Wolfall. There is no sign that the Bambers and the Wolfalls were hard up before the Civil War, and there is good reason to believe that their land sales during the Interregnum[23] were caused mainly by the sequestrations. But there is no simple explanation for the post-war sales of the Hollands and the Radcliffes, although they might well have blamed the sequestrations. Indeed, William Holland complained in 1652 about the 'great damage' caused by the seizure of some part of his estate.[24] Almost as soon as the sequestration was discharged,[25] he parted with his ancestral home to Nathaniel Gaskell of Manchester.[26] Sir Alexander Radcliffe had his Essex and Norfolk lands sequestered.[27] His lands in Norfolk were discharged as early as 1645, while his manor and rectory of Henham were freed in 1651.[28] Even so, Radcliffe had to sell Henham shortly afterwards[29] and in 1657 his son, John, parted with the Norfolk manor of Attleborough for £8,000.[30] Since neither the Hollands nor the Radcliffes had paid any composition fines, it would seem that sequestration was the only explanation for their sales. In fact there were also other reasons. Both families were in financial difficulties and were selling land before the Civil War. The Hollands mortgaged their lands to William Lever of Kersal, Gentleman, in about 1634 for £1,400 and 'did not redeeme ... according to the time limitted for the redemption'.[31] In 1636 they sold land in Clifton.[32] Alexander Radcliffe had mortgaged part of his main Lancashire estate of Ordsall to Humphrey Chetham, the moneylender, in 1634,[33] and seven years later he seems to have sold his manor of Tockholes.[34] Thus pre-war debts as well as post-war sequestrations seem to explain the decline of the Hollands and Radcliffes.

Why was sequestration not necessarily a financial tragedy? Why did so few Royalist gentlemen have their lands and incomes reduced as a result? There were perhaps two main reasons. First, some members of the Lancashire sequestration committee appear to have been lenient towards the Royalists and their families. Such were Sir Thomas Stanley of Bickerstaffe, Colonel Peter Egerton of Shaw and Edward Butterworth of Belfield, brother of Alexander the Royalist. About 1646 Thomas Birch of Birch, that dedicated political and religious revolutionary, accused them of having made 'divers undue and

unwarrantable allowances to the wives and children of notorious papists and delinqts'. Among those said to have benefited by 'myscar-
riages concerning sequestracons' were the children of Adam Hulton
of Hulton and the wives of John Westby of Mowbreck and Thomas
Tyldesley of Myerscough, then 'cheife comander in Litchfield'. In
1645 Stanley, Egerton and Butterworth apparently suspended sequestration proceedings against two other delinquent gentlemen: Henry
Butler of Rawcliffe and Ferdinando Stanley of Broughton.[35]

Secondly, many Lancashire Royalist gentry were able to rent at
least part of their estates from the sequestrators, either directly or
through friends or relatives, and often at extreme undervaluations.
By doing so they escaped considerable hardship. In 1652 William
Anderton of Anderton rented his demesne lands at Anderton and Ad-
lington, and Abraham Langton farmed his lands at Lowe.[36] In the
same year Sir William Gerard of Bryn had the satisfaction of seeing
his demesnes at Bryn and Garswood and his mills and coalmines at
Ashton-in-Makerfield leased to Roger Bradshaw of Haigh,[37] a neutral
gentleman who in fact helped many a suffering Royalist.[38] In 1653
William Norris was granted a seven-year lease of two-thirds of his
estate at Blackrod, while his friend, Nicholas Blundell, farmed for him
two-thirds of his 'small estate at Moorhouses for one yeare'.[39] The
Andertons, the Gerards, the Langtons and the Norrises were all successful in regaining their property, either from the Committee for
Compounding or from the Treason Trustees.[40] They might not have
been so successful had they been seriously harmed by the sequestration
of their estates.

Sequestration could be permanently lifted in return for a payment
known as a composition fine.[41] As we shall see, the amount and burden
of the fine varied considerably from family to family. Many Royalists
were able to pay their fines without any difficulty. Some could pay
only by selling part of their property, while others who managed to
compound for the whole of their estates were eventually forced to sell
in order to recoup themselves. These 'voluntary' private sales, unlike
the public sales of confiscated Church, Crown and delinquent property, were not invalidated at the Restoration. Thus Sir John Habakkuk considers that

... the burden of the argument that the land transactions of [the Inter-
regnum] led to permanent [social] changes seems to fall upon the royalists
whose estates were sequestered—not confiscated—and who paid a fine to
compound for their delinquency.[42]

Contemporaries certainly saw a direct connection between composition fines and private land sales. Clarendon said that the Parliamentary authorities forced the Royalists to compound at 'so unreasonable rates, that many were compelled to sell half, that they might
enjoy the other toward the support of their families'.[43] Clarendon's

views have been echoed by a number of modern historians. Dr Christopher Hill has suggested that Royalists must have sold a considerable amount of land in order to pay composition fines.[44] Dr H. E. Chesney considered that private sales were extensive and that these were partly caused by composition fines.[45] Sir Charles Firth claimed that these fines forced many delinquents to sell in a flooded market.[46] It has been said that in south-west Lancashire something in the nature of a minor social revolution took place. Mr F. Walker remarked that the Civil War itself and the heavy compounding fines forced many old Royalist land-owning families to sell land to wealthy merchants of the Manchester district.[47] Unfortunately Walker made little attempt to elaborate or substantiate his argument.

It is extremely difficult to say how much land was sold to pay composition fines, not only in south-west Lancashire but in the county as a whole. The evidence is less abundant than at first sight appears. The papers of the Committee for Compounding give very little information about private sales by Lancashire Royalist gentry. Among the Royalist family muniments in the County Record Office and other local repositories there are very few deeds of bargain and sale for the period from the Civil War to the Restoration. Among the Chancery Close Rolls, Feet of Fines in the Palatine Court of Lancaster and the conveyances at Lancashire Quarter Sessions, it is not always easy to distinguish between sales and mortgages. Even more frustrating is the knowledge that, in spite of the law requiring the enrolment of all sales of land, many transactions went unrecorded. For those reasons our statistics will tend to underestimate rather than overestimate the amount of property sold privately. Nevertheless, it must be true that only a minority of compounding Lancashire Royalists sold land.

Seventy-four Lancashire Royalist gentry regained their property by means of a composition fine, but only 11 (14 per cent) of these have been discovered selling land before the Restoration.[48] Only six of these 11 Royalists could perhaps be said to have sold for the sole purpose of paying their composition fines.[49] In 1651 Peter Heywood of Heywood, on paying the first half of his fine of £341, asked the Committee for Compounding for 'leave ... to sell lands worth £30 a year, to pay the other half'.[50] Richard Orrell of Farington had his fine set at £22 10s. 0d. in 1649,[51] and early in 1651 he sold six parcels of land in Leyland and Longton to eight local yeomen and a tailor for at least £21 14s. 2d.[52] Edward Chisnall of Chisnall, William Farington of Worden, senior, Sir George Middleton of Leighton and Richard Whittingham of Claughton also appear to have sold land because of composition fines,[53] but on a fairly small scale and apparently with no harmful effects. Indeed, only three of the 11 Royalists—Viscount Molyneux of Sefton, Mosley of Hough and Prestwich of Hulme—seem to have made *extensive* sales during the Interregnum, and it is unlikely that these were caused entirely by composition fines. Thomas Prestwich compounded for £443 in 1649,[54] yet he later sold land for amounts much larger than his fine. In 1655 and 1657 he sold small parcels of land to local men for £74, but in 1659 he parted with his manor of Sholver for £1,000. Almost immediately after the Restoration he sold his principal manor of Hulme for £1,560.[55] After that the Prestwich family disappeared from the Lancashire gentry. The eclipse of this family may have been caused less by their modest composition fine than by their generous financial aid to the king during the Civil War.[56] The Molyneuxes did not suffer nearly as seriously as the Prestwich family, but in 1655 they sold their vast Sussex lands for over £13,000.[57] These sales seem to have been caused less by their composition fine of £3,140[58] than by their prewar debts and family liabilities of £9,000.[59] Sir Edward Mosley's sale of much of his property in Leicestershire and Derbyshire for £5,350[60] seems to have been due to a combination of extravagance, dissipation, pre-war debts (£6,000),[61] and over-generous aid to the king (£20,000),[62] as well as to a huge composition fine (£4,874).[63]

Clearly, then, composition fines were neither disastrous nor the only cause of Royalist land sales. That the Lancashire Royalist gentry did not suffer unduly from these fines is further shown by the fact that after the Civil War they apparently sold rather less property than did the non-Royalist gentry. The latter were not victims of composition fines or confiscations, yet they sold lands — all in Lancashire — for at least £8,192 between the end of the Civil War and the Restoration.[64] On the other hand private sales of Lancashire property by the compounding Royalist gentry fetched only £1,872, although we do not know the purchase price of every land transaction. If, however, we add the sale of non-Lancashire property, the Royalist total rises to £7,552.[65] Even so, this is still less than the amount received by the non-Royalist gentry.

Moreover, private sales of *Lancashire* land by the Royalist gentry were not accompanied by even a minor social revolution, as is shown by Table 42. It will be noted that yeomen formed the largest single group of purchasers, although the value of the property they acquired was very small.[66] Merchants and creditors appear to have bought no property at all.[67] In brief, 'the middle sort' can hardly be said to have risen at the expense of the compounding Royalist gentry. Nor did the Parliamentarian gentry gain much at their expense. The total purchases of the three Parliamentarians—Thomas Birch of Birch, Esquire, Edward Rigby of Goosnargh, Gentleman, and John Starkie of Huntroyd, Esquire—amounted to only £500.[68]

Why did composition fines not seriously harm the Lancashire Royalist gentry and bring about a redistribution of property? Was it, as Sir John Habakkuk has suggested, because the fines were not particularly burdensome?[69] It is hard to say. So much depended upon individual circumstances. 'The real burden of the fine,' Habakkuk

TABLE 42

PURCHASERS OF LANCASHIRE LAND SOLD BY COMPOUNDING ROYALIST GENTRY, 1650–59

Classification of Purchasers	Numbers	Estates purchased			Amount paid £
		Total	Manors	Non-manors	
Lancs. gentry	3 (15%)	3 (21%)	0	3	500 (27%)
Lancs. yeomen	8 (40%)	5 (36%)	0	5	21 (1%)
Lancs. tailor	1 (5%)	1 (7%)	0	1	?
Other Lancastrians	4 (20%)	4 (29%)	1	3	351 (19%)
Non-Lancastrians	4 (20%)	1 (7%)	1	0	1,000 (53%)
Totals	20 (100%)	14 (100%)	2	12	1,872[a] (100%)

a If we added Lancashire lands sold by Royalist gentry who suffered only from sequestrations but not from fines or forfeitures, the total would reach only £1,992.

writes, 'varied considerably from family to family, according to the degree of the royalist's delinquency, the nature of his legal interest in the estate, and the possibilities of under-valuation.'[70] How far do these arguments apply to Lancashire?

First, what were the rates of assessment? In theory Royalists were fined according to the degree of their delinquency at one-tenth, one-sixth or one-third of the capital value of their estates. A Royalist whose fine was fixed at one-tenth of the capital value paid two years' annual value: at one-sixth he paid three years' and at one-third or one-quarter he paid five years' annual value. The highest of these rates were unusual in Lancashire and, with one exception, were paid only by those compounding on the third Act of Sale, 1652. The 74 Royalists with whom we are presently concerned paid a total of 82 fines and lenient assessment appears to have been common. Unfortunately it has not been possible to identify clearly the rates of 24 of those fines, but of the remaining 58 all save one were at the level of only three years' income or less.[71] This was hardly a crushing burden and no doubt goes some way towards explaining the small number of private sales in Lancashire. However, one must not paint too rosy a picture of the situation. The Royalist gentry in Lancashire seem to have been far more heavily assessed than their brethren in Bedfordshire, Northamptonshire and Yorkshire, as Table 43 shows.

The Royalists in Lancashire were more heavily assessed than those elsewhere because they were no doubt more devoted to the king's cause. Yet in spite of their zeal some of the Lancashire Royalists apparently had friends in the enemy camp who were able to mitigate their hardships. Robert Holt of Stubley had his fine rated at only one-sixth on 17 October 1646, perhaps because about a week earlier his 'old school-fellow ffrynde & acquaintance', John Bradshaw of Marple, Cheshire, the future regicide, had asked the Committee for Compounding to 'leighten or abate the ffyne'.[72]

A second and more important reason for the leniency of composition fines in Lancashire was that 60 of the 74 Royalists held all or part of their land on lease, for life or in reversion. These paid lighter fines than the minority who had absolute ownership of the whole of their estates. Among the unfortunate few was Thomas Morley of Wennington. His fine of £165, rated at one-sixth, was exactly three times his annual income of £55.[73] This was because all his lands were held in fee simple.[74] Those who belonged to the fortunate majority found the fines far less burdensome. Good examples are Thomas Heap

TABLE 43

KNOWN RATES OF FINES LEVIED ON COMPOUNDERS IN FOUR ENGLISH COUNTIES

	Under $\frac{1}{10}$	$\frac{1}{10}$	$\frac{1}{6}$	$\frac{1}{3}$	$\frac{1}{2}$	Total
Lancashire	4 (7%)	10 (17%)	43 (74%)	1 (2%)	–	58 (100%)
Bedfordshire and Northants[a]	–	17 (57%)	9 (30%)	4 (13%)	–	30 (100%)
Yorkshire[b]	2 (1%)	102 (48%)	96 (45%)	10 (5%)	2 (1%)	212 (100%)

a Habakkuk, 'Landowners', 132. Presumably Habakkuk's figures exclude compositions on the third Act of Sale.
b P. G. Holiday, 'Royalist Composition Fines and Land Sales in Yorkshire after the Civil Wars, 1645–65', Leeds Univ. Ph.D. thesis, 1966, 122. Holiday's figures specifically exclude compositions on the third Act of Sale (ibid., 102, 122).

of Pilkington, Thomas Norris of Spcke and the elder William Farington of Worden, all of whom, like Thomas Morley, had their fines rated at one-sixth. Thomas Heap's fine amounted to £101, but it was nowhere near three times his annual landed income of £45. This was because he was only the tenant of the property.[75] Thomas Norris's fine was also well below three times the annual value of his land. This was because he held only a reversionary interest in his property, which was also charged with annuities and a debt of £1,200.[76] William Farington's fine was likewise a modest one. In his case it was because he held only a life interest in most of his lands and rented the remainder.[77] Indeed, Farington was apparently so little harmed by his fine of £511 that on 18 August 1653 he was able to purchase the manor of Penwortham for £650.[78] Farington was, of course, exceptionally fortunate, but there can be little doubt that many of the Royalist gentry paid low or modest fines simply because of the legal safeguards surrounding their estates. In Lancashire a considerable amount of land seems to have been entailed, partly perhaps because the county contained many recusants who were determined to preserve their property from the full effects of the penal laws. Fortunately, the Parliamentarian rulers, being themselves mostly men of estates, respected the property rights of their opponents.[79]

A third reason for the leniency of the composition fines was deliberate undervaluation of their property by many of the Lancashire Royalists. Such deceit was not surprising, for the fine was based on the compounder's own statement of his income and liabilities and, as Sir John Habakkuk has reminded us, the possibilities of evasion were considerable.[80] At least 32 of the 74 compounding Royalists appear to have undervalued their lands, while only seven seem to have returned true particulars of their estates.[81] However moderate and reasonable their opponents may have been, the Lancashire Royalist gentry were a somewhat recalcitrant lot and, despite the heavy penalties for undervaluation, were determined to preserve their wealth by fair means or foul. The Norrises of Speke apparently had no more conscience in financial than in religious matters. William Norris renounced his Catholic religion in 1651,[82] while his son, Thomas, blatantly lied about the value of his estates. In 1650 Thomas told the Committee for Compounding that they were worth £294 per annum,[83] although in 1635 a decree of the Court of Duchy Chamber had valued them at £900.[84] In 1660 the Speke estate was set down as worth £1,200 per annum in the Royal Oak list.[85] Another Royalist who deliberately understated his landed income was Thomas Gerard of Ince. In 1647 he returned a particular which put the annual value of his lands at only £73,[86] yet in a lawsuit in 1641 his opponents said that they were worth £400 per annum.[87] Gerard's opponents may have exaggerated his wealth for their own ends, but a more objective source—the lay subsidy roll for 1641—valued his lands at £250 per annum.[88] Dishonesty was often the best policy. William Farington of Worden paid a modest fine and was able to purchase Penwortham manor, not just because his lands were partly entailed and partly rented, but also because he had grossly undervalued his property.[89]

Thus because of deliberate undervaluation, the large amount of entailed property, and low rates of assessment for delinquency, most Royalist composition fines were tolerable and private sales were very uncommon. In short, fines, like sequestrations, had little adverse effect on the economic standing of the Lancashire Royalist gentry. In Somerset, on the other hand, 'sequestrations and compositions were disasters for all but the most prosperous' Royalists.[90]

2 THE SALE AND RECOVERY OF FORFEITED ROYALIST LAND

Despite the leniency of the fines, only 74 Lancashire Royalist gentry had compounded by the end of 1652. Well over 100 Cavaliers had not even attempted to compound. Lancashire contrasts sharply with Cheshire and Nottinghamshire where the overwhelming majority of Royalists had compounded by 1652.[91] But the Royalists in Lancashire were apparently as reluctant to make their peace with Parliament as their brethren in Cornwall, where by 1649 only 57 out of 274 sequestered delinquent estates had been recovered by composition.[92] It was partly to deal with the recalcitrant non-compounder and partly to achieve financial solvency that in 1651–52 Parliament ordered the confiscation and sale of the lands of 780 Royalists in England and Wales. As well as the non-compounders, the three Acts of Sale included two other categories of Royalist: those who had combined delinquency with recusancy and those who had been the king's principal military and political advisers during the Civil Wars. Indeed, Parliament had excluded many of the more prominent Royalists from pardon as early as 1644.[93] Three Lancashire Cavaliers were named in the first Act of Sale, 16 July 1651 : James, seventh Earl of Derby, Thomas Tyldesley of Myerscough and Charles Towneley of Towneley and Norton. Four other important Lancashire Royalists were named in the second Act of Sale, 4 August 1652: Robert Blundell of Ince Blundell, Thomas Clifton of Lytham, Richard Massey of Rixton and Edward Scarisbrick of Scarisbrick. In the third Act of Sale, 18 November 1652, 213 Lancashire names appear, a far larger total than for any other English or Welsh county.[94] Most of these Lancastrians were obscure individuals and indeed a majority of them   120—were not even gentry [95] These persons were probably selected more for their Catholic Royalism than for their unwillingness or inability to compound. Altogether 100 members of the Lancashire upper classes were named in the Acts of Sale: two peers—the seventh Earl of Derby and Lord Morley and Mounteagle—and 98 gentry. Of this 100 as many as 93 were Catholic.[96] In Yorkshire—a county that bears a striking resemblance to Lancashire in its post-war social history—the vast majority of gentry who suffered from the Acts of Sale were also Catholic.[97]

As Maurice Ashley pointed out many years ago, the Acts of Sale were not fully implemented.[98] Thus the estates of 16 Lancashire gentlemen escaped confiscation altogether. Perhaps it was because in many cases their property was hardly worth confiscating, like the tiny annuity of £17 18s. 5d., which was shared by the three Grimshaw brothers of Clayton.[99] Most of the other 13 individuals were sons or younger brothers of more prominent Royalists and they too may have had little property to forfeit. Altogether the estates of 84 Lancashire Royalist gentlemen were confiscated, but, as Table 44 shows, not all were sold.

Why did so many of these Royalist properties escape sale? Why were so many estates either discharged or else not sold, and why were several Royalists able to compound for all or some of their lands? The reasons lie in the terms of the Acts of Sale. Many estates were discharged because they were entailed. Such properties could only be sold during the lifetime of the Royalist concerned. Since several Lancashire Royalists had died leaving one or more entailed estates, 21 properties were discharged by the authorities. Thus James regained the lands of his deceased father, Edward Scarisbrick, because by an indenture of 24 March 1630 part of the estate had been conveyed to his mother for life, as her jointure, and the rest to his father, also for life.[100]

Another group of Royalists or their heirs managed to prevent the sale—though not the continued sequestration—of 19 of their properties[101] by claiming various allowances, such as those to dependents,

TABLE 44

NUMBER OF ESTATES CONFISCATED BY PARLIAMENT

	Confiscated	Discharged	Not sold but remained sequestered	Compounded[a]	Sold
No. of people	84	11 (and 3 others in part)[b]	3 (and 8 others in part)[b]	9 (and 4 others in part)	59
Manors	83	7	10	2	64
Non-manors	175	14	9	13	139
Total No. of estates	258	21	19	15	203

a Six Royalists whose lands were sold, even although they had compounded, are excluded. See below, p. 151 n. 103.
b These include Thomas Dalton of Thurnham and Robert Fazakerley of Fazakerley.

heirs or creditors. A fairly typical claim was that of the children, guardians and creditors of Thomas Dalton of Thurnham. They pleaded that in October 1641 the manors of Thurnham, Over Gleaston and Bulke had been conveyed to trustees for the payment of 'several annuities charged upon the premises'. Their claim was 'allowed' by the Committee for Removing Obstructions.[102]

The third category of Royalists whose forfeited lands were not sold consisted of those who compounded on the third Act of Sale. This Act allowed the delinquents to compound for all or some of their confiscated estates within a thirty-day pre-emption period at one-third of their capital value. Thirteen Lancashire Royalist gentlemen took advantage of this provision and as a result regained two manors and 13 other parcels of land.[103] Their motives for compounding may have been similar to those of their brethren on the eastern side of the Pen-

nines. Dr Holiday has observed that in Yorkshire 29 confiscated properties were redeemed by composition and adds: 'all but two of the
[29] estates were held in fee simple and could thus have been sold
in perpetuity'.[104] In Lancashire all save one of the compounded properties were held in fee simple,[105] hence the alacrity with which the
fines were paid. Although these fines were heavy, being in theory equivalent to five times the annual value of the property, all save one
of the 13 Royalists apparently managed to retain the bulk of their
recovered estates until after the Restoration.[106] The exception
was William Norris of Blackrod, Gentleman. Almost as soon as he
had compounded, Norris seems to have sold several messuages in
Blackrod for £300,[107] and by 1680 he had sunk to the level of a
humble yeoman.[108] Although the composition fine of £127 16s. od.[109]
cannot have been solely responsible for Norris's fate, it may well have
administered the final *coup de grâce* to a gentleman subsisting on a very
low income.[110]

Altogether 41 Lancashire Cavaliers were named in the Acts of Sale
whose entire estates were either unaffected, discharged or else recovered by composition. This was indeed a very high proportion. But
let us now turn our attention to the 59 Royalists who were less fortunate, and whose lands were publicly sold by the Treason Trustees
at Drury House. The Sales Trustees appear to have disposed of 203
Lancashire properties,[111] of which 97 belonged to the Earl of Derby.
The latter is a special case requiring separate treatment, not because
of his exalted status, but because of the vastness of his estates. But
first let us examine the sales which affected the other 58 Lancashire
Royalists.

It would appear that 50 (86 per cent) of these 58 Royalists had
regained 86 (81 per cent) out of their 106 properties by the mid-
1660s.[112] The 58 Royalists in Lancashire appear to have been almost
as successful as their brethren in Yorkshire, who recovered 82 per cent
of their estates, and far more successful than the Royalists in south-
east England, who retrieved just 70 per cent of their lands.[113]

The most important question, however, is not *whether* but *when* the
English Royalists regained the bulk of their estates. Did they have
to wait for the overthrow of the Republic and the restoration of the
monarchy? They apparently had to do so in south-east England, for
there 38 per cent of the Royalists bought back only 25 per cent of
their properties before 1660.[114] But in Yorkshire at least 28 (62 per
cent) of the 45 Royalist gentry regained 69 per cent of their estates
during the Interregnum.[115] The position in Lancashire is less certain.
However, it would appear that 25 (43 per cent) of the 58 Royalists
recovered 51 (48 per cent) out of their 106 properties before the Restoration at a cost of £31,008 16s. 6d. The Royalists in Lancashire
therefore regained a smaller number of their estates than did their
brethren in Yorkshire. Nevertheless, if we concentrate on the *value*

rather than the *number* of properties repurchased, the situation in Lancashire must have been similar to that obtaining in Yorkshire, that is, just over two-thirds of Royalist land was regained before the Restoration.[116]

Most of the 25 Lancashire Royalist gentry who regained their lands before 1660 appear to have used the services of agents or trustees.[117] The best known example of a trust purchase concerns the lands of William Blundell of Crosby. In his letters he states that he bought back his lands 'with money borrowed of my friends',[118] these being his cousin, Roger Bradshaw of Haigh, and Gilbert Crouch, a well known London lawyer. The purchase price was £989 13s. 5d., of which £548 16s. 0d. was paid in 'doubled money'.[119] This suggests that Crouch had raised some of the money from the London speculators who traded in public faith bills. When Blundell's land was safely in the possession of his trustees, it was mortgaged to the extent of the debt and Roger Bradshaw managed the property until it was finally repaid in 1660.[120] Other Lancastrians regaining their estates by means of trust purchases included many of the more famous Royalist families like Anderton of Clayton, Hoghton of Park Hall, Lathom of Parbold, Massey of Rixton and Towneley of Towneley.[121] Some Lancashire delinquents recovered their land through the services of well known trustees like Joseph and Samuel Foxley, John Fullerton, George Hurd, Thomas Wharton and John Wildman. Of all the agents in the north of England, Wildman was probably the best known. This ex-Leveller was described by Mrs Lucy Hutchinson as ' . . . a greate manager of papists' interests'.[122] However, only two Lancashire Catholic Royalists seem to have regained their lands through John Wildman,[123] these being Thomas Clifton of Lytham[124] and Abraham Langton of Lowe.[125]

Three Royalist families—Pemberton of Whiston, Urmston of Westleigh and White of Kirkland[126]—seem to have regained their lands without employing agents. Young William Rishton of Pontalgh also openly repurchased his father's lands, although he apparently needed the assistance of Humphrey Weld of Dorset,[127] one of the more famous Royalist agents. Unfortunately the expense proved too much for Rishton, and in 1658 he sold Pontalgh and neighbouring properties to Richard Walmesley of Dunkenhalgh, a wealthy Catholic squire.[128] Shortly after the Restoration the Rishton family disappears from view.[129] No other Royalist repurchasing his Lancashire lands had to sell out completely before the Restoration, although Towneley of Towneley had to part with his estates in Lincolnshire.[130]

How many Lancashire Royalists recovered their estates after 1660? It is extremely difficult to say. Only two definitely did. The Gerards of Halsall were restored to their lands by a private Act of Parliament.[131] Lord Morley and Mounteagle regained his Lancashire manors of Hornby, Tatham and Farleton by borrowing £6,500 from

Lord Brudenell and negotiating with the purchaser, John Wildman.[132]

It is impossible to say exactly when 23 (40 per cent) of the Royalists regained their 30 properties. Inadequate information forbids positive assertions. All that can be confidently stated is that these Royalists could have recovered their lands at any time between 1653 and 1665. However, circumstantial and indirect evidence tentatively suggests that many, if not most, of these 23 Royalists may have retrieved their property during the Interregnum. It is not fanciful to suggest that a Papist delinquent like James Bradley of Brining may have recovered his land, for it was bought from the Treason Trustees in 1653 by a fellow Catholic, Bartholomew Hesketh of Aughton.[133] The Catholic Talbots of Salesbury may also have regained their property before the Restoration, for it was purchased in 1654 by Adam Bolton of Dunkenhalgh,[134] who was himself a Papist[135] and a loyal steward of the Catholic Walmesleys.[136] Catholic solidarity[137] must have saved a number of Lancashire Royalist estates during the Interregnum.

There is another group of Royalists about whom we know virtually nothing. Some or all of the lands of five other Royalists were sold by the Sales Trustees, but we do not know *whether*, let alone *when*, they ever regained them.[138]

Only three of the 58 Royalists lost their entire estates.[139] In each case pre-war debt seems to have been the main cause of their ruin, the Commonwealth confiscations being merely the final *coup de grâce*. John Robinson of Old Laund evidently engaged George Hurd, a London merchant, to purchase his confiscated property,[140] but he apparently failed to raise the necessary money. This is hardly surprising, for his annual income was only about £69[141] while his debts amounted to £1,092.[142] Hence his lands were sold in 1654 to a London gentleman named Henry Druell for £900.[143] One Royalist, Edward Langtree of Langtree, apparently tried unsuccessfully to regain his forfeited lands through the medium of Joseph and Samuel Foxley.[144] But with an annual income of at most £150[145] and debts of at least £1,200,[146] he was forced to sell his equity of redemption in 1655 to one of his creditors, Francis Rockley of Rockley, Yorkshire.[147] After that the Langtree family disappeared from the ranks of the Lancashire gentry. The third Royalist who seems to have lost all his lands was Robert Shireburn of Little Mitton. It is most unlikely that he or his descendants ever recovered them, either before or after the Restoration, in view of the serious financial position of the family. Robert's debts amounted to £2,722 at the time of the Civil War,[148] while the annual income of the Shireburn family fell from £350 in 1626 to £125 in 1663.[149] Hence they had little option but to sell their title in 1665 to Alexander Holt, a London goldsmith,[150] who had already acquired the property from the Treason Trustees.[151] The fate of John Robinson, Edward Langtree and Robert Shireburn was indeed tragic. But these gentlemen were the exceptions to the rule, which is that in Lancashire the Royalist gentry were highly successful in regaining their forfeited lands. (See Table 45.)

Since a majority of the Lancashire Royalists recovered most of their lands, the sale of their property can hardly have had important social consequences. Table 46 shows that few individuals or groups were able to add to their estates at the expense of the Royalist gentry. It will be noted that in Lancashire a majority of those purchasing delinquents' lands were relatives, agents or possible agents of the Royalists. This is

TABLE 45

ROYALIST PROPERTY REGAINED BEFORE AND AFTER 1660

| | Estates sold | | | | |
	Total	Manors	Non-manors	Amount paid to Treason Trustees £ s. d.[a]	Nos. of Royalists affected
Property regained before 1660	51 (48%)	30	21	31,008 16 6 (69·1%)	25 (43%)
Property regained after 1660	5 (5%)	5	0	3,686 15 2 (8·2%)	2 (3%)
Property regained at an uncertain date	30 (28%)	5	25	6,334 6 2 (14·1%)	23 (40%)
Property never regained	15 (14%)	3	12	2,989 12 7 (6·6%)	3 (5%)
Untraceable property	5 (5%)	0	5	880 18 4 (2·0%)	5 (9%)
Totals	106 (100%)	43	63	44,900 8 9 (100%)	58 (100%)

a In the case of 25 of the 80 land transactions we are ignorant of the purchase price.

at variance with Dr H. E. Chesney's belief that London merchants and speculators figured prominently among purchasers of Royalist property throughout England.[152] As Table 46 shows, Londoners acquired very little Lancashire Royalist property: 11 per cent calculated by the value, and less than 9 per cent calculated by the number, of the properties sold. Indeed, even these figures tend to exaggerate their share. Six Londoners bought Royalist land in Lancashire from the Sales Trustees, but apart from Alexander Holt, the only one who made a large purchase was John Wildman, who paid £3,686 15s. 2d. for Lord Morley and Mounteagle's manors of Hornby, Tatham and

Farleton.[153] The other four London purchasers were Henry Druell, Thomas Wharton, Joseph Clifton and John Fullerton. Druell made a moderate purchase, paying £900 for the lands of John Robinson of Old Laund.[154] Thomas Wharton was normally a Royalist agent, and when he bought Mickleheyes from the Sales Trustees, he may have done so on behalf of its former owner, Edward Rishton.[155] Unfortunately Rishton's lands cannot be traced after the Restoration, so we cannot say for certain whether Wharton retained them or the Royalist regained them. John Fullerton and Joseph Clifton both bought the Goosnargh lands of Henry Butler of Rawcliffe for only

TABLE 46

CLASSES OF PURCHASERS OF CONFISCATED ROYALIST LAND

		Estates sold			Amount paid to Treason Trustees		
Purchasers	Numbers	Total	Manors	Non-manors	£	s.	d.
1. Royalists' relatives	5 (5·7%)	4 (3·8%)	1	3	520	8	9 (1·2%)
2. Royalist agents	29 (33·3%)	43 (40·6%)	27	16	29,427	17	1 (65·5%)
3. Possible Royalist agents	20 (33·3%)	30 (28·3%)	5	25	6,334	6	2 (14·1%)
4. Creditors	3 (3·5%)	5 (4·7%)	3	2	420	13	6 (1·0%)
5. Parliamentary grantee	1 (1·2%)	2 (1·9%)	2	0	—		
6. London merchant	1 (1·2%)	3 (2·8%)	2	1	193	1	0 (0·4%)
7. London gentry	5 (5·7%)	6 (5·6%)	3	3	4,794	15	2 (10·7%)
8. Other gentry	1 (1·2%)	1 (0·9%)	0	1	67	9	4 (0·1%)
9. Lancs. gentry	4 (4·6%)	4 (3·8%)	0	4	1,973	16	7 (4·4%)
10. Lancs. yeomen	5 (5·7%)	4 (3·8%)	0	4	708	8	8 (1·6%)
11. Other Lancastrians	4 (4·6%)	4 (3·8%)	0	4	459	12	6 (1·0%)
Totals	87 (100%)	106 (100%)	43	63	44,900	8	9 (100%)

£208 in 1654,[156] but within two years they had sold them for £260 to the elder Richard Shuttleworth of Gawthorpe.[157] Whether Fullerton and Clifton were speculators or merely agents for Shuttleworth is uncertain.[158]

If Chesney emphasised the role of London merchants and speculators in the purchase of Royalist land, R. H. Tawney stressed the part played by creditors. 'Among the purchasers of the confiscated estates,' he wrote, 'not a few ... were creditors entering on properties long mortgaged to them.'[159] But because of the small number of Lancashire Royalists who were seriously in debt,[160] creditors seem to have bought extremely little delinquent land. Indeed, Table 46 exaggerates the amount they obtained. Although William Thornton of Grantham bought Padiham and Bradley mills[161] and John Crispe acquired the manors of Cliviger and Towneley from the Treason Trustees,[162] they very soon conveyed them to two London merchants, Benjamin Martin and Francis Bramwell, who purchased them on behalf of the Royalist Towneleys of Towneley.[163] Even Edward Langtree's lands did not remain for long in the hands of the creditor-purchaser, Francis Rockley of Rockley.[164]

In her study of land sales in south-east England Dr Joan Thirsk showed that a large amount of Royalist property was acquired by local gentry, yeomen, artisans and tenants.[165] But Table 46 shows that few gentry or yeomen bought land which had belonged to the 58 Lancashire delinquents. Merchants and artisans were conspicuous by their absence. Even tenants bought remarkably little land, acquiring only six (5 per cent) of the 106 Royalist properties and spending a mere £1,793 19s. 11d.[166]

Lastly, it should be noted that few enemies of the *ancien régime* obtained Lancashire Royalist property. Mary Deane, widow of Admiral Deane, General-at-Sea, was granted by Parliament the lands of Charles Gerard of Halsall.[167] But apart from Richard Shuttleworth of Gawthorpe, only three Lancashire Parliamentarian gentry seem to have purchased. These were the elder John Braddyll of Portfield, Robert Cunliffe of Sparth and Edward Robinson of Euxton.[168]

To sum up: the sales of the lands of the 58 Lancashire Royalists have very little social or political significance. It is impossible to speak of a transfer of property from the gentry to the 'middle sort', or from Royalists to Parliamentarians. Moreover, the sales of Royalist land in Lancashire (excluding the Earl of Derby's property) appear very like those in Yorkshire and very unlike those in south-east England, as Table 47 shows.

Finally, what were the main reasons for the success of the Lancashire Royalists in regaining the bulk of their lands? One reason was surely that most Royalist gentry were in a fairly healthy financial state. In 1642 only a small minority were seriously in debt[169] and the Civil Wars ruined but a few.[170] Hence they were in a strong position to recover their confiscated property. Indeed, a prosperous lawyer like Robert Blundell of Ince Blundell was able to regain his patrimonial estate as early as February 1653 through the medium of William West of Middleton.[171]

A second reason for the success of the Lancashire Royalist gentry was that much of their property was legally safeguarded. Exactly half the 58 Royalists whose lands were forfeited had some type of reversionary claim recognised on 54 of their 106 properties (32 manors and 22 non-manors).[172] Such estates could be sold only for the lifetime of the present owners, and this obviously reduced their market value, thereby enhancing the Royalists' chances of repurchasing them. Thus when the manors of Windleshaw and Ashton were sold in 1653 for the life of Sir William Gerard the latter had no difficulty in regaining them through the agency of Samuel Row of Westminster.[173]

A third reason why most Lancashire Royalists successfully re-covered their lands was that they did not have to compete for them against wealthy London businessmen. This was because during the second half of the seventeenth century rich Londoners were finding it increasingly possible to maintain power and status without acquir-ing large landed estates.[174] London merchants were quite prepared to buy property in the metropolis and in the surrounding districts,

TABLE 47

PURCHASERS OF ROYALIST LANDS IN LANCASHIRE, YORKSHIRE
AND FOUR SOUTH-EASTERN COUNTIES[a]

	Parcels of land sold		
Purchasers	Lancashire	Yorkshire	South-east England
Royalist relatives or agents	47 (44%)	91 (58%)	9 (25%)
Possible Royalist agents	30 (28%)	14 (9%)	–
Parliamentary grantees	2 (2%)	5 (3%)	4 (11%)
Creditors	5 (5%)	18 (12%)	4 (11%)
Local buyers	12 (11%)	13 (8%)	13 (36%)
Non-local buyers	10 (10%)	15 (10%)	6 (17%)
Totals	106 (100%)	156 (100%)	36 (100%)

a Holiday, thesis, Table XVI, p. 193; Joan Thirsk, 'The Sale of Delinquents' Estates during the Interregnum and the Land Settlement at the Restoration', London Univ. Ph.D. thesis, 1950, Table IV, p. 130. Dr Thirsk's figures refer to only four of her 12 southern counties: Essex, Hertfordshire, Kent and Surrey

as Dr Thirsk has shown.[175] But they were less willing to invest in real estate in outlying provinces like Lancashire and Yorkshire.[176] It is sig-nificant that the only Londoner who permanently settled on the Lan-cashire Royalist property he had bought was himself of Lancashire extraction.[177] Alexander Holt, who obtained Robert Shireburn's lands and whose family held them until the eighteenth century, was related to the Holts of Gristlehurst.[178] Moreover, it should be noted that Londoners were not always interested in owning forfeited land when the job of conveyancing was itself so profitable. The peculiar economic circumstances that resulted from the Civil War offered great opportunities to enterprising attorneys and businessmen. Hence it is not surprising that most Londoners who bought delinquent land were not prospective country gentlemen, still less speculators, but agents acting for the Royalists.

A fourth reason for the success of the Lancashire Royalists was that they did not have to bid for their property against land-hungry tenants. It was only the first Act of Sale, 1651, which assisted tenants to buy their land by guaranteeing them pre-emptive rights for thirty days after the announcement of each sale.[179] Since only one of the 58 Royalists—Towneley of Towneley—appeared in the first Act, this considerably reduced the amount of property that could be sold to tenants.[180] Even Towneley lost property to only five of his tenants,[181] for his London agents were able successfully to frustrate the efforts of the rest to acquire their holdings.[182]

A fifth reason why most Lancashire Royalists did not permanently lose their forfeited property was that most of it lay in the northern and western parts of the county, that is, in the predominantly Royalist and Catholic areas.[183] The Lancashire victims of the Acts of Sale were surrounded by sympathisers and supporters. A number of those who bought on behalf of the Royalists were themselves Royalists, like John Fleetwood of Penwortham, who joined with John Wildman and Henry Colbron of London in helping Thomas Clifton of Lytham to regain his four manors.[184] Edward Midgall of Blackhall was able to recover his lands through the services of a neighbouring Royalist yeoman, Thomas Threlfall of Goosnargh.[185] We have noticed, too, how a sense of religious solidarity may have prompted several Catholics to rescue the forfeited estates of a number of papist delinquents.[186] Thus the Lancashire Royalist gentry were not short of friends, and in this respect they seem to have been more fortunate than the Earl of Derby, the sale of whose estates we must now examine.

3 THE SALE OF THE LANDS OF THE EIGHTH EARL OF DERBY

John Seacome, a historian of the Stanleys, wrote a depressing account of the family after the Civil Wars. On succeeding to his estates, Charles, son of the 'martyr' earl, found:

... the ancient House of Lathom demolished ... the House of Knowsley in little better condition ... and what was yet more deplorable near one half of the estate possessed by his father sequestered and sold, and a little, or very small part of it, ever recovered ...[187]

Seacome was no doubt referring to all forfeited Stanley estates and not just to those in Lancashire. But the earl's losses were undoubtedly greater in some counties than in others. In north Wales Charles Stanley lost three confiscated Flintshire manors to Commonwealth purchasers.[188] In Cheshire he may have lost most of his estates.[189] In Lancashire the situation is extremely uncertain, but it would be an exaggeration to say that only 'a little, or very small part of [the Earl's estate was] ever recovered'. Twenty-one of the 26 Lancashire manors of the Earl of Derby were definitely sold by the Treason Trustees,[190] but only one of them—Broughton in Lonsdale—was not eventually regained. On the other hand, the Stanleys seem to have lost a very considerable number of small properties.

It is very difficult indeed to discover exactly when the Stanleys regained their 20 manors and 16 other parcels of land.[191] The evidence is often so flimsy that no statement can be too cautious. But it may be very tentatively suggested that the Derbys probably retrieved 10 manors and six other properties before the Restoration. Like the other 58 Lancashire Royalists, the Earl of Derby relied heavily on the services of London agents.[192] He apparently regained Skelmersdale manor through John Owen, a London Welshman, who paid £2,641 19s. 7d.[193] Upholland manor was repurchased for him in March 1653 by William Cox, a London merchant, at a cost of £745 13s. 2d.[194] In September 1653 the earl used the services of Anthony Samwell of Westminster and Henry Nevile of Billingbeare, Berkshire, who bought his manors of Lathom, Knowsley, Childwall, Burscough, Much Woolton and Little Woolton, for £7,500 18s. 7d.[195]

It is almost impossible to say *when* and *how* the Stanleys regained their other properties (10 manors and 10 non-manors). It is easy to establish the fact, but extremely difficult to trace the process, of recovery. But it is most unlikely that Charles Stanley would have regained his manors of Treales, Bretherton, Bolton and Bury before the Restoration because each of them was sold to a strong supporter of the Republic.[196] Treales was granted to John Parker of the Middle Temple and his wife Margaret, widow of the Leveller, Colonel Thomas Rainborough.[197] The manor was probably given to Margaret for Rainborough's war services to Parliament. Bretherton was bought for £550 by John Cliffe, a county committeeman.[198] Bolton, together with non-manorial property in Halliwell and Salford, was acquired for £290 19s. 10d. by Charles Worsley of Platt, the future Major-General.[199] He also obtained the manor of Bury for £287 18s. od.[200] Three smaller pieces of property, also sold to Parliamentary soldiers, were apparently regained after 1660.[201]

One hardly dare even suggest when the remaining 12 properties of the Earl of Derby were regained, so flimsy and vague is the evidence. But it is more likely to have been before than after the Restoration. This is suggested by the names of those who purchased from the Treason Trustees. Gilbert Mabbott of London, who bought the manor of Weeton,[202] was probably acting as an agent of Charles Stanley. In the Stanley papers Mabbott is not named as purchasing for himself any of the family property during the Interregnum, nor is he mentioned as an agent for any of the earl's tenants.

The Earl of Derby lost his manor of Broughton and anything up to 60 other parcels of land.[203] Many, though not all, of these properties were lost through sheer miscalculation. Partly to pay off the debt owing to the Commonwealth on the lands repurchased and partly to regain his other confiscated estates, Charles Stanley resorted to a multiplicity of conveyances. He asked many of his tenants to buy their farms from the Treason Trustees and granted them a release of the property in return for a sum of money equivalent to three years' purchase.[204] 'Severall tennants of the manor of Upholland purchased their severall tenements at the request of the aforesaid Earle'.[205] But most of the tenants who bought at Derby's request lived in the Bury or Pilkington areas.[206] One of these tenants was Richard Meadowcroft, Gentleman, who, along with Edward Shacklock of Moston, bought premises called Warton in Pilkington from the Treason Trustees in December 1653. The purchasers also had a conveyance from the Earl of Derby.[207] After the Restoration the eighth earl tried to regain the property which his tenants had bought. But the tenants did not co-operate as he had hoped, and a petition sent to the House of Lords in 1660 successfully frustrated his attempts. The tenants were allowed to remain in possession because Derby's conveyances were regarded as in the nature of voluntary sales.[208] In short, 'The Stanleys' own cleverness told against them'.[209]

Thus the late seventeenth century, no less than the late sixteenth century, witnessed the 'crisis of the aristocracy' in Lancashire.[210] Ernest Broxap wrote that 'feudalism' in Lancashire died with the

TABLE 48

LANCASHIRE PROPERTY REGAINED OR LOST BY THE
EIGHTH EARL OF DERBY

	Estates sold			Amount paid to Treason Trustees £ s. d.[a]
	Total	Manors	Non-manors	
Property regained before 1660	16 (16·5%)	10	6	14,638 8 9 (37·7%)
Property regained after 1660	8 (8·2%)	4	4	1,638 9 1 (4·2%)
Property regained at an uncertain date	12 (12·4%)	6	6	3,887 11 2 (10·0%)
Property lost or untraceable	61 (62·9%)	1	60	18,680 9 4 (48·1%)
Totals	97 (100%)	21	76	38,844 18 4 (100%)

a In the case of 25 of the 90 land transactions we are ignorant of the purchase price.

execution of the seventh Earl of Derby.[211] It might perhaps be truer to say that it died with the forfeiture and reduction of his estates. Nevertheless, we must not exaggerate the decline in the territorial possessions of the Stanleys. After the Restoration they still held vast estates, both inside and outside Lancashire. However, Table 48 shows that, while not disastrous, their losses of Lancashire property were still quite considerable.

The loss of so many of the Derby properties meant that there was bound to be a certain transfer of wealth from the aristocracy to other social groups. Table 49 classifies the main purchasers of the Derby estates. It will be noted that the Earl of Derby's agents were the largest group of purchasers, buying at least 37 per cent of his property from the Treason Trustees.[212] Apart from these agents, the table either exaggerates, minimises or completely masks the share of some categories of purchasers. Although only two Parliamentary grantees obtained land, 16 Lancashire Parliamentarians or supporters of the Republic[213] (10 gentry and six plebeians) gained at the earl's expense. On the other hand non-Lancastrians bought considerably less and Lancastrians considerably more than the table implies. At first sight it might appear that a 'foreigner', Edward Lee of Sunderland, acquired the earl's manor and castle of Broughton for £2,860 12s. 11d.[214] But in 1658 Broughton passed to a local gentleman, Colonel Roger Sawrey.[215] Londoners also bought far less land than might be supposed. Three of the 13 who purchased already rented their property,[216] while the other 10 appear to have been agents acting for the earl's tenants. One such trustee was Robert Ainsworth, a City merchant, who acquired Derby property in Elton hamlet, Bury, from the Treason Trustees,[217] but 'only in trust for the sd Thomas Symonds', a local clothier and tenant.[218] Another agent may have been Peter Legay of London, Merchant. On 7 June 1654 Legay bought in his own name from the Sales Trustees the manor of Pilkington and 'sevrall messuages lands tenements ... scituate ... in the Manor of Bury'.[219] But very soon afterwards Legay seems to have parcelled out some of the lands among several of the tenants.[220] Some of the tenants' agents were, of course, Lancastrians, like Thomas Eckersall and Roger Booth of Bury, who bought at least two properties 'in discharge of a trust in them reposed'.[221] A total of about sixty-five tenants of the Earl of Derby seem to have purchased through agents.[222] Another 31 bought directly from the Sales Trustees.[223] Sums paid by the tenants ranged from a modest £37 9s. 6d. paid by Thomas Harrock of Little Woolton, Yeoman, for a barn in his neighbourhood[224] to £1,337 paid by Sir Thomas Stanley, a Parliamentary leader, for Cross Hall.[225] Altogether tenants acquired, directly or indirectly, a substantial share of the lands of the Earl of Derby. Table 50 does not take account of resales.[226] But if we included such sales, the number of Derby tenants buying land would rise from 96 to about 130.[227]

TABLE 49

Purchasers	Numbers	Estates sold			Amount paid to Treason Trustees £ s. d.
		Total	Manors	Non-manors	
1 Royalist agents	11 (12·4%)	16 (16·5%)	10	6	14,638 8 9 (37·7%)
2 Possible Royalist agents	8 (9·0%)	12 (12·4%)	6	6	3,887 11 2 (10·0%)
3 Parliamentary grantees	2 (2·2%)	1 (1·0%)	1	0	—
4 London merchants	8 (9·0%)	8 (8·2%)	0	8	6,250 5 10 (16·1%)
5 London gentry	5 (5·6%)	6 (6·2%)	0	6	1,839 6 10 (4·7%)
6 Other gentry	1 (1·1%)	1 (1·0%)	1	0	2,860 12 11 (7·4%)
7 Lancs. gentry	19 (21·4%)	19 (19·6%)	3	16	4,266 9 3 (11·0%)
8 Lancs. yeomen	13 (14·6%)	17 (17·5%)	0	17	2,024 17 0 (5·2%)
9 Lancs. merchants	2 (2·2%)	2 (2·1%)	0	2	132 8 7 (0·3%)
10 Other Lancastrians	20 (22·5%)	15 (15·5%)	0	15	2,944 18 0 (7·6%)
Totals	89[a] (100·0%)	97 (100·0%)	21	76	38,844 18 4 (100·0%)

a This is a very conservative total because in some cases many purchasers were concealed behind one or two trustees. See above, p. 133.

Why did Charles Stanley lose considerably more of his property to other social groups and individuals than did most of the other 58 Royalists? As we have observed, one reason was his own miscalculation, his misplaced trust in his tenants. But apart from his own failures and shortcomings, his own defects of personality, the earl was not favoured by circumstances. He lost several of his properties because there was a ready market for them. Why was this?

First, it should be observed that the earl's name was in the Act of Sale, 1651. This enabled many of his tenants to buy directly from the Treason Trustees by exercising their pre-emptive rights. On the other hand the tenants of the other Royalists—except Towneley of Towneley—had no such rights, because their landlords appeared in the Acts of 1652.

TABLE 50

CLASSES OF PURCHASERS OF THE EIGHTH EARL OF
DERBY'S LANCASHIRE LANDS: II

Purchasers	Amount paid to Treason Trustees £ s. d.
Royalist agents or possible agents	18,525 19 11 (17·7%)
Tenants	13,904 2 1 (35·8%)
Others	6,414 16 4 (16·5%)
Total	38,844 18 4 (100·0%)

A second reason is an economic one. It is significant that a considerable amount of the Derby property that was lost lay in Bury and Pilkington, a pastoral–textile region.[228] Dr Joan Thirsk has observed that pasture farming was more profitable than corn-growing during the second half of the seventeenth century.[229] The small gentry, yeomen and tenants were in a better position to buy lands in south-east Lancashire than they were in the arable or mossland parts of the county, where most of the other 58 Royalists had their estates.

A third reason is a political one. As we observed, most of the lands of the 58 Cavaliers lay in the Royalist and Catholic parts of Lancashire. Here the delinquents were able to rescue some of their estates through the help of friends, neighbours and co-religionists. By contrast, many of the estates lost by the Stanleys were in the largely Parliamentarian hundred of Salford, where their enemies abounded and little help was forthcoming.[230] Indeed, far from wishing to help the Stanleys, 60 Parliamentarian tenants in the Bury and Pilkington district frankly

admitted that they wished to purchase their holdings. In a petition
(of 1653?) to the House of Commons they lamented that as a result
of 'serving the Parliamt ffaithfully ... some of their leases are much
weakened'. Fearing for their tenurial security if 'the said Earl [of
Derby] should be compounded with', they requested that if Parliament should 'resolve to set' his 'lands upon sale', they might 'have
the first choice in the purchase thereof'.[231] Faced with such frightened
and politically hostile tenants, it is not surprising that the Earl of
Derby lost so much of his south-east Lancashire property.

Such were some of the reasons for the reduction of the Earl of
Derby's estates. The consequences   at least in south-east Lancashire—may have been far-reaching. It is conceivable that the weaken-
ing of aristocratic rule in the Bury area, through the partial break-
up of the Derby estates, accelerated the growth of the small farmer
class, and laid the foundations for the rise of modern industry.[232]

4 THE DECLINING ROYALIST GENTRY, 1660–1700

We must now consider the possible long-term, as opposed to short-
term, consequences of the sequestrations, composition fines and sales
for the Lancashire Royalist gentry and aristocracy. Dr Christopher
Hill has suggested that some Royalists who recovered their confiscated
lands in or before 1660 ran into debt in doing so, and that many have
been forced to sell again before the end of the seventeenth century.[233]
But in Lancashire only a small minority of the delinquents seem to
have resold their recovered property. William Blundell of Crosby was
'overcharged with debt' through having to pay £989 for the repurchase of his forfeited estate and a further £1,167 for recusancy fines
unpaid since Elizabethan times. In spite of this he does not seem to
have sold any of his recovered property, and by 1660 he was no longer
seriously in debt.[234] The Blundells were more fortunate and more typical than the Andertons of Clayton, who, after regaining their confiscated manors of Whittle-le-Woods, Clayton and Bardsea in 1654,[235]
sold Whittle in 1666, Clayton in 1683,[236] and retained only their outlying manor of Bardsea in north Lonsdale. Of the 50 Royalists who
had regained their forfeited estates, only eight (16 per cent) were
forced to sell all or a substantial part of their property before 1700.[237]
Eleven estates (eight manors, three non-manors) were affected and
their sale reduced the proportion of confiscated property which had
been recovered from 81 per cent to 70 per cent. This still left a considerable amount in Royalist hands at the end of the century and
compares favourably with the situation in Yorkshire, where 67 per
cent of confiscated estates were recovered and remained in the hands
of their original owners until well into the 1680s.[238]

Confiscation had been the most severe penalty imposed upon the
Royalists. But many had experienced the sequestration of their estates

and/or composition fines. These fines, it has been suggested, led to much borrowing and subsequent indebtedness. Professor G. E. Aylmer has said that 'the lasting effects of this indebtedness may have been delayed as late as the 1670s and even beyond, when many middling and lesser ex-Cavalier families were in great economic difficulties, and in some cases had to sell up'.[239] How many Lancastrians who compounded for delinquency had to sell their land between 1660 and 1700, and how many of these sellers had also been heavy borrowers? Ninety-three Lancashire Royalist gentry compounded for their estates after the Civil War.[240] But only 19 (20 per cent) of these or their descendants had to sell all or a large amount of their property between 1660 and 1700.[241] Of those 19 only one can be proved to have borrowed heavily.[242] He was Francis Sherrington of Boothes. His lands were sequestered for delinquency after the Civil War. Between 1646 and 1650 he borrowed at least £2,433 from London lawyers and merchants,[243] and then paid his composition fine. Between 1685 and 1690 Sherrington sold his manor of Tyldesley, together with property in Westleigh and Pennington.[244] But his heavy borrowings and subsequent sales cannot have been caused solely by his composition fine, for it amounted to only £373.[245]

Altogether 221 Lancashire Royalist gentry were severely penalised for their delinquency. But only 30 (13·5 per cent) of these or their heirs apparently sold all or a substantial part of their property between 1660 and 1700.[246] So it would seem that sequestrations, composition fines and forfeitures did not cause many Royalists or their relatives to sell land, even in the long run.

Who gained most at the expense of the minority of ex-Royalist gentry selling land after 1660? Table 51 reveals that it was their fellow gentry, to judge by the numbers who purchased and by the amount and value of the property acquired. But it is also worth noting the fairly large sum spent on land—£8,685—by Lancashire merchants. This is hardly surprising, for the post-Restoration period witnessed a great expansion of the Lancashire textile industries[247] and of Liverpool's overseas trade, especially with the American colonies and the West Indies.[248] There was therefore more surplus capital to invest in real estate. It would, of course, be a gross exaggeration to suggest that the late seventeenth century saw the rise of the Lancashire bourgeoisie, but it is clear that they bought considerably more Royalist land after the Restoration than during the Interregnum.[249] On the other hand, as might be expected, former Parliamentarian[250] gentry families seem to have spent less on Royalist property between 1660 and 1700 than they did between 1644 and 1659. In the shorter and earlier period they paid £5,373[251] but in the longer and later period only £4,713.[252]

The land market is not, of course, the only index of social change. Income and status also need to be taken into account. To discover the landed wealth of the post-Restoration gentry would be a vast undertaking which falls outside the scope of this book.[253] Nevertheless, it is possible to say something about the status of former Royalist families during the later decades of the seventeenth century. Such sources as the Schedule of Contributors to the 'Free and Voluntary Gift', 1661, the Lay Subsidy Rolls, 1663–64, the Hearth Tax Assessments, Ladyday 1664 and Ladyday 1666, Blome's List of Gentry, 1673, and the List of Lancashire Freeholders, 1695,[254] show that 99 (56 per cent) of the 177 Royalist families were no longer officially regarded as members of the Lancashire gentry by the end of the

TABLE 51

PURCHASERS OF LAND BELONGING TO EX-ROYALISTS OR THEIR
DESCENDANTS, 1660–1700

| | | Estates purchased | | | |
| | | | | | |
Classification of Purchasers	Numbers	Total	Manors	Non-manors	Amount paud £
Peer	1 (2%)	1 (2%)	1	0	?
London gentry[a]	4)9%)	4 (9%)	3	1	3,960 (12·0%)
Other gentry	4 (9%)	4 (9%)	1	3	1,860 (5·6%)
Lancs. peer	1 (2%)	1 (2%)	1	0	?
Lancs. gentry	15 (35%)	15 (34%)	5	10	14,151 (42·4%)
Lancs. yeomen	2 (5%)	2 (4%)	1	1	4,205 (12·4%)
Lancs. merchants	6 (14%)	8 (18%)	3	5	8,685 (26·0%)
Lancs. craftsmen	2 (5%)	2 (4%)	0	2	100 (0·3%)
Other Lancastrians	At least 8 (19%)	8 (18%)	1	7	432 (1·3%)
Totals	At least 43 (100%)	45 (100%)	16	29	33,393 (100·0%)

a Three were lawyers and one was a money-lender.

seventeenth century. This was an enormous proportion. However, before drawing any conclusions from these figures it is worth noting that other groups of gentry also suffered heavy losses during the late seventeenth century. We have seen that a very high proportion of families who had supported Parliament or the Republic—56 per cent—had disappeared from the Lancashire gentry by 1695.[255] Among families who had changed sides or been divided during the Civil War, as many as 46 per cent had sunk into obscurity by the same date. What is even more significant is that among the silent majority of the Lancashire gentry—the 456 families who cannot be found supporting either side during the Civil War[256]—a mere 26 per cent still enjoyed gentle status in the palatinate in 1695.[257] Of course several new families rose to fill many of the gaps left by the disappearance of the old. But in the middle and later seventeenth century the general decline of the whole Lancashire gentry class is unmistakable.[258] As we observed in Chapter I, the gentry comprised a smaller proportion of the Lancashire population in 1695 than in 1642.[259]

Thus it was not only the Royalists but all groups of gentry who declined between the outbreak of the Civil War and the end of the seventeenth century. Hence the anti-Royalist legislation cannot have been solely responsible for the loss of property and prestige by so many ex-Cavaliers. Undoubtedly some Royalist families might not have declined had it not been for political oppression. When the Civil War broke out the Lathoms of Parbold seem to have been in a fairly healthy financial state.[260] However, in 1654 their manors of Allerton and Parbold were confiscated and sold by the Treason Trustees. They were able to repurchase Allerton for £2,749 12s. 2d. through John Sumner of Midhurst, Sussex,[261] and Parbold for £3,931 through George Hurd, a well known London agent.[262] But the cost proved too great. Allerton remained mortgaged to the Sumner family until 1670, when the Lathoms sold the manor to two Lancashire merchants, Richard and Thomas Percival, for £4,755, of which sum Charles, son of John Sumner, received £3,300 and the Lathoms the remainder.[263] Shortly after Parbold was retrieved by Hurd it was mortgaged for £2,000 to John Crispe, a well known London money-lender.[264] But the Lathoms were unable to pay off their mortgage, and Crispe finally foreclosed in 1660.[265] Even before losing Parbold the Lathoms had apparently lost their gentility,[266] and although they still continued to live in the district, they disappeared into mediocre obscurity. The Lathoms would without doubt have blamed the agrarian legislation of the Revolution for their plight.

Apart from financial penalties imposed by their enemies, what else caused Royalists to sell land or lose status during the late seventeenth century? The cost of military aid to Charles I during the Civil War may have been important in some cases. Edward Tyldesley of Myerscough sold Entwisle Hall and adjoining property to land-hungry tenants between 1657 and 1670.[267] This cannot have been solely due to the continual sequestration of the Tyldesley estates, and the consequent reduction of revenue, between 1643 and 1652.[268] The main reason may have been that Edward's father, Thomas Tyldesley, 'had raised men at his own charge at the beginning of the war'.[269] Apparently Thomas Tyldesley raised his own regiment and train bands for Charles I.[270] This must have been a costly item. Royalist families like the Tyldesleys were no different from Parliamentarian families like the Moores of Bank Hall in that their post-war debts were caused largely by their wartime expenses.

A main cause of the decline of some Royalist families in the post-Restoration period seems to have been their pre-war financial state. Both the Penkeths of Penketh and the Tarbocks of Tarbock had disappeared from the ranks of the Lancashire gentry by 1673, although they do not seem to have sold any land after the Civil War. It was said that, through their loyalty to Charles I, the Penkeths were 'reduced to a very poore condition', having, in 1682, 'not above five acres'.[271] If that was all that they possessed, it is not surprising that they lost their gentle status. Yet neither the Penkeths nor the Tarbocks seem to have had any financial penalty imposed upon them by Parliament after the Civil War. Both families had already lost most of their property under James I.[272] Even without the Civil War and the defeat of the king they would have lost their gentility. Another Royalist family which finally disappeared from the ranks of the Lancashire gentry was Radcliffe of Ordsall. After selling outlying estates during the Interregnum,[273] they finally parted with their ancestral home in 1662.[274] Unlike the Penkeths and the Tarbocks, some of their lands had been sequestered by Parliament.[275] But as we previously observed, pre-war debt as well as post-war sequestration was probably responsible for their decline.[276]

Another reason for the collapse of some Royalist families was post-Restoration extravagance. The eclipse of the Catholic Osbaldestons of Osbaldeston may have been partly due to penal taxation both before and after 1660, but it was also caused by the improvidence of the last male representative.[277]

Some Royalist families declined through sheer bad luck. The Rigby family of Burgh and Layton, although selling lands in 1655 and 1667,[278] seem to have actually improved their condition after the Restoration, when an Alexander Rigby acquired a considerable fortune through trade and marriage and became High Sheriff of Lancashire in 1690 and a knight in 1695. But during the War of the League of Augsburg he apparently lost £40,000 when one of his ships was seized by the enemy. It was this incident which seems to have ruined the Rigby family.[279]

The most important reason for the eclipse of so many Royalist gentry families in the later seventeenth century was not economic but demographic. Of the 99 Royalist families who disappeared from the Lancashire gentry between 1661 and 1695, 29 did so through failure to produce male heirs. Such was the fate of the prominent Cansfields of Robert Hall and the more obscure Doughtys of Thornley. Whether natural extinction itself was partly related to economic decay, as Sir John Habakkuk has suggested,[280] it is impossible to judge. But the fact remains that failure of the male line was of crucial importance in the decline not only of the Royalist but also of the Parliamentarian gentry. About 117 gentle families had supported Parliament or the English Republic. Sixty-six of these families had disappeared from the Lancashire gentry by 1695 and of these 19 (28 per cent) did so through failure to produce male heirs.[281]

To sum up: the Parliamentarian sequestrations, fines and forfeitures had only limited social and economic consequences for the Royalist gentry, both in the long and the short term. The decline of the Cavalier families in the later seventeenth century was due primarily to other factors, the most important being the lack of heirs, which affected the Parliamentarian gentry almost as much.

5 THE SUCCESSFUL ROYALIST GENTRY, 1660–1700

Having dealt with the unsuccessful Royalist gentry, let us now turn our attention to the successful. Why did so many families not only regain but retain their lands until the end of the seventeenth century? Was it due to such economic factors as royal bounty, office-holding, marriage, trade, industry and agriculture? Let us first consider royal bounty. At the Restoration many Royalists clamoured for compensation for their losses during the Civil War and Interregnum. Many of them grossly exaggerated the sacrifices they had made for the king. Sir George Middleton of Leighton described in great detail how he had lost £38,530 'by reason of his loyalty' to the Stuarts. His military and other wartime expenses came to £7,600, damage to his property amounted to £7,000, while fines for delinquency and recusancy had cost him £14,000. Middleton also alleged that he had lost £9,930 as a result of legal battles with his tenants, who had been inspired by his Parliamentarian enemies, Thomas Fell of Swarthmoor and William West of Middleton.[282] Evidently Charles II was unmoved by this sad story, for Middleton received not a farthing in compensation. But he was not the only unlucky petitioner. Indeed, Lancashire Royalists who obtained rewards from the restored monarch were few, and those who benefited most were the peerage. In 1661 Charlotte, Countess of Derby, received an annual pension of £1,000 and her nephew, Edward Stanley, got £500 per annum.[283] Charles Gerard of Halsall, created Baron Gerard of Brandon in 1645, was treated extremely generously, perhaps because he had served the king so faithfully. In 1662 he was granted a pension charged on the customs. In March 1665 he was given an annual pension of £1,000 to retire from the post of Colonel of the Life Guard, which Charles II desired to confer on the Duke of Monmouth. His retirement, however, did not take place until 1668, when, according to Samuel Pepys, he received £12,000.[284] None of the Lancashire gentry was well rewarded, except Sir Gilbert Gerard, youngest brother of Baron Charles Gerard, who by 1677 was said to have 'got by the Court and the late bishop of Durham (whose daughter he married) £30,000'.[285] But the other gentry obtained very small sums, like Richard Kirkby of Kirkby, who had just '£500 in boons',[286] and the widow of Thomas Tyldesley of Myerscough, who was granted an annuity of only £200.[287] Charles II and Parliament made feeble attempts to assist the poorer Royalists. In 1662 an Act was passed reserving £60,000 to be distributed among

loyal and Indigent officers.[288] But since there were 5,353 such officers
in England and Wales,[289] the sum was totally inadequate, and
Richard Butler of Myerscough was lucky to receive £16.[290] How
much, if anything, the other 145 Lancashire Indigent officers
obtained, it is impossible to say.[291] Finally, only one Lancashire
Royalist gentleman seems to have been rewarded with a lease of
Crown land. In 1664 John Byrom of Salford was granted for 31 years
'certain waste ground and Incroachmts in the Manno[r] of Salford' for
an annual rent of £1 4s. od. and an entry fine of only £4 6s. 8d.[292]

After the Restoration Charles II rewarded some of his followers
with offices. Here again it was the Lancashire peerage and not the
Lancashire gentry who benefited. The eighth Earl of Derby was
granted the office and revenues of Chamberlain of the county palatine
of Chester for his life and that of his son.[293] Caryll, viscount Molyneux
of Sefton, was appointed for life Butler of the county palatine of Lancaster and Steward of Blackburn hundred, Tottington, Rochdale and
Clitheroe.[294] Charles Gerard of Halsall was given a number of posts,[295]
the most important being those of Colonel of the King's Life Guard[296]
and Gentleman of the Bedchamber.[297] Very few of the Lancashire
Royalist gentry received posts from the king. The royal army was
small at the Restoration,[298] so not many were able to obtain commissions. Sir Gilbert Gerard of Halsall and Richard and Roger Kirkby
of Kirkby Ireleth were among the fortunate few. Gerard became a
lieutenant in the King's Life Guard, while Richard Kirkby was made
a captain, and his son Roger an ensign, in the Coldstream Guards.[299]
Nor did many of the Lancashire Royalist gentry obtain civilian posts.
The most fortunate belonged to families which had engaged in plots
against the Republic. Thus Sir Gilbert Gerard became a Gentleman
of the Privy Chamber-in-Ordinary,[300] while James Halsall of Melling
was appointed Cupbearer-in-Ordinary even before the Restoration.[301]

Only 17 (9 per cent) of the 180 Royalist families in Lancashire
appear to have received royal bounty or offices at the Restoration.[302]
This was even worse than the situation in Yorkshire, where 11 per
cent of Royalist families benefited from the king's generosity.[303] Many
Lancashire Royalists must have been bitterly disappointed that their
loyal services had been so ill rewarded. Whether their resentment
helped to strengthen the Whig opposition to the Stuarts in the later
years of the seventeenth century it is hard to say.[304] But it is interesting
that eight of the 16 Lancashire Whig M.P.s between 1679 and 1702
were drawn from ex-Royalist families.[305] On the whole, however, it
would perhaps be true to say that Charles II's generosity—or lack
of it—had little effect on the economic state or political behaviour
of the Lancashire gentry during the late seventeenth century.[306]

If royal munificence did not aid the financial recovery of many Lancashire Royalists, neither did holy matrimony. Not many Royalists

or their sons seem to have married wealthy heiresses after the Civil War. One of the few who did was Charles Anderton of Lostock, who, by marrying Margaret, eldest daughter of Lawrence Ireland of Lydiate, acquired the manors of Lydiate, Cunscough and Aughton, together with lands in Egargarth, Maghull and Aintree.[307] Also advantageous was the acquisition of a large marriage portion. According to Sir John Habakkuk, the portion increased in relation to the jointure during the later seventeenth century.[308] The Faringtons of Worden seem to have benefited from this trend. When in 1672 George Farington married Elizabeth Whitmore of Thurstington, Cheshire, he received a portion of £700, which was barely nine times the jointure he conferred of £80.[309] But when in 1685 his nephew, William Farington, married Elizabeth Swettenham of Somerford Booths, he acquired a portion of £2,000, which was twenty times the jointure of £100.[310] Marriage must certainly be a partial explanation of the prosperity of the Faringtons in the second half of the seventeenth century. For some of the poorer Royalists a large marriage portion may have been essential not so much to their prosperity as to their very survival. Before the Civil War the annual income of the Gorsuch family was probably only about £50.[311] In 1664 they possessed merely six hearths.[312] They had recovered their confiscated estates, probably in 1655.[313] But the cost[314] might have been a great burden to the family had it not been for the marriage of James Gorsuch in 1677. In that year Gorsuch received a marriage portion of £400 in return for settling a jointure of only £30 per annum on his Yorkshire bride, Abigail Metham of Metham.[315] It will be noted that the portions provided in the last two marriage settlements exceeded the national average. In the later seventeenth century the standard ratio was £100 jointure for every £1,000 portion.[316] This was precisely the ratio in the marriage settlement drawn up by Viscount Caryll Molyneux and Lord Henry Arundel in 1675. Caryll's son and heir, William, was to receive a dowry of £10,000 in return for settling on Bridget, his wife, a jointure of £1,000 per annum.[317] William's marriage portion of £10,000 may well have assisted the financial recovery of the Molyneux family in the late seventeenth century, but, as we shall see, this was by no means the only, or even the main, explanation. Indeed, it is doubtful if the economic recuperation of more than a handful of Lancashire Royalists really depended on marriage.

Trade seems to have helped the Lancashire Royalists even less than marriage. Indeed, the proportion of Royalist families engaged in commerce appears to have been even smaller after than before the Civil War. Only four gentlemen of Royalist stock seem to have been overseas merchants after the Restoration. Charles Gerard of Halsall became a member of the Royal Africa Company in about 1662.[318] William Blundell of Crosby and Henry Blundell of Ince Blundell were both profitably engaged in trade with the Barbadoes during the

1660s.[319] Alexander Rigby of Burgh, son of Cornet Rigby,[320] acquired a considerable fortune in foreign trade before his unfortunate bankruptcy in 1696.[321]

Royalists who prospered through industry after the Civil War were about as few as those who thrived by trade. One enterprising industrialist was Sir Thomas Preston of Furness Abbey, who exploited his iron mines to the full during the mid-1660s. Sir Thomas not only operated new pits but sold the processed ore to customers both in the immediate vicinity and in Cheshire, Staffordshire and distant Ireland. His profits were quite substantial.[322] Thomas Preston was, however, a somewhat isolated figure. No other Royalist family seems to have been profitably engaged in the iron trade after the Civil War. Nor can coal mining have brought much wealth to many former Royalists. Sir William Gerard of Bryn apparently showed a growing awareness of the value of coal,[323] while the Grimshaws of Clayton kept careful coal-mining accounts.[324] Yet there is no clear evidence that either the Gerards or the Grimshaws derived much of their total income from coal mining.[325]

Royal bounty, office-holding, marriage, trade, industry: these helped but few of the Lancashire Royalist gentry. Those who recovered in the late seventeenth century did so by exploiting their main source of livelihood: agriculture.

In 1682 John Houghton, the agricultural writer, spoke of

... the great improvements made of lands since our inhuman civil wars, when our gentry, who before hardly knew what it was to think, then fell to such an industry and caused such an improvement, as England never knew before.[326]

Houghton had in mind new agricultural techniques, such as improved stock breeding, intensive crop cultivation, fertilisers and drainage. But in Lancashire there was little sign of an agricultural revolution in the late seventeenth century. It is true that in 1651 Samuel Hartlib praised the pasture farmers of Lancashire and other northern counties for their careful cattle breeding and rearing.[327] But little progress was made in arable farming, if we exclude the field cultivation of potatoes.[328] In fact most changes in the early modern period had occurred before the Civil War. Marling was already traditional in the palatinate and as early as the period 1560–90 most farmers in the Lancashire plain successfully marled in the ordinary course of business.[329] Lime was also used in parts of Lancashire before the Civil War,[330] so in the 1650s Roger Bradshaw of Haigh was doing nothing new when, on behalf of William Blundell of Crosby, he limed the 'Hall Croft' field at the high cost of £8 per acre.[331] Improvements had also been made from the mosses before 1642,[332] but during the late seventeenth century the only ex-Royalist family which apparently undertook any major drainage operation was Fleetwood of Penwortham. About 1692

Thomas Fleetwood, employing 2,000 men, drained Martin Mere by a new straight cut through the enclosed salt marsh near present-day Southport, converting a fishing lake to arable winter ground.[333] This was not a lasting success, for Martin Mere became a lake once again in 1755, when the sea flooded in.[334] In fact, most of the extensive marshlands of Lancashire were not successfully drained until the late eighteenth and early nineteenth centuries.[335]

'Improvements' cost money and were beyond the financial reach of most of the Lancashire gentry. Royalists who survived or thrived after the Civil War did so less by experimenting with new farming techniques than by increasing their ancient sources of revenue: tithes, rents and entry fines. Some delinquents who had suffered financially from the anti-Royalist legislation were tempted to squeeze the utmost out of their tenants and others. 'Papists and malignants compound and they oppress their poor tenants,' thundered the Reverend Richard Heyricke in 1646.[336] One oppressive malignant was Thomas Preston of Holker, the lay impropriator of Cartmel parish. After paying a heavy composition fine of £1,592 in 1649,[337] he tried to recoup himself by increasing the rate of tithes. This aroused so much opposition that well over 100 of the Cartmel parishioners refused to pay.[338] The Molyneuxes of Sefton paid a composition fine of £3,140,[339] so it is not surprising to find rents on their Sefton lands gradually rising between 1660 and 1670.[340] The Molyneuxes also tried to alter copyholds to their own advantage and were accordingly sued by their tenants in 1657.[341] Of course, other financially embarrassed landlords besides Royalists tended to adopt a harsh attitude towards their tenants. Edward Moore of Bank Hall, son of the regicide and inheritor of debts of £10,000,[342] advised his son in 1667 to

Serve God and make much of your own; and as the new leases fall out, raise your rents according to my directions, that you may have something to live on like other neighbouring gentlemen.[343]

Most Lancashire landlords apparently found it difficult to follow Moore's advice. Rents were generally fixed by manorial custom or by the terms of long leases, so it was almost an achievement for the Cliftons of Lytham to be able to raise their Pentecost and Martinmas rents in Kirkham from £2 6s. 7d. in 1664 to £2 7s. 6d. in 1677.[344] Leases for lives with low annual rents and high entry fines still prevailed in south-west Lancashire and the Fylde during the late seventeenth century, and, as in Bedfordshire and Northamptonshire, little attempt was made to replace them by short-term leases at rackrents.[345] The only way the Lancashire Royalists could increase the revenue from their tenants was by imposing even higher entry fines, and indeed this is what many of them seem to have done. If we compare Table 52 with Table 7 above, we shall see that Cavalier families—except the Cliftons of Lytham—were levying considerably higher fines on their tenants in the 42 years after than in the 42 years preceding the Civil War.

As in the pre-Civil War period some gentry levied much higher fines than others, and these exactions varied considerably from one year to another and from one holding to another, even when imposed by the same landlord. However, the average fine on Royalist estates between 1646 and 1688 was as high as 50 times the annual rent, whereas between 1600 and 1642 it was 35 times. It is obviously very difficult to make an exact comparison between Royalist leasing policy in the pre-war and post-war period because we know virtually nothing

TABLE 52

FINES EXACTED BY SOME EX-ROYALIST FAMILIES, 1646–88[a]

Royalist lessors	No. of leases	Total rents £ . s. d.			Total fines £ s. d.			Average fine as multiple of rent
Blundell of Crosby	22	11	3	7	904	3	4	80·8
Chorley of Chorley	26	14	8	1	822	19	2	57·1
Clifton of Lytham	40	19	1	9	761	3	4	39·9
Eccleston of Eccleston	45	34	12	9	1,085	3	4	31·3
Farington of Worden	40	35	1	7	2,317	17	0	66·0
Gerard of Bryn	18	9	1	7	718	3	4	79·0
Hesketh of Rufford	27	15	3	4	564	6	8	37·2
Hoghton of Park Hall	10	3	2	5	284	17	6	91·3
Molyneux of Sefton	104	73	0	2	3,357	3	7	45·9
Scarisbrick of Scarisbrick	29	21	6	10	1,101	0	0	51·1
Totals	361	236	0	1	11,916	17	3	50·5

a For sources, see above, p. 14 n.

about the fines levied in the early seventeenth century by the Ecclestons, Faringtons, Gerards, Hoghtons and Molyneuxes. But it is likely that all these families made greater demands on their tenants in the later seventeenth century. Certainly on the Molyneux estates the upward trend of fines, though slight, is unmistakable (see Table 53).

These rising entry fines were not the only reason for the economic survival and revival of the Molyneuxes in the late seventeenth century. Higher rents, marriage and possibly office-holding also contributed to their prosperity. But increasing fines should perhaps rank first among the causes of the financial recovery not only of the Molyneuxes but of several other Lancashire Royalist families after the Civil War. The upward movement of fines—to which no serious opposition was recorded[346]—may possibly have been more common in Lancashire than in many other parts of England during the late seventeenth century.[347] It is also worth noting that, apart from London and Middlesex, Lancashire was one of the few English counties whose population seems to have significantly increased between the Restoration and the Glorious Revolution.[348] A growing population must have forced up entry fines. Thus, demographic factors as well as their own post-war difficulties may explain the agrarian policy of many Lancashire Royalist families.

CONCLUSION

After the Civil War 71 per cent of the Lancashire Royalist gentry were victims of Parliamentary sequestrations, composition fines and forfeitures. But few of these declined socially or economically as a result. During the Interregnum sequestrations caused only a handful of Royalists to lose income or sell land. Likewise composition fines caused few private sales, and indeed more property—at least in Lancashire—seems to have been sold by non-Royalists than by Royalists between 1646 and 1659. Exactly 100 members of the Lancashire upper classes had their lands declared forfeited to the State, but, for various reasons, only 59 of them had their estates publicly sold during the Interregnum. Almost half the property in the palatinate that was sold by the Treason Trustees belonged to the Earl of Derby.[349] Yet in spite of their wealth, the Stanleys apparently failed to regain a considerable amount of their Lancashire property. By contrast, most of the other 58 Royalists or their heirs retrieved the bulk of their estates, mainly, it would seem, before the Restoration. Indeed, it could perhaps be said that in the case of land transactions, no less than in the realm of politics and religion, mid-seventeenth-century Lancashire was England in miniature. For sales of confiscated Royalist land in south-east Lancashire which mainly belonged to the Earl of Derby—resembled those in south-east England, with local gentry, yeomen and tenants, as well as Royalist agents, acquiring most of the

TABLE 53

FINES EXACTED BY THE MOLYNEUXES OF SEFTON IN FOUR DECADES

Dates of leases	No. of leases	Total rents £ s. d.	Total fines £ s. d.	Average fine as multiple of rent
1650–59	29	17 17 6	761 12 9	42·6
1660–69	27	18 16 0	850 7 4	45·1
1670–79	13	12 10 2	592 0 0	47·3
1680–88	35	23 16 6	1,153 3 6	48·7

property. On the other hand, the sales in north and south-west Lancashire mirrored those in Yorkshire, with most of the land apparently being bought by the Royalists themselves.

Even in the long run the anti-Royalist legislation had limited economic consequences, for only a small percentage of the Lancashire Cavalier families had to sell all or a substantial amount of their property between 1660 and 1770. On the other hand many lost status even if they did not sell land, and by the end of the seventeenth century 56 per cent of the Royalist families had disappeared from the ranks of the Lancashire gentry. (But so had the same proportion of their political opponents.) What apparently caused the eclipse of so many Royalist families was not so much Roundhead oppression as military aid to Charles I, pre-war debts, post-war extravagance, sheer bad luck and, above all, failure to produce male heirs. The other 44 per cent of the Royalist families successfully maintained their position during the late seventeenth century. Royal bounty, office-holding, generous marriage portions, trade and industry undoubtedly helped some. But what probably saved a greater number of Royalist gentry from social and economic perdition was more efficient estate management. This involved not so much the introduction of new farming techniques as the raising of entry fines, which a growing population made possible.

NOTES

[1] R. Allen Brown, *The Normans and the Norman Conquest* (1969), 206–7; G. W. O. Woodward, *The Dissolution of the Monasteries* (1966), passim; A. Nevins and H. S. Commager, *America: the Story of a Free People* (Oxford, 1976), 92–3; The economic fate of the French nobility was less serious. See R. Forster, 'The Survival of the Nobility during the French Revolution', *Past and Present*, No. 37 (1967), 71–86. In Ireland the Catholic share of land fell from 59 per cent in 1641 to 22 per cent in 1665. See Karl S. Bottigheimer, 'The restoration land settlement in Ireland: a structural view', *Irish Historical Studies*, xviii, 1972, 1.
[2] C. Hill, *Puritanism and Revolution*, 155–6.
[3] Stone, *Causes*, 49.
[4] 'Restoration Land Settlement', 323 and n. 33.
[5] 'Land Sales', 76 seq.
[6] P. G. Holiday, 'Royalist Composition Fines and Land Sales in Yorkshire after the Civil Wars, 1645–65', Leeds Univ. Ph.D. thesis, 1966, 295–302; Joan Thirsk, 'The Sale of Delinquents' Estates during the Interregnum and the Land Settlement at the Restoration', London Univ. Ph.D. thesis, 1950, 317, 336–42, 347–8.
[7] 'Landowners', 130–51.
[8] Twenty-eight of the 312 participated only in the Third Civil War. The other 284 consisted of the three Lancashire peers, 272 gentry and nine Side-changers who had all supported the king at some time or other between 1642 and 1648.
[9] These 42 *exclude* two Royalists who were executed—the seventh Earl of Derby and John Gerard of Halsall, the Royalist plotter—and *include* 17 who also had their lands sequestered and/or included in the Acts of Sale. For a full list of Royalist casualties see Blackwood, D.Phil. thesis, App. V.
[10] These lucky Royalists were overwhelmingly Protestant, and included several younger sons, like Henry Nowell of Read, or gentlemen who were perhaps too obscure to attract the attention of the Parliamentarian authorities, like William Powell of Newton.
[11] G. M. Trevelyan, *England under the Stuarts* (19th edn., 1947), 191.

[12] Of the 69 committeemen who served at some time or other between 1643 and 1653 only seven can be confidently called radicals. On the moderate Parliamentarians see above, p. 74 seq.

[13] For examples of leniency see above, pp. 114–15.

[14] C.A.M., i, 47. Quoted in Morrill, *Cheshire*, 116–17.

[15] Twenty-two apparently escaped sequestration, 21 were sequestered or resequestered, the Earl of Derby was executed, and one gentleman—John Clifton of Lytham—was killed at Brindle.

[16] See Broxap, 34, 188–9, 191–4.

[17] T. Heywood, ed., *The Norris Papers*, Chet. Soc., O.S., Vol. 9, 1846, 14.

[18] P.R.O., SP23/201/159.

[19] P.R.O., E179/132/337; 132/349.

[20] According to the subsidy rolls the incomes of the Byroms and the Southworths fell by a half and those of the Bannisters, Holts, Kirkbys and Middletons by more than a half. These indicate serious financial losses, even when full allowance is made for the tendency of subsidy assessments to decline during the seventeenth century. For details of their losses see P.R.O., E179/131/317; 131/334; 132/337; 132/349; 132/350; L.R.O., DDX 3/96.

[21] For pre-war sales by the Byroms and Southworths see Blackwood, D.Phil. thesis, App. II. For references to the Middletons see ibid., 107 and n. 5.

[22] They were either discharged without being fined or no record exists of their fines.

[23] For details of their sales see Blackwood, App. X.

[24] P.R.O., SP23/90/951.

[25] Ibid.

[26] B. Holland, *The Lancashire Hollands* (1917), 293. The Hollands retained their manor and some land until about 1670, when the heiress married Humphrey Trafford of Trafford (ibid., 285–6, Proceedings in Trans. L. & C. Antiq. Soc., Vol. 3 (1885), 170).

[27] C.C.C., i, 95, 116. His Lancashire lands apparently escaped sequestration, probably through the influence of Humphrey Chetham, his mortgagee (C. P. Hampson, *The Book of Radclyffes* (Edinburgh, 1940), 166).

[28] C.C.C., i. 116, iv. 2617.

[29] Thos. Wright, *Hist. of the County of Essex* (1836), ii, 146; V.C.H., iv, 212, n. 99.

[30] L. G. Pine, ed., *Burke's Landed Gentry* (17th edn., 1952), 2113.

[31] P.R.O., SP23/118/698.

[32] P.R.O., PL17/128/19.

[33] Raines and Sutton, *Life of Humphrey Chetham*, Chet. Soc., N.S., Vol. 49, 114–15.

[34] P.R.O., PL17/139/142.

[35] Liverpool Record Office, Moore Deeds and Papers 1152 (unfoliated). In their apparent reluctance to put through the sequestration of the Royalists, Stanley, Egerton and Butterworth resembled some of the Parliamentarian gentry of East Anglia (Holmes, 191–2).

[36] P.R.O., SP28/211: Account Book 1652, fos. 15, 20.

[37] Ibid., f. 52.

[38] A. J. Hawkes, 'Sir Roger Bradshaigh of Haigh, Knight and Baronet, 1628 1648', in *Chetham Miscellanies*, N.S. VIII, Chet. Soc., N.S., Vol. 109, 1945, 9, 12–13. See also above, p. 124 and below, p. 152 n. 124.

[39] P.R.O., SP28/218 (unfoliated).

[40] See above, pp. 123, 124, 129 and below, p. 151 n. 107.

[41] Composition fines, like confiscations, generally, though by no means always, followed sequestration.

[42] 'Landowners', 130.

[43] *Rebellion*, v, 129. Quoted in Habakkuk, 'Landowners', 131.

[44] *The Century of Revolution* (Edinburgh, 1961), 147. See also Hill, *Puritanism and Revolution*, 164.

[45] 'The Transference of Lands in England, 1640–1660', T.R.H.S., 4th Ser. xv, 1932, 183, 189, 204–5, 207.

[46] 'The Royalists under the Protectorate', E.H.R., lii, 1937, 639–40.

[47] *Hist. Geog. of S.W. Lancs.*, 132.

[48] Nineteen Royalist gentlemen who compounded on the third Act of Sale, 1652, are excluded from these calculations. For details see Blackwood, D.Phil. thesis, 260 n. 1.

[49] Alexander Rigby of Burgh may have sold Carleton Hall for the same reason, since his sale price (£400) only just exceeded the amount of his fines (£381). See L.R.O.,

QDD 51/16; C.C.C., iii, 1650. One compounding Royalist—Roger Nowell of Read—sold lands for an unspecified sum, so it is difficult to speculate about his motives. For details of the sales see Blackwood, D.Phil. thesis, App. X, 1.

[50] C.C.C., iii, 1789. Even if the lands sold for as little as 15 or 16 years' purchase because of the depressed state of the post-war land market, the sale price must have easily covered the cost of the composition fine. For land prices see C. Clay, 'The Price of Freehold Land in the Later Seventeenth and Eighteenth Centuries', Ec.H.R., 2nd Ser., xxvii, 1974, esp. pp. 173–6.

[51] C.C.C., iii, 2057.

[52] The prices are not given in two of the six deeds, but they must have raised Orrell's total receipts to well over £22. For details see Blackwood, App. X, 1.

[53] The amounts were lower than the sale prices see Blackwood, loc. cit. For fines see C.C.C., iii, 1784, 1860; SP23/48/195; 248/86.

[54] C.C.C., ii, 1443.

[55] Shaw, *Annals of Oldham*, i, 149; E. Butterworth, *Hist. Sketches of Oldham* (Oldham, 1856), 42; P.R.O., C54/4025/1; H.L.R.O., Private Act, 13 Car. II, cap. 2.

[56] V.C.H., iv, 337 and n. 21. The actual amount of their aid is not stated.

[57] L.R.O., DDM 1/60. The General Account, 1655, lists the creditors who received payment from the sales.

[58] *Roy Comp. Papers*, iv, 152.

[59] T. E. Earle and R. D. Radcliffe, 'The Child Marriage of Richard Second Viscount Molyneux', Trans. Hist. Soc., L. & C., Vols. 43–44 (1893), 252–3, 265.

[60] For details see Blackwood, App. X, 1.

[61] J. Booker, *Hist of Didsbury and Chorlton*, Chet. Soc., O.S., Vol. 42, 1857, 147 seq.; Raines and Sutton, op. cit., 116–17; P.R.O., LC4/202, f. 272.

[62] J. Wheeler, *Hist of Manchester* (1836), 51. This figure seems incredibly high.

[63] C.C.C., ii, 1061; P.R.O., C231/6.

[64] A number of the non-Royalist sellers were, however, gentlemen whose lands had been sequestered for 'recusancy only'. These neutral Catholics received £5,682. For details of sales by non-Royalists see Blackwood, D.Phil. thesis, App. IX.

[65] For details of these sales see ibid., App. X. Since the Molyneuxes of Sefton were peers, their transactions are excluded from these calculations. So is the sale of Hulme by Thomas Prestwich, since it took place after the Restoration.

[66] It is just possible that the four non-Lancastrians (a physician and three gentlemen) listed in Table 42, who bought the manor of Sholver, may have been acting on behalf of yeomen in the Oldham area.

[67] These classes have been regarded as the main beneficiaries of the private sales of Royalist land. See Chesney, 'The Transference of Lands', 186; Hill, *Puritanism and Revolution*, 165. Nathaniel Gaskell of Manchester, purchaser of Clifton Hall from the Hollands, may have been a merchant. But even he did not buy from a compounding Royalist. See above, p. 114. Apart from Gaskell, James Jolly of Droylsden seems to have been the only Lancashire merchant buying privately from the Royalist gentry between 1644 and 1659. But his 'victim'—Thomas Charnock of Leyland—sold *before* he was sequestered. For details of all private Royalist land sales see Blackwood, App. X.

[68] For full details see ibid., App. VIII.

[69] 'Landowners', esp. pp. 132, 136.

[70] Ibid., 136.

[71] This conclusion, together with the main arguments in the two following paragraphs, is based on a close study of the papers of the Committee for Compounding.

[72] P.R.O., SP23/3/262; 189/520, 523.

[73] *Roy. Comp. Papers*, iv, 194. In this and the following three cases income is that given in the particulars of estate values among the Royalist Composition Papers. For a discussion of these papers as evidence of income see Blackwood, 'Economic State', pp. 54–5.

[74] *Roy. Comp. Papers*, iv, 194.

[75] Ibid., iii, 174–5.

[76] P.R.O., SP23/208/661, 663.

[77] C.C.C., iii, 2025; *Roy. Comp. Papers*, ii, 287–8.

[78] L.R.O., DDF 1385. Farington had rented the manor since 1611 (L.R.O., DDF 1366).

[79] Mr J. Brownbill wrote that 'However much in matters of religion the Parliamentarians might regard themselves as "not under the law", when property was concerned they were rigorists' (Intro. to *Roy. Comp. Papers*, vi. pt. i, 33–4).

[80] 'Landowners', 134.

[81] We are ignorant as to whether the remaining 35 compounding Royalists told the truth because, apart from their particulars, there is no means of measuring the value of their estates.

[82] G. Chandler, *Liverpool* (1957), 143.

[83] P.R.O., SP23/208/661–3.

[84] P.R.O., DL5/32, f. 107.

[85] Heywood, ed., *The Norris Papers*, p. xii.

[86] P.R.O., SP23/201/45.

[87] P.R.O., DL1/367; 368.

[88] P.R.O., E179/132/340.

[89] See Blackwood, 'Cavalier and Roundhead Gentry', 84; id., 'Economic State', p. 55.

[90] Underdown, *Somerset*, 128. Unfortunately Underdown gives no statistical details.

[91] Morrill, *Cheshire*, 204; A. C. Wood, *Nottinghamshire in the Civil War* (Wakefield, 1971), 141.

[92] For an account of Royalist compositions in Cornwall, see M. Coate, *Cornwall in the Great Civil War and Interregnum, 1642–1660* (2nd edn., Truro, 1963), 237.

[93] See details of the Propositions of Uxbridge, 1644, in S. R. Gardiner, ed., *Constitutional Documents of the Puritan Revolution, 1625–1660* (3rd edn., Oxford, 1906), 278 seq. The Lancastrians named were James, seventh Earl of Derby, Thomas Tyldesley of Myerscough and John Girlington of Thurland. In the Propositions of Newcastle, 1646, Caryll Molyneux of Sefton and John Preston of Furness Abbey were added to the Lancashire names of those excluded from pardon (ibid., 299). In fact the estates of Girlington, Molyneux and Preston were never confiscated.

[94] Yorkshire—with 118 names—had the second largest total (A. & O., ii, 623 seq.).

[95] For the Lancastrians named in the three Acts of Sale, see ibid., ii, 520–1, 591, 623–35.

[96] The seven non-Catholics were the Earl of Derby, Henry Doughty of Thornley, Charles Gerard of Halsall, John Greenhalgh of Brandlesome, Gilbert Hoghton of Wheelton, William Radclffe of Foxdenton and John Robinson of Old Laund.

[97] Holiday, 'Land Sales', 73.

[98] *Financial and Commercial Policy under the Commonwealth and Protectorate* (1934), 42 n. 5.

[99] P.R.O., SP/218 (unfoliated). Thomas, Nicholas and Robert Grimshaw nevertheless remained under sequestration (*Roy. Comp. Papers*, vi. pt. ii, 410).

[100] C.C.C., iv, 2492–3.

[101] This figure includes four manors of the Earl of Derby: Breightmet, Halewood, Great Sowerby and Little Sowerby.

[102] P R O , Index 17349, f. 28; J. Ry. Lib., English MS. 213, f. 43 seq.

[103] For some unaccountable reason six other Royalists paid their composition fines, had their lands discharged and yet almost immediately afterwards had them sold by the Treason Trustees.

[104] 'Land Sales', 74–5.

[105] The only lands which were entailed belonged to the deceased John Molyneux of Newhall. They had been mostly settled on his widow (C.C.C., iv. 3171–2; P.R.O., Index 17349, f. 54).

[106] William Anderton of Anderton and Thomas Nelson of Fairhurst sold small pieces of property. For details see Blackwood, D.Phil. thesis, App. X.

[107] L.R.O., QDD63/19d. It is not completely certain that Norris was selling his lands. The alacrity with which he conveyed his recovered property and the fact that the purchaser may have been a well known London agent also suggests that Norris may have been simply raising a mortgage so as to repay the money borrowed to pay his fine.

[108] H.L.R.O., Main Papers (2nd List of Popish Recusants in Lancashire, 6 December 1680), unfoliated after f. 19.

[109] C.C.C., iv, 3134.

[110] It was probably at most £33 15s. od. per annum. See P.R.O., SP23/226/211–13, 216–18.

[111] These 203 properties exclude land held by 16 plebeian Royalists and also the manor of Rochdale, which belonged to the Byrons of Newstead Priory, Nottinghamshire.

[112] Apart from Royalist family muniments listed in the Bibliography, the evidence for this statement is to be found mainly in the following sources: P.R.O., E179/250/

5; E179/132/349; 132/350; L.R.O., DDX 3/96; 3/97; Raines, ed., *Visitation 1664–65 by Dugdale*, Chet. Soc., O.S., Vols. 84, 85, 88; V.C.H., iii–viii, and various county, parish and printed family histories. Very useful are P.R.O., E179/250/11; 250/9: Hearth Tax Assessments, Ladyday 1664 and Ladyday 1666. These show, for example, whether or not the Royalist or his heir was occupying the manor house. For a fuller discussion of sources see Blackwood, D.Phil. thesis, 272 n. 2.

[113] Holiday, 'Land Sales', 76 seq.; Thirsk, 'Restoration Land Settlement', 323 and n. 33.

[114] Thirsk, art. cit., 321.

[115] Holiday, art. cit., 77–8, 84, 91. This percentage excludes Yorkshire land recovered by composition.

[116] See above, Table 45, for the number and value of the Lancashire properties purchased. Unfortunately Dr Holiday did not estimate the value of Royalist property regained and lost in Yorkshire.

[117] Eighteen of the trustees were Londoners, nine were Lancastrians and two were from other counties.

[118] M. Blundell, ed., *Cavalier: Letters of William Blundell to his Friends, 1620–1698* (1933), 40–1.

[119] L.R.O., DDBl 30/25. 'Doubling' meant that a state creditor, on advancing a sum equal to his original loan, plus accumulated interest, could have the whole amount charged against purchases of confiscated property.

[120] M. Blundell, op. cit., 41 seq.; L.R.O., DDBl 30/26.

[121] For Anderton of Clayton and Lathom of Parbold see above, pp. 136, 139. For the Masseys of Rixton see P.R.O., C54/3759/10; A. C. Tempest, 'The Descent of the Mascys of Rixton', Trans. Hist. Soc., L. & C., Vol. 39 (1887), 132–4. For Houghton of Park Hall see P.R.O., C54/3791/6; L.R.O., DDAl 4; J. Ry. Lib. English MS. 213, fos. 41, 50; Wigan Cen. Lib., D/D/An/20/83. For evidence that Towneley regained his manors of Cliviger, Hapton and Towneley, see L.R.O., DDTo I/8 (unfoliated).

[122] Lucy Hutchinson, *Memoirs of the Life of Colonel Hutchinson*, 198.

[123] Dr M. Ashley suggests that Wildman made 15 purchases in Lancashire (*John Wildman* (1947), 72). But Dr Ashley based his conclusions on a study of *The Calendar of the Committee for Compounding*. The Close Rolls (P.R.O., C54) suggest that Wildman made only four purchases of Royalist land in Lancashire.

[124] P.R.O., C54/3763, 3, 4. These two conveyances show that Wildman, together with Henry Colbron of London and John Fleetwood of Penwortham, bought Clifton's four manors of Clifton, Little Plumpton, Westby and Lytham for £4,523 7s. 9d. That the Clifton family regained their estates before the Restoration is shown by the fact that in the middle and late 1650s they were granting leases in Clifton and Salwick (e.g., L.R.O.. DDCl 1294–6, 1467–70, 1472). At the same time Clifton's friends, John Fleetwood of Penwortham and Roger Bradshaw of Haigh, were granting leases of some of the Clifton property in Lytham, doubtless on the instructions of the family (L.R.O., DDCl 1704–11, 1713, 1715, 1718). Fleetwood—a delinquent—had been one of the guardians of Bradshaw, a crypto-Royalist (Hawkes, 'Sir Roger Bradshaigh of Haigh, etc.', p. 9).

[125] P.R.O., C54/3804/16. Wildman bought the manor of Hindley for £515 7s. 2d. in 1653. Some months later we find Langton selling closes in Hindley for £78 to a local farmer, a possible indication that he had regained his lands before the Restoration (L.R.O., QDD 63/16).

[126] P.R.O., C54/3832/34; C.C.C., iv, 2630; *Roy Comp. Papers*, vi. pt. ii, 304–5.

[127] P.R.O., C54/3762/9.

[128] L.R.O., DDPt 46/1 (Walmesley Commonplace Book), f. 24.

[129] V.C.H., vi, 401.

[130] For details see Blackwood, D.Phil. thesis, App. X.

[131] P. H. Hardacre, *The Royalists during the Puritan Revolution* (The Hague, 1956), 157. Their Lancashire lands comprised the manors of Halsall and Downholland.

[132] W. H. Chippindall, ed., *Hornby Manor Estates*, Chet. Soc., N.S., Vol. 102, 1939, 7.

[133] C.C.C., iv, 3010. Hesketh was a convicted recusant in 1641 (P.R.O., E377/49).

[134] P.R.O., C54/4029/44.

[135] *Miscellanea*, C.R.S., Vol. 6 (1906), 147 n. 3.

[136] G. A. Stocks and J. Tait, eds., *Dunkenhalgh Deeds*, in *Chetham Miscellanies*, N.S. IV, Chet. Soc., N.S., Vol. 80, 1921, 13.

[137] See Blackwood, 'Marriages', 326–7.

[138] These Royalists were Henry Butler of Rawcliffe, Gervase Clifton of Lytham, Richard Eyves of Fishwick, Edward Rishton of Michelheys and John Turner of Tunstall.

[139] Two other Royalists failed to regain *some* of their lands. John Lathom of Ashhurst apparently lost Damhouse to Thomas Wolfall of Wolfall, a fellow Royalist, who had a claim on the property (*Roy. Comp. Papers*, iv, 68). The Towneleys of Towneley seem to have lost eight small parcels of land in Cliviger, Hapton, Ightenhill and Towneley, mostly to tenants. (P.R.O., C54/3757/5, 7; 3762/17, 19; 3765/30; L.R.O., DDTo I/8 (unfoliated)).

[140] P.R.O., C54/3793/20.

[141] See particulars of his estate in *Roy. Comp. Papers*, v, 155–6.

[142] P.R.O., C54/3793/20. See also Blackwood, 'Economic State', p. 80.

[143] P.R.O., C54/3784/2.

[144] P.R.O., C54/3800/8.

[145] P.R.O., E179/131/335. See also Blackwood, atr. cit., 59.

[146] Wigan Cen. Lib., D/D/An/20/189.

[147] T. C. Porteus, *A Hist. of Standish* (Wigan, 1927), 148. Francis Rockley told the Committee for Removing Obstructions that by statute merchant Langtree owed him £1,200, i.e. just over £600 (P.R.O., Index 17349, f. 48). For some of Langtree's other borrowings see P.R.O., LC4/203, f. 254; 204, f. 94.

[148] P.R.O., C54/3786/15; 3793/16; 3799/5.

[149] According to the lay subsidy rolls. See P.R.O., E179/131/317; 132/350.

[150] V.C.H., vi. 389, vii. 322.

[151] He had bought Catterall manor himself (P.R.O., C54/3786/15), but he seems to have obtained various lands in Catterall and Claughton, together with the manor of Little Mitton, through agents (P.R.O., C54/3793/16; 3799/5).

[152] 'The Transference of Lands', 195–6.

[153] P.R.O., C54/3794/20.

[154] P.R.O., C54/3784/2.

[155] C.C.C., iv, 2531.

[156] P.R.O., C54/3833/14.

[157] P.R.O., C54/4005/14.

[158] After 1656 the property cannot be traced.

[159] 'The Rise of the Gentry', Ec.H.R., xi, 1941, 12.

[160] See Table 25.

[161] P.R.O., C54/3761/9.

[162] L.R.O., DDTo I/8 (unfoliated).

[163] Ibid.; P.R.O., C54/3972/28. These are the only cases where land was repurchased for a Lancashire Royalist at second hand.

[164] The Langtree estate was certainly in the hands of Edward Standish, a former Royalist, by 1670 (Porteus, loc. cit.).

[165] 'Sale of Lands', 188–207. Many of the purchasers bought at second and third hand as well as direct from the Treason Trustees (ibid. 206–7). But in Lancashire, as in Yorkshire, there does not seem to have been much traffic in confiscated Royalist land, except that belonging to the Earl of Derby.

[166] The reasons are discussed above, p. 130.

[167] P.R.O., C54/3798/8. For an account of Richard Deane see D.N.B., v, 704–8.

[168] Robinson bought as one of Richard Chorley's tenants. For details of this and the other purchases see above, p. 92, and Blackwood, D.Phil. thesis, App. VIII.

[169] See above, Table 25.

[170] Mainly those who had given generously to the king. See above, pp. 117, 139.

[171] Gibson, *Lydiate Hall*, 120; L.R.O., DDIn 69/14.

[172] For reversionary charges and valid entails recognised by the Committee for Removing Obstructions see P.R.O., Index 17349, passim; *Roy. Comp. Papers*, ii, 280 seq., iii, 213–14; C.C.C., iv, 2493, 2568–9, 2621, 3151; P.R.O., C54/3759/10.

[173] P.R.O., C54/3789/3. The leases of the Gerard family for the late 1650s show that they had obviously regained their manors before the Restoration (L.R.O., DDGe(E) 244; 800; 804; 1233; 1316; 1499).

[174] E. A. Wrigley, 'A Simple Model of London's Importance in Changing Society and Economy, 1650–1750', *Past and Present*, No. 37 (1967), 54.

[175] Thirsk, 'Sale of Lands', 200; id., thesis, 159. Dr R. G. Lang has shown that among the small minority of Jacobean London merchants who left the City, most retired to

estates in the Home Counties ('Social Origins and Aspirations of Jacobean London Merchants', Ec.H.R., 2nd Ser., xxvii, 1974, 45 and n. 5).

[176] This statement is qualified but not contradicted by the fact that Londoners bought a considerable amount of Church and Crown land in Lancashire during the Interregnum. See above, Chapter III, section 3.

[177] Perhaps the only other genuine London purchaser was Henry Druell, who obtained John Robinson's land. But by 1666 Druell was no longer living in the district according to the Hearth Tax returns (P.R.O., E179/250/9).

[178] V.C.H., vi, 389; T. D. Whitaker, *Hist. of the Original Parish of Whalley and the Honor of Clitheroe*, ed., J. G. Nichols and P. A. Lyons (4th edn., 1876), ii, 24.

[179] I am grateful to Sir John Habakkuk for reminding me about this important fact.

[180] In practice tenants could buy the lands of Royalists named in the other Acts of Sale provided they did so at second hand or through agents at first hand. But direct purchases were much more difficult. Hence, apart from Towneley of Towneley only two of the 58 Lancashire Royalist gentry—Richard Chorley of Chorley and Richard Eyves of Fishwick—had their lands sold to tenants by the Treason Trustees. The Chorleys regained their property a year later, however. See above, p. 96. It is not known whether Richard Eyves eventually recovered his lands in Aughton, which were sold in 1653 to John Duxbury, a yeoman tenant, for £307 17s. 1d. (P.R.O., C54/3762/6).

[181] See P.R.O., C54/3757/5, 7; 3762/17, 19. Dr Joan Thirsk kindly drew my attention to the last indenture.

[182] See the undated petition of the Towneley tenants to the Lord Protector among the partially classified Towneley Papers in the L.R.O., DDTo I/8.

[183] Of the 58 Royalists whose forfeited land was sold, only Janion of Blackrod, Robinson of Old Laund, and Towneley of Towneley lived in the Parliamentarian regions of Lancashire, that is, Salford hundred and eastern 'Blackburnshire'.

[184] P.R.O., C54/3763/3, 4.

[185] P.R.O., E134/18 and 19 Chas. II/H.3.

[186] See above, p. 125.

[187] *Hist. of House of Stanley*, 384.

[188] Hardacre, op. cit., 158; also p. 99.

[189] Dore, *The Civil Wars in Cheshire*, 97–8. Mr Dore admits that the Interregnum land sales in Cheshire require more investigation (ibid.).

[190] The manors of Breightmet, Halewood, Great Sowerby and Little Sowerby escaped sale, probably because they formed part of the jointure lands of the Countess of Derby (*Roy. Comp. Papers*, ii, 225). It is uncertain whether the manor of Bolton-cum-Adgarley was ever sold.

[191] See Table 48 for details of the properties regained by the Earl of Derby. The main evidence used to establish the facts of recovery is as follows: P.R.O., C54 (for 'resales'); PL17; L.R.O., DDK; V.C.H., iii–viii.

[192] Only one of his manors was repurchased for him by a Lancastrian. The younger Henry Ogle of Whiston, a former Royalist, bought the manor of Rainford in 1654 (P.R.O., C54/3800/20).

[193] L.R.O., DDK 1602/3.

[194] P.R.O., C54/3797/21. Upholland was undoubtedly again in the earl's possession by 1655. See P.R.O., C54/3834/33.

[195] P.R.O., C54/3760/7; L.R.O., DDK 1472/1. See also C.S.P.D., 1653–4, pp. 368–9; V.C.H., iii, 110, 164 n. 8, 252.

[196] It is of course true that some former enemies of Charles I acted as agents for the Royalists, e.g. John Wildman.

[197] P.R.O., C54/3786/1.

[198] P.R.O., C54/3793/10. Cliffe was named as a member of the county assessment and militia committees in the late 1650s (A. & O., ii, 1071, 1371, 1434). Nicholas Rigby of Harrock may have been Cliffe's agent (*Roy. Comp. Papers*, ii, 240).

[199] P.R.O., C54/3757/6.

[200] P.R.O., C54/3767/11.

[201] For details see Blackwood, D.Phil. thesis, 287 n. 8.

[202] P.R.O., C54/3902/31.

[203] Probably not all these 60 properties were permanently lost. About fifteen parcels of land were resold, but the ultimate destiny of the other 45 estates is unknown.

[204] Thirsk, 'Restoration Land Settlement', 324.

[205] L.R.O., DDK 702/9.

[206] See Stanley of Knowsley Papers in L.R.O., esp. DDK 702/5, 8 and 9.

[207] L.R.O., DDK 1474/2.

[208] Thirsk, 'Restoration Land Settlement', 324; Hardacre, op. cit., 154.

[209] M. P. Schoenfeld, *The Restored House of Lords* (The Hague, 1967), 115.

[210] For the economic state of the Stanleys under Elizabeth I see B. Coward, 'Disputed Inheritances', B.I.H.R., xliv, 1971, 211–14.

[211] Broxap, 4–5.

[212] Calculated by the value, not by the number, of the properties.

[213] This figure includes two side-changers, Alexander Greene and John Hartley, both of Manchester. For details of the purchases made by the 10 gentry see above, pp. 89, 92, and Blackwood, D.Phil. thesis, App. VIII.

[214] P.R.O., C54/3762/3. Lee also had a conveyance from Charles Stanley (L.R.O., DDK 702/9), so this was another property which Charles lost through his own 'cleverness'. He was still hoping to regain it in 1685 (ibid.).

[215] Koop, *Broughton in Furness*, 19, 61.

[216] These were Thomas Barlow, citizen and sadler, Captain Geoffrey Fleetwood and James Fletcher, merchant (P.R.O., C54/3671/2, 8; 3794/3). It may be significant that they all had Lancashire surnames.

[217] P.R.O., C54/3790/13.

[218] P.R.O., C54/4024/31.

[219] P.R.O., C54/3796/35; 3794/1. Dr Thirsk kindly drew my attention to these indentures.

[220] L.R.O., DDK 701/3; 702/8; 741/10; 1473/7.

[221] L.R.O., QDD 63/12d, 18d.

[222] L.R.O., DDK 741/7; 1474/2 and 3; and sources cited in notes 218, 220–1.

[223] For details see *Roy. Comp. Papers*, ii, 232–3, 236, 239; L.R.O., DDK 1472/2; 1474/1; P.R.O., C54/3671/2, 8; 3673/14, 15; 3764/6, 11; 3765/9; 3767/8, 9; 3768/7; 3789/11; 3790/14; 3792/24, 25; 3794/24; 3798/5; 3833/10; 3837/24; 3895/3.

[224] P.R.O., C54/3767/9.

[225] C54/3794/24.

[226] It is often very difficult to distinguish between a resale and a release of a trust.

[227] Unfortunately most of the indentures of resales have been lost. But the Stanley papers give the names of just over 110 tenants acquiring their holdings during the Interregnum, mostly in the Bury and Pilkington area. A careful scrutiny of these papers suggests that about thirty-five tenants may have bought at second or third hand. See DDK 701/3; 702/5, 8–9; 741/7 and 10; 1453/2; 1472/2; 1473/1, 5 and 7; 1474/1–3.

[228] See M. Gray, *Hist. of Bury, 1660–1876* (Bury, 1970), 16.

[229] Thirsk, 'Agriculture and Social Change', 100–1.

[230] Any lands regained by the earl in Salford hundred were due not to the help of friendly neighbours but to the professional services of London agents like Peter Legay, who purchased the manor of Pilkington 'upon speciall trust and confidence' of Charles Stanley (L.R.O., DDK 702/20).

[231] L.R.O., DDK 12/7. Not all the earl's tenants in the Bury–Pilkington area acquired their freeholds. A minority of at least 40 were named as 'noe purchasers' (L.R.O., DDK 702/21). None of these was a Parliamentarian and indeed one was Captain William Kay of Cobhouse, Yeoman, a prominent Royalist. It is possible that many of the other non-purchasing tenants were either Royalists or 'neuters'.

[232] Dr Joan Thirsk has written that one of the most powerful pre-conditions for industrialisation in the eighteenth century was 'surely the success of the small part-farming, part-industrial family of pastoral England in the seventeenth century', and that these small farmers 'were not people who depended on the gentry'. (Horn and Thorn in Staffordshire: the Economy of a Pastoral County', *North Staffordshire Journal of Field Studies*, ix, 1969, 14.)

[233] See *Puritanism and Revolution*, 195 and n. 3; *The Century of Revolution*, 147, 200–1.

[234] Blundell, ed., *Cavalier*, 41; L.R.O., DDBl 30/25; 30/26.

[235] Through the services of Richard Bell, a London merchant. See *Roy. Comp. Papers*, i, 82; P.R.O., C54/3844/23.

[236] P.R.O., PL17/177/88; V.C.H., vi, 31 and n. 6.

[237] Sales of very small pieces of property are excluded from these calculations. For details of the sales between 1660 and 1700 see Blackwood, D.Phil. thesis, App. X, 2. See also ibid., 295 n. 6.

[238] Holiday, 'Land Sales', 92. Dr Holiday gives the amount as approximately three-quarters, but he is including land recovered by composition.

[239] *The Struggle for the Constitution* (2nd edn., 1968), 166.

[240] This figure includes 19 Royalists who compounded on the third Act of Sale as well as those paying their fines before 1653.

[241] Sales of small pieces of property are again excluded from these calculations. For details of the sales see Blackwood, App. X, 2; also ibid., 296 n. 4.

[242] Many more must have done so whose borrowings are unrecorded.

[243] P.R.O., LC4/202, f. 327; 203, f. 67; C193/42 (unfoliated). See also the following recognisances: P.R.O., C54/3359/177; 3491/208; 3572/226.

[244] V.C.H., iii, 425, 429; P.R.O., PL17/225/65.

[245] C.C.C., ii, 1192.

[246] For the Royalists concerned see Blackwood, App. X, 2; also ibid., 297 n. 4.

[247] Wadsworth and Mann, *The Cotton Trade and Industrial Lancs.*, 71 seq.

[248] Clemens, 'The Rise of Liverpool, 1665–1750', Ec.H.R., 2nd ser., xxix, 1976, 211 seq.

[249] Compare Table 49 above, and Blackwood, App. X, 2.

[250] The term 'Parliamentarian' is not used here in the broad sense as in chapter III but confined to the 91 families who had participated in the Civil War.

[251] This includes lands belonging to the Earl of Derby and all other Royalist gentry property bought first or second hand at the public and private sales.

[252] See Blackwood, App. X, 2. £4,713 is a conservative total because in several post-Restoration transactions involving an ex-Parliamentarian or his descendant we are ignorant of the purchase price.

[253] Dr M. J. Galgano has studied the economic state of some of the leading Catholic gentry in Lancashire and four other north-western counties. See 'Restoration Recusancy in the North-west of England: a Social History, 1658–1973', Vanderbilt Univ. Ph.D. thesis, 1971, Chapter IV.

[254] For references see above, p. 108 n. 214–18.

[255] See above, pp. 97–9.

[256] The 26 families who supported the Republic but not Parliament in the Civil War are excluded.

[257] Of these 456 families 76 disappeared from the gentry between 1664 and 1695 and 260 between 1642 and 1664. See above, pp. 100–1.

[258] 171 families rose to gentility between 1642 and 1664 and another 381 between 1665 and 1695. But these were outnumbered by the 318 families who lost their gentility between 1642 and 1664 and by the 346 who disappeared from the gentry between 1665 and 1695. Of the 346 disappearing families, 152 belonged to the 171 new families of the 1640s and 1650s. For sources see above, p. 108 n. 214–18. For further details of gentry numbers see below, p. 161 seq. and Appendix I.

[259] See above, p. 5. Some of the gentry who 'disappeared' may have simply left the county while retaining their gentility. The Gerards of Halsall and the Chadwicks of Healey are good examples. But such families as these cannot have been numerous.

[260] There is no evidence that the family was seriously in debt or selling even small parcels of land at any time between 1630 and 1642.

[261] P.R.O., C54/3782/20; V.C.H., iii, 130 and n. 6.

[262] P.R.O., C54/3767/1.

[263] R. Stewart-Brown, *Hist. of Allerton* (Liverpool, 1911), 21; T. Heywood, 'On the Family of Percival, of Allerton, Lancashire', Trans. Hist. Soc. L. & C., Vol. 1 (1848–49), 62–4.

[264] P.R.O., PL17/156/141; C54/3820/15; LC4/204, f. 25.

[265] V.C.H., vi, 179–80.

[266] They are not named in Blome's list of 1673.

[267] J. C. Scholes, *Documentary Notes relating to Turton* (Bolton, 1882), Nos. 5 and 54.

[268] *Roy. Comp. Papers*, vi, pt. i, 19–20.

[269] Clarendon, *Rebellion*, v, 186.

[270] J. Lunn, *Hist of the Tyldesleys of Lancs.*, 74.

[271] HMC 35; *Kenyon*: 144: Peter Bold to Roger Kenyon, 3 July 1682.

[272] See above, p. 59.

[273] See above, p. 114.

[274] Manch. Cen. Ref. Lib., L3/1/2/11/14–21.

[275] These were in Essex and Norfolk, not in Lancashire. See above, p. 114.

[276] See above, p. 114.

[277] W. W. Longford, 'Some Notes on the Family of Osbaldeston', Trans. Hist. Soc., L. & C., Vol. 87 (1935), 69. See also Blackwood, D.Phil. thesis, 302 n. 7.

[278] For these lands the Rigbys received £913 (L.R.O., QDD 51/16; 59/3).
[279] V.C.H., vi, 212; J. Venn, *Annals of a Clerical Family* (1904), 257; H. Fishwick, *Hist. of Bispham*, Chet. Soc., N.S., Vol. 10, 1887, 100 seq.
[280] See intro. to M. E. Finch, *The Wealth of Five Northamptonshire Families, 1540–1640* (Northamptonshire Record Society, Vol. 19, 1956), p. xiii.
[281] Evidence for failure of the male line is to be found in the V.C.H., iii–viii, and various parish and family histories. Among families which had changed sides or been divided during the Civil War only four (16 per cent) had failed in the male line by 1695. How many of the other 456 Lancashire gentry families failed to reproduce themselves it is impossible to say. Most of these families are so obscure that little is known about their demographic history. But it would be surprising if there was not a high rate of natural extinction among them also.
[282] L.R.O., DDTo H/4 (unfoliated): A pticuler of the Expences Charges & losses wch Sr George Middleton of Leighton ... Knt and Bart hath suffered (N.D.).
[283] W. A. Shaw, ed., *Calendar of Treasury Books* (1904), i, 194.
[284] D.N.B., vii, 1094–5.
[285] A. Browning, ed., *English Historical Documents, 1660–1714* (1953), 248.
[286] Ibid., 242.
[287] Shaw, ed., *Cal. Treasury*, i, 528.
[288] *Statutes of the Realm*, 14 Car. II, cap. 8. See also 15 Car. II, cap. 3.
[289] *A List of Officers claiming to the Sixty Thousand Pounds, etc.* (1663), cols. 1–160.
[290] J. Lunn, *A Short Hist. of Tyldesley* (Tyldesley, 1953), 73.
[291] Fifty-three of the 146 Lancashire Indigent officers were gentry.
[292] P.R.O., LR2/56 (unfoliated).
[293] Schoenfeld, op. cit., 120.
[294] Somerville, *Office-holders in the Duchy and County Palatine of Lancaster*, 125, 138–9.
[295] See D.N.B., vii, 1094–5.
[296] J. Childs, *The Army of Charles II*, 261.
[297] E. S. de Beer, ed., A List of the Department of the Lord Chamberlain of the Household, autumn 1663, B.I.H.R., xix (1942–43), 14.
[298] Childs, op. cit., esp. chapters I and II.
[299] C. Dalton, ed., *English Army Lists and Commission Registers, 1661–1714* (1892), i, 1, 105; Childs, 39.
[300] Beer, op. cit., 16.
[301] B.L., Egerton MS. 2551 (Nicholas Papers), f. 13. In 1664 James Halsall was made Scout-Master General, an office connected with the Army (Childs, 261).
[302] This excludes those who might have received rewards as Indigent Officers.
[303] Holiday, thesis, 309 10.
[304] In about 1728 Thomas, Earl of Ailesbury, wrote that Whigism originated among disappointed Royalists. See Joan Thirsk, *The Restoration* (1976), 7.
[305] Not all such Whigs were frustrated men. The Gerards of Halsall produced two Whig M.P.s yet they had been well rewarded with money and offices at the Restoration. Of the seven Lancashire Tory M.P.s, one belonged to a former Parliamentarian family and four were of Royalist stock. For a list of Lancashire Whig and Tory M.P.s in the late seventeenth century see Pink and Beavan, *Parliamentary Representation of Lancs.*, 78–81, 121–2, 156–9, 192–4, 228 31, 257–8, 284–6. I have excluded 'carpetbaggers' from all calculations.
[306] Further research is needed on the political aspects of this subject which really lies outside the scope of this book.
[307] Gibson, *Lydiate Hall*, 27, 46.
[308] 'Marriage Settlements in the Eighteenth Century', T.R.H.S., 4th Ser., xxxii, 1950, 20 seq.
[309] L.R.O., DDF 1115.
[310] L.R.O., DDF 1124.
[311] B.L., Add. MS. 36924, f. 98: Lay Subsidy Assessment, 1628. The P.R.O. Lay Subsidy Roll for 1641 is partially damaged.
[312] P.R.O., E179/250/11.
[313] L.R.O., DDSc 28/33.
[314] Gorsuch's lands in Scarisbrick and Burscough were purchased from the Treason Trustees for £302 11s. 0d. (P.R.O., C54/3790/5). But this takes no account of possible agents' fees and other expenses.
[315] L.R.O., DDSc 28/34.
[316] Habakkuk, 'Marriage Settlements', 25.

[317] L.R.O., DDM 17/155.

[318] D.N.B., vii, 1094.

[319] Galgano, thesis, 224–5.

[320] Cornet Alexander Rigby had served under Thomas Tyldesley of Myerscough in 1651 (Fishwick, *Hist. of Bispham*, 99).

[321] See above, p. 140.

[322] M. J. Galgano, 'Iron-mining in Restoration Furness: the Case of Sir Thomas Preston', *Recusant History*, xiii, 1976, 212–15.

[323] Galgano, thesis, 222.

[324] L.R.O., DDLx 4/6: Colliery accounts, 3 August 1661. See also DDLx 4/2–5.

[325] After noting the small sums recorded in the admittedly incomplete accounts of 1661, I am rather sceptical of the estimate that in 1678 Grimshaw's colliery at Clayton-le-Moors was worth the clear yearly profit of £196. See P.R.O., PL6/33/29.

[326] *A Collection for the Improvement of Husbandry and Trade* (1728 edn.), iv, 56. Quoted in Thirsk, *Restoration*, 159.

[327] Samuel Hartlib, *His Legacie* (1651), 96. See Thirsk, 'Agriculture and Social Change', 96.

[328] Potatoes were first introduced in North Meols in the late seventeenth century, but whether by the Royalist Hesketh family is unknown. See F. A. Bailey, *A Hist. of Southport* (Southport, 1955), 24.

[329] E. Kerridge, *The Agricultural Revolution* (1967), 246.

[330] Long, thesis, 90.

[331] Blundell, ed., *Cavalier*, 41.

[332] Long, op. cit., 78–9.

[333] R. Millward, *Lancashire: An Illustrated Essay on the History of the Landscape* (1955), 52.

[324] Ibid.

[335] See T. W. Fletcher, 'The Agrarian Revolution in Arable Lancashire', Trans. L. & C. Antiq. Soc., Vol. 72 (1962), 96 seq.

[336] *Queen Esther's Resolve* (1646), 26. Quoted in Hill, *Puritanism and Revolution*, 167.

[337] C.C.C., ii. 1164, v. 3268.

[338] For details see Blackwood, 'Agrarian Unrest', 72–3.

[339] *Roy. Comp. Papers*, iv, 152.

[340] Galgano, thesis, 248–9.

[341] Ibid., 233.

[342] T. Heywood, ed., *The Moore Rental*, Chet. Soc., O.S., Vol. 12, 1847, p. xlvii.

[343] Ibid., 119. Quoted in Hill, op. cit., 168.

[344] Their Kirkham tenants numbered 22 in 1664 and 21 in 1677. See L.R.O., DDCl 455 (unfoliated).

[345] For the situation in Bedfordshire and Northamptonshire see H. J. Habakkuk, 'English Landownership, 1680–1740', Ec.H.R., x, 1939–40, 14–17. Signs of rack rents on Lancashire estates are very few. The Tenants' Book of Little Crosby, 1659–1728, contains seven references to rack rents during the late seventeenth century (L.R.O., DDBl 54/41, fos. 3, 6, 10, 13, 14, 50, 60). But a careful examination of this book shows that the beneficial lease was still the normal tenure on the lands of William Blundell of Crosby (1620–98), who remained a benevolent landlord.

[346] At least, not after 1660. For evidence of landlord–tenant conflict in Lancashire before the Restoration see above, p. 145, and Blackwood, 'Lancs. Cavaliers', 17–31.

[347] Entry fines were apparently higher in Lancashire than in Cumberland and Staffordshire (Galgano, thesis, 286).

[348] For the population of Lancashire see above, p. 3. For London's population see Wrigley, 'London's Importance, etc.', *Past and Present*, No. 37 (1967), 44–9.

[349] Plebeian Royalist property is of course excluded from this calculation.

CHAPTER V

CONCLUSION

What main conclusions emerge from our study of the Lancashire gentry during the period of the Great Rebellion? The first and most obvious point to note is that the Lancashire gentry were essentially rural. Of the 774 gentle families in 1642, only 12 per cent were town dwellers. The gentry were also more numerous in lowland than in highland zones, in arable than in pastoral regions.

Economically the Lancashire gentry in 1642 were heterogeneous and poor even by northern standards. Most of them were 'mere' gentry, deriving the bulk of their income from the land or, more specifically, from rents, fines, tithes, demesne farming and coal mining. Despite their poverty, only a very small proportion of younger, and elder, sons seem to have pursued a career, trade and the law being apparently the most profitable occupations. There was considerable social mobility in early Stuart Lancashire, despite an apparently inactive land market. Large numbers of families entered and left the Lancashire gentry between 1600 and 1642, yet few appear to have risen or declined economically *within* the gentry.

The main social characteristics of the Lancashire gentry on the eve of the Civil War were their poor educational standards and their geographically and socially restricted marriages, while the greater gentry were also noted for their long pedigrees and long associations with Lancashire. Only a very small number of gentlemen alive in 1642 had apparently received any kind of higher education or had attended schools outside the palatinate. Moreover, most Lancashire gentlemen married locally and within their class. Yet despite their parochial education and marriages, despite their status consciousness, the Lancashire gentry lacked the cohesion and local patriotism of the Kentish gentry. This was probably because they were deeply divided on religious grounds. Unfortunately we are ignorant of the religious attitudes of a majority of the Lancashire gentry in 1642. But there can be no doubt that the main religious protagonists among them were the Roman Catholics and the Puritans, the former outnumbering the latter by about two to one.

During the Civil War the Lancashire gentry were also sharply divided, although a majority cannot be placed on either side. Among the minority who did participate the Royalists outnumbered the Parliamentarians by about two to one. Yet the Royalist gentry failed to hold Lancashire for the king mainly, it would seem, because of popular opposition to their recruiting drive, the large passive element among them and the depletion of their forces by the large numbers of officers and men fighting outside the county. Socially and economically no great gulf separated the Royalist and Parliamentarian gentry. Neither in terms of age, younger sons, lineage, status, office-holding or even of economic state does there seem to be any sharp contrast between the two groups. There were only two major differences: first, the Parliamentarian gentry were apparently better educated than the Royalist gentry, and, secondly, most of the former were Puritan and most of the latter were Papist. Religion was undoubtedly an important factor in determining political loyalties.

During and after the Civil War the Lancashire Parliamentary gentry do not appear to have been seriously split between extremists of the left and right. Most were moderate men who co-operated with the government until the late 1650s, largely, it would seem, through a strong fear of Royalism. But after the death of Oliver Cromwell an equally strong fear of social and religious anarchy caused the moderate gentry to support Booth's uprising in 1659 and to welcome the Restoration in 1660.

During the Interregnum the greater gentry ceased to dominate local government. They lost their monopoly of the Bench and their majority on the county committee. The most active and dedicated officials were the lesser gentry. However, this was a minor, not a major, social revolution. In Lancashire power did not pass to the 'middle sort', as happened in Westmorland,[1] and local government was still gentry government.

After the Civil War few Parliamentarian gentry gained and few Royalist gentry lost land. Only a very small number of Parliamentarian gentry bought confiscated and privately sold land and nearly half of this property apparently returned to the original owners at the Restoration. Few Royalists appear to have sold land privately as a result of sequestrations and composition fines, and most of those whose estates were publicly sold regained them, largely, it would seem, before the Restoration. Even after the Restoration few ex-Royalist families seem to have sold much land because of their sufferings during the Interregnum. The Earl of Derby was rather less fortunate than most of the Royalist gentry. Although he retrieved all but one of his confiscated manors, he appears to have lost a considerable number of small properties.

A striking feature of the later seventeenth century is the decline of both the Royalist and Parliamentarian gentry. Fifty-six per cent of both Royalist and Parliamentarian families had disappeared from the gentry by 1695. The social eclipse of the Parliamentarian families seems to have been caused by failure of the male line, debt, loss of their Interregnum purchases and, above all, by loss of local power at the Restoration. The social demise of the Cavalier families was apparently caused less by anti-Royalist legislation than by military aid to Charles I, pre-war debt, post-war extravagance and, above all, by failure to produce male heirs.

After the Civil War a new gentry emerged in Lancashire, although few of them were ex-Parliamentarians. But between 1642 and 1664 far more families left than entered the Lancashire gentry, and the overwhelming majority of the disappearing gentry had apparently taken no part in the Civil War. These 'neutral' gentry were considerably poorer than the Royalist and Parliamentarian gentry[2] and hence may have suffered more severely from the economic crisis of the late 1640s.[3]

It is clear that the Lancashire gentry were not a finite, but an everchanging, group of families. Throughout the seventeenth century large numbers of families entered and left the Lancashire gentry. However, Table 54 shows that it was only during the period of the

TABLE 54

THE NEW AND DISAPPEARING GENTRY IN SEVENTEENTH CENTURY LANCASHIRE

	1600–42	1643–64	1665–95
Nos. of families entering the gentry	289	171	381
Nos. of families disappearing from the gentry	278	318	346

For sources for this and Tables 55 and 56, see above, pp. 30 n. 35–40, 108 n. 214–18. For full details of gentry numbers in Lancashire during the seventeenth century, see below, Appendix I.

Great Rebellion that the 'disappearing' gentry outnumbered the new gentry. The social origins of the new gentry families are extremely hard to discover, but it is likely that a majority were of yeoman stock.[4] At any rate only a minority were of urban origins, especially after the Restoration. But during the period of the Great Rebellion town dwellers formed a *substantial* minority of the new gentry. (See Table 55.)

To sum up: the Great Rebellion in Lancashire saw neither the enrichment of the old, nor the emergence of a new, Parliamentarian gentry. Nor did it see the impoverishment of the Royalist gentry. Rather it witnessed the disappearance of many 'neutral' gentry families, the rise of an urban gentry and the decline of the gentry as a whole.

However, the greatest amount of social change in Lancashire seems to have occurred after the Restoration, when more families entered and left the gentry than at any other time in the seventeenth century.[6] This may occasion surprise, for the late seventeenth century has been

TABLE 55

ORIGINS OF NEW GENTRY FAMILIES IN SEVENTEENTH CENTURY
LANCASHIRE

	Families of rural origin	Families of urban origin	Total number of new families
1600–42	237 (82·0%)	52 (18·0%)	289 (100·0%)
1643–64	124 (72·5%)	47 (27·5%)	171 (100·0%)
1665–95	358 (94·0%)	23 (6·0%)	381 (100·0%)

regarded as a time of social stability, not of social mobility.[7] At least
it has been considered a stable period for the aristocracy and greater
gentry.[8] But this does not seem to have been entirely true of Lancashire. It is, of course, undeniable that throughout the seventeenth century the 'disappearing' gentry were mostly lesser gentry. But in the
post-Restoration period a far from negligible proportion belonged to
the greater gentry. Table 56 gives details.

TABLE 56

FAMILIES DISAPPEARING FROM THE LANCASHIRE GENTRY
DURING THE SEVENTEENTH CENTURY

	Lesser gentry families	Greater gentry	Total number of families disappearing from the gentry
1600–42	255 (91·7%)	23 (8·3%)	278 (100·0%)
1643–64	296 (93·1%)	22 (6·9%)	318 (100·0%)
1665–95	275 (79·5%)	71 (20·5%)	346 (100·0%)

Yet far more important than the disappearance or emergence of
this or that group of gentry families was the overall decline of the
Lancashire gentry during the seventeenth century. In 1600 Lancashire may have had a larger gentry population than most other English
counties. But between 1600 and 1695 the gentry declined from 763
to 662 families, or from 3·2 to 1·6 per cent of the Lancashire population.[9] This was perhaps the main social change in seventeenth century
Lancashire, a change accelerated but not originated by the Great
Rebellion.

NOTES

[1] Phillips, 'County Committees, etc.', North. Hist., v (1970), 56—7. See also pp. 40–4.

[2] According to the lay subsidy rolls the average annual landed income in 1642 of 72 gentry families who had supported Parliament during the Civil War or the Republic afterwards was £232. The average income of 120 Royalist gentry families was £331. 220 'neutral' gentry families had an average income of only £113 in 1642. For references see above, p. 30 n. 39.

[3] It is generally agreed that small landowners are more vulnerable than large landowners to an agricultural depression.

[4] The surnames suggest that throughout the seventeenth century few of the new gentry were of non-Lancashire origins.

[5] Part of the explanation is that during the 1640s and 1650s the term 'Gent.' was used very loosely in the towns. See Aylmer, The State's Servants, 180, 394–5.

[6] See Table 54 and Appendix I. The fact that the term 'Gent.' was used more loosely during the late seventeenth century does not weaken the argument that there was more social mobility in Lancashire after than before the Restoration.

[7] See Stone, 'Social Mobility', esp. p. 60 seq.

[8] See esp. Habakkuk, 'English Landownership', 2–17.

[9] For details see above, p. 5, and below, Appendix I. There may of course have been a growing reluctance to acquire or even to retain gentle status in a century of increasing taxation. But this cannot entirely explain the fall in the numbers of gentry families.

APPENDIX I

SOCIAL MOBILITY AMONG THE LANCASHIRE GENTRY DURING THE SEVENTEENTH CENTURY

Number of families in 1600	Number of families in 1642	Number of families in 1664	Number of families in 1695
763 Less: 278 no longer gentry	485 Less: 137 no longer gentry	348 Less: 139 no longer gentry	209
Add: new gentry	289 Less: 181 no longer gentry	108 Less: 55 no longer gentry	53
	—	—	
	774	456	
	Add: new gentry	171 Less: 152 no longer gentry	19
		—	—
		627	281
		Add: new gentry	381
			—
			662

For sources see above, pp. 30 n. 35–40, 108 n. 214–18.

APPENDIX II
THE SOCIAL STATUS OF LANCASHIRE ARMY OFFICERS SERVING IN THE CIVIL WARS, 1642–48

1. *The Parliamentarian Officers*

Note. The following gentry appear under both cavalry and infantry officers: Major-General Ralph Assheton of Middleton, Esquire, Colonel Alexander Rigby of Goosnargh, senior, Esquire, Colonel Nicholas Shuttleworth of Gawthorpe, Gentleman, and Lieutenant-Colonel Alexander Rigby of Goosnargh, junior, Gentleman. For sources see above, p. 66 n. 11

(a) *Cavalry officers*

Rank	Numbers	Esqrs	Gents	Gentry?	Plebs
Major-General	I	I	o	o	o
Colonel	5	I	3	o	I
Lt. Col.	2	o	I	o	I
Major	2	o	I	o	I
Capt.	17	2	9	3	3
Lieut.	6	o	2	3	I
Cornet	2	o	o	I	I
Quartermaster	2	o	o	o	2
Total	37 (100%)	4 (11%)	16 (43%)	7 (19%)	10 (27%)

(b) *Infantry officers*

Rank	Numbers	Barts	Esqrs	Gents	Gentry?	Plebs
Major-General	I	o	I	o	o	o
Colonel	10	2	4	3	o	I
Lt. Col.	5	o	2	2	o	I
Major	4	o	o	4	o	o
Capt.	46	o	I	17	3	25
Lieut.	5	o	o	3	o	2
Ensign	3	o	o	I	I	I
Gent. of Arms	I	o	o	o	I	o
Total	75 (100%)	2 (3%)	8 (10%)	30 (40%)	5 (7%)	30 (40%)

(c) *Other officers*

Rank	Numbers	Esqrs	Gents	Gentry?	Plebs
Colonel	4	3	0	1	0
Lt. Col.	4	1	1	0	2
Major	2	0	1	0	1
Capt.	33	2	15	4	12
Lieut.	4	0	0	0	4
Other Officers	2	0	0	0	2
Total	49 (100%)	6 (12%)	17 (35%)	5 (10%)	21 (43%)

2. *The Royalist officers*

Note. The following gentry appear under both cavalry and infantry officers: General James Stanley, seventh Earl of Derby, Major-General Charles Gerard of Halsall, Esquire, Major-General Thomas Tyldesley of Myerscough, Esquire, Colonel Richard Molyneux, second Viscount Maryborough, Colonel Edward Rawsthorne of Newhall, Esquire, and Colonel Thomas Prestwich of Hulme, Esquire. For sources see above, p. 66 n. 11.

(a) *Cavalry officers*

Rank	Numbers	Peers	Barts	Esqrs	Gents	Gentry?	Plebs
General	4	1	1	2	0	0	0
Colonel	10	2	0	7	1	0	0
Lt. Col.	3	0		2	1	0	0
Major	4	0	0	2	2	0	0
Capt.	35	0	0	7	15	3	10
Lieut.	23	0	0	0	8	5	10
Cornet	21	0	0	1	5	4	11
Quartermaster	27	0	0	0	5	4	18
Total	127 (100%)	3 (2%)	1 (1%)	21 (16%)	37 (29%)	16 (13%)	49 (39%)

(b) *Infantry officers*

Rank	Numbers	Peers	Kt	Esqrs	Gents	Gentry?	Plebs
General	3	1	0	2	0	0	0
Colonel	9	1	1	4	3	0	0
Lt. Col.	4	0	0	2	2	0	0
Major	3	0	0	1	2	0	0
Capt.	37	0	0	7	12	6	12
Lieut.	20	0	0	0	7	2	11
Ensign	9	0	0	1	0	2	6
Gent. of arms	3	0	0	1	2	0	0
Total	88 (100%)	2 (2%)	1 (1%)	18 (21%)	28 (32%)	10 (11%)	29 (33%)

(c) *Other officers*

Rank	Numbers	Esqrs	Gents	Plebs
Colonel	1	1	0	0
Capt.	26	8	12	6
Lieut.	3	0	3	0
Total	30 (100%)	9 (30%)	15 (50%)	6 (20%)

APPENDIX III
STATISTICAL ANALYSIS OF THE ACTING MAGISTRATES, 1646–59[1]

	The Lancashire magistracy	
	1646–48	*1649–59*
1. Total number of justices	32	40
2. Status:		
Greater gentry (barts, kts, esqrs)	28 (87·5%)	22 (55%)
Lesser gentry (gents)	4 (12·5%)	14 (35%)
Plebeians	–	4 (10%)
3. Younger sons	4 (12%)	4 (10%)
4. Total receiving higher education	17 (53%)	15 (37%)
5. Soldiers in Civil Wars (1642–48)	20 (62%)	21 (52%)
6. Puritans	24 (75%)	31 (80%)
7. Served as J.P.s 1625–42	16 (50%)	–
8. Served as J.P.s 1646–48	–	18 (45%)
9. Served on county committee 1643–48	25 (78%)	–
10. Served on county committee 1649–53	–	22 (55%)
11. Of recent gentry stock (i.e. since 1603)	2 (6%)	6 (15%)
12. Urban dwellers	1 (3%)	5 (12%)
13. Merchants	1 (3%)	2 (5%)
14. Lawyers	7 (22%)	5 (12%)
15. Paid office-holders 1625–42		
(excluding sheriffs)	3 (9%)	2 (5%)
16. Financial difficulties, 1630–42	3 (9%)	3 (7%)

[1] *Sources.* For status, see above, p. 30 n. 35–40; younger sons, p. 54 n.; education, p. 24 n.; soldiers, p. 66 n. 11; Puritans, p. 36 n. 196; pre-war J.P.s, p. 32 n. 80; post-war J.P.s, p. 102 n. 8; county committeemen, p. 102 n. 8; Stuart gentry, p. 30 n. 36–40; mercantile and legal activities, p. 17 n.; pre-war office, p. 17 n.; pre-war debts, p. 19 n.

APPENDIX IV
STATISTICAL ANALYSIS OF THE ACTING COUNTY COMMITTEEMEN, 1643–53[1]

	The Lancashire Committeemen	
	1643–48	*1649–53*
1. Total number of committeemen	41	45
2. Status:		
Greater gentry (barts, kts, esqrs.)	26 (63·4%)	18 (40%)
Lesser gentry (gents)	15 (36·6%)	20 (44·4%)
Plebeians	–	7 (15·6%)
3. Younger sons	8 (19%)	4 (9%)
4. Total receiving higher education	21 (51%)	16 (35%)
5. Soldiers in Civil Wars (1642–48)	22 (53%)	20 (44%)
6. Puritans	31 (75%)	35 (77%)
7. Served as J.P.s 1646–48	25 (61%)	–
8. Served as J.P.s 1649–59	–	22 (49%)
9. Of recent gentry stock (i.e. since 1603)	3 (7%)	7 (15%)
10. Urban dwellers	5 (12%)	6 (13%)
11. Merchants	2 (5%)	5 (11%)
12. Lawyers	7 (17%)	6 (13%)
13. Paid office-holders 1625–42 (excluding sheriffs)	5 (12%)	3 (6%)
14. Financial difficulties, 1630–42	3 (7%)	1 (2%)

[1] *Sources.* See above, Appendix III, n. 1.

SELECT BIBLIOGRAPHY: Manuscript Sources

A record of the sources used in this book is contained in the footnotes, hence it has been thought unnecessary to add a bibliography of printed works. But to elucidate some of the arguments in the text, a separate list of the manuscript sources is given here. This includes all family muniments consulted; otherwise only documents cited specifically in this book are listed. The estate papers (with the names of the relevant families in brackets) which yielded particularly valuable material are followed by an asterisk *. P or R denotes a family which was mainly or entirely Parliamentarian or Royalist during the Civil War.

Bodleian Library, Oxford

Oxford University Archives, Matriculation Register PP, 1615-47

British Library, London

Additional MS. 9354—St Omer Composition Lists, 1622-70
Additional MS. 30208—An Alphabetical Account of the Land Revenues belonging to the Crown ... since 1650
Additional MS. 34013—List of Suspected Persons in Various English Counties, 1655
Additional MSS. 36924-7—The Norris Papers, vols. i–iv*. As well as the papers of the Norris family,[R] vol. i includes the 1628 Lay Subsidy Assessment (West Derby hundred)
Egerton MS. 2551—The Nicholas Papers
Harleian MS. 1912—Gray's Inn Barristers, Admissions, etc.
Harleian MS. 2112—Collection of Law Papers concerning Chester by R. Holme
Lansdowne MS. 1218—Commission of the Peace, 1561
Royal MS. 18.D.iii—List of J.P.s in various counties (including Lancashire), c. 1592

Chetham's Library, Manchester

Bailey Transcripts, Bundle 17—The Protestation returns, 1641-42
MS. A.3, 90—Letter Book of Sir Ralph Assheton of Whalley,[P] 1648
MS. C.8, 13—Towneley Deeds
Raines MS. xxx—Miscellaneous Papers

Downham Hall, Clitheroe

Court Rolls of the Manor of Downham, 21 October 1645-18 October 1655 (Assheton of Whalley[P])

Gonville and Caius College, Cambridge

MS. 'Liber Matriculationis', 1560–1678

Guildhall Library, London

Guildhall MS. 5576/1—Fishmongers' Company, Freemen and Apprentices, vol. i, 1614–50

Guildhall MS. 11593—Grocers' Company Register of Apprentices, vol. i, 1629–66

Royal Contract Estates: Sales Contracts, 1628–77; also Draft Deeds 52 and 53

House of Lords Record Office, Houses of Parliament

Main Papers—Two Lists of Popish Recusants in Lancashire, December 1680

Private Acts of Sale post-Restoration

Inner Temple Library

Admissions to the Inner Temple to 1659 (typescript, 1954)

John Rylands Library, Manchester

English MS. 213—Letters and Papers concerning Lancashire Catholics, mainly seventeenth century

Lancashire County Record Office, Preston

Estate and Family Muniments

Alison of Park Hall, DDAl* (Hoghton of Park Hall[R])
Blundell of Ince Blundell, DDIn (Blundell of Ince Blundell[R])
Blundell of Little Crosby, DDBl* (Blundell of Crosby[R])
Braddyll of Portfield, DDBr (Braddyll of Portfield[P])
Bretherton of Hey, DDBr (Bretherton of Hey[R])
Cavendish of Holker, DDCa (Preston of Holker[R])
Clifton of Lytham, DDCl* (Clifton of Lytham[R])
Farington of Worden, DDF* (Farington of Worden[R])—these papers include the lay subsidies for Lancashire, 1593
Fitzherbert-Brockholes, DDFz (Brockholes of Claughton[R])
Gerard of Ashton-in-Makerfield, DDGe* (Gerard of Bryn[R])
Hesketh of Rufford, DDHe* (Hesketh of Rufford[R])
Hoghton of Hoghton, DDHo (Hoghton of Hoghton Tower[R])
Hopwood of Hopwood, DDHp (Hopwood of Hopwood[P])
Kenyon of Peel, DDKe* (Assheton of Whalley[P])
Lord Lilford of Bank Hall, DDLi (Atherton of Atherton[P])
Mather of Lowick, DDLk (Ambrose of Lowick[R])
Molyneux of Sefton, DDM* (Molyneux of Sefton[R])
Petre of Dunkenhalgh, DDPt* (Walmesley of Dunkenhalgh)
Rawsthorne of Hutton, DDR (Rawsthorne of New Hall[R])

Scarisbrick of Scarisbrick, DDSc* (Eccleston of Eccleston,[R] Scarisbrick of Scarisbrick[R])

Stanley of Knowsley, DDK* (Earls of Derby[R])—these papers include the List of Lancashire Freeholders, 1695

Tatton of Cuerden, DDTa* (Charnock of Astley[R], Parker of Extwisle[P])

Towneley of Towneley, DDTo* (Middleton of Leighton[R], Towneley of Towneley[R])

De Trafford of Trafford, DDTr (Trafford of Trafford)

Trappes-Lomax of Clayton-le-Moors, DDLx* (Grimshaw of Clayton[R])

Lancashire Quarter Sessions Records

QDD—Deeds of Bargain and Sale
QSC—Commissions of the Peace
QSR—Quarter Sessions Rolls

Miscellaneous Documents

Ancient Deeds, DX
Documents Purchased, DP
National Trust, DDN—Sir Gilbert Hoghton's Lieutenancy Book. Includes muster rolls, 1632; List of Amounderness Freeholders, 1633
Probate Records
(i) Diocese of Chester
(ii) Archdeaconry of Richmond
Smaller Deposits, DDX—includes Salford Hundred Exchequer Lay Subsidy Rolls, 1663 and 1664

Liverpool Record Office

Moore Deeds and Papers* (Moore and Bank Hall[P])

Manchester Central Reference Library

Carill Worsley Papers, M35 (Worsley of Platt[P])
Radcliffe Papers, L3 (Radcliffe of Ordsall[R])

Public Record Office, London

Chancery

C54—Close Rolls (Deeds of Bargain and Sale and Recognisances)
C181/4—Crown Office, Miscellaneous Books (Lancashire Sewers Commissioners 1629–34)
C193/12/2—Crown Office, Miscellaneous Books (Justices of the Peace, 1626–30)
C193/13/3—Crown Office, Miscellaneous Books (Justices of the Peace, 1649–50)
C193/41–42—Crown Office, Miscellaneous Books (Entry Books of Writs of Statute Staple)
C231—Crown Office, Docquet Books

Court of Wards and Liveries

Wards 5—Feodaries' Surveys
Wards 9—Miscellaneous Books, including Entry Books of Contracts for Wardships and Leases

Crown Estate Office

CRES 6/2—Entry Books and Registers: Surveyor-General's Book of Constats, 1660–61

Duchy of Lancaster

DL1—Pleadings (Bills, Answers and Replications)
DL4—Depositions
DL5—Entry Books of Decrees and Orders
DL7—Inquisitions post-mortem
DL42—Miscellaneous Books
Duchy of Lancaster Index to Patents 1558–1760

Exchequer

E121—King's Remembrancer, Certificates as to the Sale of Crown Lands
E134—K.R., Depositions
E179—K.R., Lay Subsidy Rolls, 1626, 1641, 1663; Schedule of Contributors to the 'Free and Voluntary Gift', 1661; Hearth Tax Assessments, Ladyday 1664, Ladyday 1666
E190—K.R., Port Books
E377—Lord Treasurer's Remembrancer, Recusant Rolls, Pipe Office Series
E379—L.T.R., Sheriffs' Accounts of Seizures

Land Revenue Office

LR2/56—Miscellaneous Books, 'Lands Demised by the Crown, 1640–67'
LR2/266—Miscellaneous Books, Papers concerning the Crown Lands at the Restoration

Lord Chamberlain's Office

LC4—Entry Books of Recognisances

Palatinate of Lancaster

PL6—Chancery Bills
PL17—Prothonotary's Records, Feet of Fines

Prerogative Court of Canterbury

PROB 11—Registered Copy Wills, 1384–1858

Signet Office

Indexes 6801–11—Docquet Books, 1603–44

State Paper Office

SP12—State Papers Domestic, Elizabeth I
SP16—State Papers Domestic, Charles I
SP18—State Papers Domestic, Interregnum
SP19—Committee for Advance of Money
SP23—Committee for Compounding
SP28—Commonwealth Exchequer Papers
SP29—State Papers Domestic, Charles II
Index 17349 (Claims to Delinquents' Lands)

Sidney Sussex College, Cambridge

MS Register, vol. i, 1598–1706

Wigan Central Library

Anderton Deeds and Papers, D/D/An* (Anderton of Birchley,[R] Anderton of Clayton,[R] Anderton of Euxton[R])
Dicconson–Wrightington Deeds (Wrightington of Wrightington[R])

INDEX